Hands-On Object-Oriented Programming

Mastering OOP Features for Real-World Software Systems Development

Anil Kumar Rangisetti

Apress®

Hands-On Object-Oriented Programming: Mastering OOP Features for Real-World Software Systems Development

Anil Kumar Rangisetti
Kurnool, Andhra Pradesh, India

ISBN-13 (pbk): 979-8-8688-0523-3   ISBN-13 (electronic): 979-8-8688-0524-0
https://doi.org/10.1007/979-8-8688-0524-0

Copyright © 2024 by Anil Kumar Rangisetti

This work is subject to copyright. All rights are reserved by the Publisher, whether the whole or part of the material is concerned, specifically the rights of translation, reprinting, reuse of illustrations, recitation, broadcasting, reproduction on microfilms or in any other physical way, and transmission or information storage and retrieval, electronic adaptation, computer software, or by similar or dissimilar methodology now known or hereafter developed.

Trademarked names, logos, and images may appear in this book. Rather than use a trademark symbol with every occurrence of a trademarked name, logo, or image we use the names, logos, and images only in an editorial fashion and to the benefit of the trademark owner, with no intention of infringement of the trademark.

The use in this publication of trade names, trademarks, service marks, and similar terms, even if they are not identified as such, is not to be taken as an expression of opinion as to whether or not they are subject to proprietary rights.

While the advice and information in this book are believed to be true and accurate at the date of publication, neither the authors nor the editors nor the publisher can accept any legal responsibility for any errors or omissions that may be made. The publisher makes no warranty, express or implied, with respect to the material contained herein.

Managing Director, Apress Media LLC: Welmoed Spahr
Acquisitions Editor: Melissa Duffy
Development Editor: Laura Berendson
Coordinating Editor: Gryffin Winkler
Copyeditor: Kim Burton

Cover designed by eStudioCalamar

Cover image by Vinicius "amnx" Amano on Unsplash (unsplash.com)

Distributed to the book trade worldwide by Apress Media, LLC, 1 New York Plaza, New York, NY 10004, U.S.A. Phone 1-800-SPRINGER, fax (201) 348-4505, e-mail orders-ny@springer-sbm.com, or visit www.springeronline.com. Apress Media, LLC is a California LLC and the sole member (owner) is Springer Science + Business Media Finance Inc (SSBM Finance Inc). SSBM Finance Inc is a **Delaware** corporation.

For information on translations, please e-mail booktranslations@springernature.com; for reprint, paperback, or audio rights, please e-mail bookpermissions@springernature.com.

Apress titles may be purchased in bulk for academic, corporate, or promotional use. eBook versions and licenses are also available for most titles. For more information, reference our Print and eBook Bulk Sales web page at http://www.apress.com/bulk-sales.

Any source code or other supplementary material referenced by the author in this book is available to readers on GitHub (https://github.com/Apress). For more detailed information, please visit https://www.apress.com/gp/services/source-code.

If disposing of this product, please recycle the paper

*To my teachers, Dr. Bheemarjuna Reddy and
Shri Badrinadh Garu, for identifying my strengths,
giving me wonderful opportunities to work with them,
and guiding me to achieve my goals.*

*To my lovely wife, Sravani, for being a wonderful partner
and supporting me in all situations. Without her love and
support, I could not accomplish it.*

Table of Contents

About the Author xiii

About the Technical Reviewer xv

Acknowledgments xvii

Introduction xix

Chapter 1: The Importance of Object-Oriented Programming 1

Algorithms vs. Software...2
    Algorithm Characteristics 2
    Write an Algorithm..3
    Software 5
    Software Development Challenges...6

Introduction to OOP Concepts 7
    Class 7
    Objects 13
    Inheritance 16
    Polymorphism...18

How OOP Approaches Simplify the Software Complexity 19

Systematically Modeling Real-World Entities into Software 21
    Hands-on Activity: Online Shopping 23
    Hands-on Activity: Simple Adventurous Game 33

Summary..39

Practice: Hands-on Activities 40

v

TABLE OF CONTENTS

Chapter 2: Start Learning OOP Using C++ 43
C++ OOP Constructs 44
    C++ Specific Programming Constructs 45
Model Real-World Entities Using C++ Classes 64
Interacting with Objects 77
Object Access Control Modes 87
Hands-on Activity: Smart Applications 100
Summary 109
Practice: Hands-On Activities 110

Chapter 3: Systematically Starting and Stopping Software Objects 113
Software Objects Startup and Shutdown Sequences 114
    Starting a Software Application 115
    Closing a Software Application 118
Constructors for Handling Startup Sequences 120
    Constructors in C++ 120
    C++ Supporting Constructors 123
    C++ Compiler Providing Constructors 128
    Hands-on Activities for Practicing Constructors 130
The Importance of Destructors for Doing Graceful Shutdowns 139
    Destructors in C++ 139
    Hands-on Destructors 143
Hands-on Activity 1: Constructors 150
Hands-on Activity 2: Destructors 162
Summary 166
Practice: Hands-on Activities 167

TABLE OF CONTENTS

Chapter 4: Exploring Important C++ Features 169
C++ Friend Classes and Functions 170
    C++ Friend Functions 171
    C++ Friend Class 174
Hands-on Activity: When to Use C++ Friend Concepts 177
Best Practices in Passing Arguments 188
    Arguments Passing Activities 190
Sharing Data of Objects Using C++ Static 200
Restricting Accidental Changes Using C++ const 208
    C++ Const and Pointer Usage Activities 212
Summary 225
Practice: Hands-on Activities 225

Chapter 5: Quickly and Systematically Model Real-World Problems into Software 227
Modeling Real-World Problems into Software Design 228
    A Simple Gaming Application 229
Modeling Game World Entities Using C++ Classes 235
Game Implementation Using C++ Classes 244
Model Application Entities Using C++ Classes 255
    Basic Tasks Related to a Shopping Application 270
    Basic Customer Interactions in a Shopping Application 274
    Basic Shopkeeper Interactions in a Shopping Application 278
    Simulating Shopping Application Tasks 282
Summary 288
Practice: Hands-on Activities 288

TABLE OF CONTENTS

Chapter 6: Quick Software Development Using OOP 291
The Importance of Inheritance 292
    Inheritance Approaches 294
    Issues in Combining Inheritance Approaches 299
    Access Controls and Inheritance 301
    Constructors and Destructors Working Order in Inheritance Context 306
Practicing the Reduce and Reuse Principle 311
Building New Software Building Blocks Versions Easily 323
Combine or Connect Objects Wisely 335
    Object Composition: Special Gaming Weapon 336
    Object Composition and Aggregation 342
    Hands-on Activity: Inheritance and Object Association 349
Summary 359
Practice: Hands-on Activities 359

Chapter 7: Easy-to-Use Software Development Using OOP 361
The Importance of Polymorphism 362
    Function Overloading 363
    Function Overriding 367
Overloading Operators to Deal with Complex Objects Computations 371
    How to Overload Operators 372
    Practice Operator Overloading Usage 374
Generic Functions and Data Structures 381
    Practice with Generic Functions 383
    Generic Data Structures 388
    Practice Implementing a Generic Data Structure 389
Using Dynamic Polymorphism for Offering Common Interfaces 395

TABLE OF CONTENTS

    The Importance of Virtual Functions..396

    The Importance of Pure Virtual Functions and Abstract Classes.................401

    Practice with Dynamic Polymorphism..403

Summary..408

Practice: Hands-on Activities 409

Chapter 8: Design Patterns...411

Introduction to Design Patterns 412

    Creational Patterns..412

    Structural Patterns 413

    Behavioral Patterns 414

Learning Creational Design Patterns 415

    The Factory Method..418

    The Singleton Pattern...423

Structural Design Patterns...428

    The Facade Pattern 432

    The Proxy Server Pattern...440

Behavioral Design Patterns..445

    The Chain of Responsibility Pattern..450

    The Template Method 458

Summary..465

Chapter 9: Event-Driven Programming...467

The Importance of Event-Driven Programming...468

    Key Concepts...469

    Advantages and Use Cases 473

Structure 474

    Using C++ for Events and Event Handlers 476

    Implementing Application Events and Subscribing to Classes....................480

TABLE OF CONTENTS

Quick Practice 483
Hands-on Activity: Design a Simulator 491
    IoTSensorsHandler Events 492
    SmartVehiclesHandler Custom Events 497
    SmartApplication Simulation 501
Summary 504
Practice: Hands-on Activities 504

Chapter 10: A Brief Introduction to OOP in Python and Solidity 507

Other Important OOP Languages 508
    The Importance of Python Programming 508
    The Importance of Solidity Programming 510
Python Basic Programming Constructs for OOP 511
    Python Basic Programming Constructs 511
    Python OOP Constructs 515
    Python OOP Constructs for Inheritance 519
    Python OOP Constructs for Polymorphism 521
Practicing OOP in Python 526
    Using Python for Encapsulation and Data-Hiding Features 526
    Using Python to Implement Inheritance 532
    Using Python for Polymorphism 538
Solidity Basic Programming Constructs for OOP 541
    Solidity Basics 541
    Solidity Inheritance Programming 546
    Solidity Polymorphism Programming 549
Practicing OOP in Solidity 552

TABLE OF CONTENTS

Using the Remix Editor for Practicing Solidity 553
Practicing with Smart Contracts 556
Extending Smart Contracts Using Inheritance 562
Using Solidity for Polymorphism 568
Summary 573

Index 575

About the Author

Dr. Anil Kumar Rangisetti received his PhD in computer science and engineering from the Indian Institute of Technology (IIT) Hyderabad. He has nearly 10 years of teaching and research experience in computer science and engineering. During his career, he worked at prestigious Indian institutions such as IIIT Dharwad, SRM-AP, and GMR, and at software development and research labs such as Aricent. Currently, he is an assistant professor in the CSE Department at IIITDM, Kurnool. He trains students in OOP languages and how to use advanced simulators (NS-3), Docker, and networking tools for developing applications, and he has guided many undergraduate and postgraduate students in their projects.

Broadly, Dr. Rangisetti's research interests include Wi-Fi technologies, next-generation mobile networks, software-defined networking (SDN), network functions virtualization (NFV), and cloud computing. He also writes and reviews books on computer science technologies and programming languages, and he is the author of *Advanced Network Simulations Simplified* (Packt, 2023).

About the Technical Reviewer

Saravan Nanduri is a seasoned senior full-stack web developer with nearly two decades of experience in the information technology sector, specializing in developing object-oriented applications. Having worked with prestigious companies such as Tech Mahindra and Accenture, Saravan brings expertise to every project he undertakes.

After graduating with computer science and engineering degrees in 2005, Saravan embarked on a remarkable journey leading him to the United States in 2015, where he worked for government agencies before assuming the role of senior software engineer at SS&C Innovest in 2019.

With a solid foundation in computer science, Saravan is adept at architecting and implementing both client and web-based enterprise applications. His proficiency spans a wide spectrum of technologies, including C++ and Microsoft .NET frameworks, such as C# and MVC.

Beyond his professional endeavors, Saravan values relationships and camaraderie.

Acknowledgments

First, I would like to thank Apress for accepting my book idea and giving me this wonderful opportunity. I would especially like to thank Melissa Duffy for keenly going through the book proposal and suggesting to me how to make the book proposal interesting and perfect. Melissa's support and encouragement throughout the book-writing process is highly helpful. Melissa's simple suggestions improved the quality of the book's content.

I want to thank Nirmal Selvaraj for his continuous support in the entire review and the book contents finalization process. His timely help and support helped me to finish on time.

I thank the book's technical reviewer, Sarvan Nanduri, for his valuable time and suggestions in all hands-on activities and technical concepts. His keen observations helped me correct all kinds of errors and incorporate necessary topics to improve the book's quality tremendously.

I would like to thank every member of the Apress for supporting me in writing this book. I would love to work with the Apress team again.

I give my heartfelt thanks to all my students for their interest in attending my lectures and working with me. All my students' curiosity, comments, and suggestions helped me to write this book.

Finally, I thank all my family members, friends, and colleagues for their love and support.

Introduction

Object-oriented programming (OOP) is an essential skill for implementing extendible, reusable, and easy-to-use software systems. To develop any application software or system software, learning OOP concepts and programming is necessary. OOP basic principles help in easily handling a wide variety of real-world software systems (games, application software, novel systems) implementations. This book blends OOP concepts and programming activities for active learning. All hands-on activities and real-time scenarios are described with step-by-step procedures in terms of designing, programming, and evaluations.

You will learn OOP features through real-world examples and practice through C++ programming hands-on activities. You will also learn advanced design and development skills, such as design patterns and event-driven programming for handling novel systems design and development. Finally, you are briefly introduced to OOP features practice through other important OOP languages: Python and Solidity.

This book is organized into three parts. In Part 1 (Chapters 1–4), you learn and practice OOP concepts using C++ for solving real-world software development problems.

Part 2 (Chapters 5–7) explains how to model real-world problems into reusable, extendible, and easy-to-use software development blocks using OOP concepts such as inheritance, object associations, and polymorphism.

INTRODUCTION

In Part 3 (Chapters 8–10), you learn how to use design patterns and event-driven programming for handling complex software system object creation, behavior, and interactions. Finally, you are introduced to OOP using Python and Solidity.

By the end of this book, you will have learned how to design and implement a variety of real-world software systems from scratch using OOP principles, design patterns, and event-driven programming skills.

CHAPTER 1

The Importance of Object-Oriented Programming

Object-oriented programming (OOP) is essential for handling challenges in developing flexible, extendible, reusable, and easy-to-use software systems. OOP approaches simplify the complexity of modeling real-world application concepts into software building blocks.

OOP offers powerful programming constructs and principles to deal with the complexity of software development. OOP constructs such as classes help you to systematically map real-world entities, and it helps in hiding the implementation details of the entities, controlling their data access, and simplifying the software system interactions, activities, and tasks. Moreover, OOP principles such as inheritance and polymorphism help you to develop reusable and easy-to-use software systems.

Learning OOP helps you deal with the complexity of any software, such as e-commerce applications, system software (e.g., device drivers, compilers, operating systems, databases), next-generation applications such as IoT, industrial IoT (IIoT), smart applications, and many more. To appreciate the importance of learning OOP, this chapter discusses the following topics.

CHAPTER 1   THE IMPORTANCE OF OBJECT-ORIENTED PROGRAMMING

- Algorithms vs. software
- Software development challenges
- Introduction to OOP concepts
- How OOP approaches simplify the software complexity
- Systematically modeling real-world entities into software

Algorithms vs. Software

Before exploring software, you should know how to start writing a program for solving well-defined problems, such as mathematical, computational, searching, and sorting problems. Solving these problems through a program involves considering all necessary inputs and defining a logical sequence of computational steps to get the desired results. Formally, it is known as writing an algorithm.

This section briefly introduces the following topics.

- Algorithm characteristics
- Writing an algorithm
- Software characteristics
- Software development challenges

Algorithm Characteristics

An algorithm defines a logical sequence of instructions or commands to solve a problem. For instance, algorithms are highly suitable for implementing programs to solve specific problems such as searching, sorting, data structures accessing problems, computational problems, and many mathematical problems. Algorithms can be easily converted into computer programs using basic programming constructs such as data structures, conditional statements, loops, and functions.

- Simple modeling approaches such as flow charts are helpful to write algorithms.
- Algorithms' logical sequence of steps can be converted into programs using procedural program languages such as C.
- An algorithm's success mainly depends on its performance. Algorithm performance is usually defined in terms of space and time complexity.
- Developing efficient algorithms is all about reducing space and time complexity. For example, many sorting algorithms have evolved to reduce time complexity from bubble sort ($O(n^2)$) to quick sort ($O(\log n)$). Here, the time complexity is represented in Big O notation to represent the upper bounds of algorithms.
- Algorithms can be developed into programs with smaller teams or individuals.
- Procedural-oriented programming languages (e.g., C) are sufficient to convert algorithms into programs.

Next, let's look at how to write an algorithm and convert it into a program using procedural programming language constructs.

Write an Algorithm

Let's solve a problem related to searching for an element from any given list of elements.

- Input: List of elements (list [0 to n]) and a searching element (key)
- Output: Element found (True), Element not found (False)

1. Index=0
2. Traverse through the list of elements until the list ends.

   Check the following conditions:

   In case key presents in the list:

   return True

   otherwise

   Go to 2:

3. If list ends:

   return False

Now it can be easily converted into any procedural-oriented program constructs such as if-else, for loop, and functions ().

For example, let's write a C function to solve the search problem.

```c
int search(int list [], int n, int key)
{
  int i=0;
  for (i=0;i<n;i++)
  {
    if (list[i] == key)
      return 1;
  }
  return 0;
}
```

CHAPTER 1   THE IMPORTANCE OF OBJECT-ORIENTED PROGRAMMING

You have seen how easy it is to convert a well-defined algorithm into a program using procedural language programming constructs. Next, let's quickly explore software and its characteristics.

Software

Software is evolved to solve a variety of real-world complex problems, which range from system software (editors, compilers, operating systems, databases, protocol stacks, etc.) to application software (e-commerce, online reservations, entertainment software, gaming applications, etc.) and current trending smart applications such as drone applications, IoT, and smart cities.

Unlike well-defined problem-solving using algorithm approaches, software development must follow suitable systematic software engineering procedures and models (e.g., waterfall model, iterative, spiral, and DevOps) to ensure the following features.

- Verifying and validating all requirements of stakeholders
- Reliable in terms of fault tolerance and zero downtime
- Scalable software components to meet the dynamic demands of users
- Flexible software components in terms of making necessary changes or introducing new features
- Extendible software components for producing new versions of the software to meet market needs or introducing innovative features

Besides these features, software success depends on the following.

- How quickly it can be developed and tested
- An easy-to-use interface

CHAPTER 1   THE IMPORTANCE OF OBJECT-ORIENTED PROGRAMMING

- How quickly modifications can be made
- Multiple teams able to work on components in parallel
- Reusable and easily extendible software components

Software Development Challenges

By following suitable software engineering principles and models, it is possible to get all requirements from users involved in using the software. However, translating user requirements into software design blocks is not straightforward. For example, in e-commerce applications, a few basic requirements are that software users should interact with the system easily to browse items, select items into their basket, and place an order.

These requirements cannot be easily translated into software by following algorithm design principles and procedural-oriented programming constructs. Unlike algorithms, software development involves a lot of ambiguity to be dealt with. It is very challenging to completely map all real-world entities, their transactions, and all requirements into software.

You face the following challenges when you want to develop software using algorithm and procedural programming approaches.

- It is highly challenging to model all real-world entities, requirements, and constraints in a limited number of phases.

- It is highly difficult to deal with initial ambiguity (getting ready with initial designs and models) and define logical steps.

- Starting points are not evident in implementing the system components.

- It is difficult to connect software components for integrating the complete system.
- It is difficult to develop scalable, flexible, and extendible software components.
- It is unrealistic development and release deadlines.
- It is unpredictable software success.

Next, you are introduced to OOP concepts and how OOP features are helpful for software development.

Introduction to OOP Concepts

OOP offers excellent features to simplify software development by converting high-level requirements and design processes into software implementation.

- Class
- Data abstraction
- Encapsulation
- Data hiding
- Inheritance
- Polymorphism

Let's go over OOP basic programming constructs called *classes*.

Class

A class is the most important programming construct of the OOP. It helps you easily model any real-world entity (a customer, a drone, or any transactions) into a software block. OOP basic construct called class is defined with its related data (data members or fields) and member functions for accessing its data members. This book uses "data members" and "fields" synonymously. The class structure is shown in Figure 1-1.

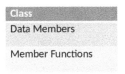

Figure 1-1. *Class structure in OOP*

For instance, customer entities related to an online shopping context can be easily modeled, as shown in Figure 1-2.

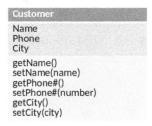

Figure 1-2. *Online shopping application example class: Customer*

Let's inspect the Customer class definition carefully. The data members section includes the customer's name, phone number, and address.

Under the member functions section, you define corresponding access functions for each data member, such as get and set functions. Usually, the "get" member functions are defined to retrieve data members' values, and set member functions are defined to update the values of data members. For example, the City field of the Customer class, getCity(), is useful for retrieving a customer entity's city, and setCity(city) is useful for setting or updating a customer entity's city.

Having the necessary set and get member functions defined in the class, you can later easily include complex online shopping application tasks. For instance, in online shopping applications, customer phone verification and update tasks can be easily done using getPhone#() and setPhone#() member functions. Similarly, other member functions are useful for accessing the respective data of the Customer class.

Next, let's look at another example in a gaming application context: modeling a duck character into software as a class (see Figure 1-3).

Figure 1-3. *Gaming application example class: Duck*

The Duck class includes a duck identifier (id), its location (x,y), and its state (dead or alive). For accessing these data members corresponding set and get member functions are defined inside the class.

Now, checking whether a duck is live or dead can be easily done by accessing the duck state using its getState() member function. Similarly, you can easily track duck position (x,y) using get and set location functions.

Another interesting example of class structure is IoT sensor modeling, as shown in Figure 1-4.

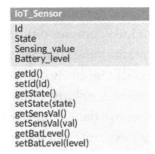

Figure 1-4. *Smart application example class: IoT_Sensor*

The IoT_sensor class includes data members related to the sensor identifier (Id), its State (sensing, sleeping, and dead), Sensing_value, and Battery_level. Under member functions, sections corresponding to set and get functions are defined for accessing the data members.

Suppose you want to keep a particular sensor in a sleep state in your IoT application. It can be easily done by accessing the sensor state using setState(state) member function. Similarly, you can access a sensor's battery status using getBatLevel() and setBatLevel(level) functions.

Besides simplifying modeling real-world entities, classes are powerful programming constructs whose definition captures the following important OOP principles.

Data Encapsulation

If you are an experienced C programmer, you can easily understand structure data type helps you to combine related data elements under a single structure variable. However, you cannot control its data and their related accessing functions together into a structure.

The following is an example.

```
struct customer
{
  char  name[30];
```

```
    int phone;
    char address[30];
};
```

Any function can use `struct customer` variables to change internal data of the customer variable as follows.

```
void function1 (struct customer c1)
{
/* It can access customer data */
}
void function2 (struct customer c1)
{
/* It can access customer data */
}
```

Passing a c1 variable to any C functions, then those functions can change the corresponding `struct customer variable`'s data members. It means you are not able to combine data and their accessing functions. It can lead to no control over the sensitive data of real-world entities.

Interestingly, OOP classes allow you to combine related data and its member functions into a `Class` definition. It is known as data encapsulation. Then, you can model a specific real-world entity from the `class` by creating an object and interacting with the object through `class` member functions.

You can observe their data and respective accessing functions from the example classes—Customer, Duck, and IoT_Sensor. As discussed, tasks related to the corresponding entities can only be done through their class member functions. For example, the `IoT_Sensor` entity's `Sensing_value` access can be changed through its object and class member functions: `setSenseValue()` and `getSenseValue()`.

CHAPTER 1   THE IMPORTANCE OF OBJECT-ORIENTED PROGRAMMING

Data Abstraction

Having encapsulated data types support such as classes in OOP, accessing variables of the complex data types also gets simplified. In your program, you define objects (variables) for the respective Class (complex data type) and invoke necessary member functions from the objects to access their details. For example, to set an IoT sensor state to "sleep," you can easily do it with the following lines of code.

```
IoT_Sensor i1;
i1.setState(2);    // Example, 0: Dead, 1: Sensing, 2: Sleeping.
```

Similarly, you can check whether the duck is alive with the following lines of code.

```
Duck d1;
int state = d1.getState(); //1: Alive 2: Dead
if (state == 2)
  cout<<d1.getId()<<"is dead";
```

To access the IoT_sensor or Duck details, focus on their objects and accessing functions, not their implementation details. You need not know its internal details to access a complex data type.

By checking these examples, you can understand that OOP classes greatly simplify accessing complex entities' data using its related member functions defined inside the class.

Data Hiding

You have observed how to combine class data and its member functions to simplify accessing its objects. Besides these features, the OOP class offers a powerful way to control access to an object's data.

It means controlling objects data members access from the outside of a class. It can be achieved by attaching access control modes (access specifiers) with data and member functions of a class. OOP languages generally offer three access specifiers: public, private, and protected access.

- **Public access**: Data and member functions defined under the public section can be accessed by any function through the respective class objects.
- **Private access**: Data and member functions defined under the private section are allowed to be accessed by only member functions of the class.
- **Protected access**: Data and member functions defined under the protected section are allowed to be accessed by only member functions of the class and its inherited classes.

You have just seen how to limit an object's data access using the OOP access specifiers. Later chapters discuss an object's data access control in detail. Now that you have explored the OOP basic construct class, let's discuss instances and variables of the `class` data type.

Objects

Objects are powerful ways to create software components and implement tasks, transactions, activities, operations, and functions. For example, it is easier to model the real-world entities such as customers and their transactions or related activities as objects to develop an online shopping application.

Object is an instance of a class, it contains data members and member functions. Hence, any interactions related to the object are done through the class member functions.

In OOP, for example, having a `class` defined for customers simplifies online shopping customer entities as `Customer` objects. Then, all the following tasks implementaion gets simplified: registering a customer, updating customer details, and checking customer details by creating and interacting with customer objects.

Moreover, an object's powerful combination with its data and accessing functions helps you easily realize several identical software components.

The following are examples.

- A `Drone` class that creates multiple drones is nothing but defining multiple drone objects.

- A `Robot` class that creates multiple robots is nothing but defining multiple robot objects.

Similarly, think of real-world applications entities modelling such as e-commerce, gaming, and system software.

Objects Details

To understand an object, you can view it as a variable of a particular data type. Similarly, an object is a variable of the `class` data type. In OOP, objects are instances of classes. During program execution, objects are created by allocating necessary memory space for their data member's access.

For example, to create a variable of `int`.

```
int a; // int is data type and a is variable
```

Similarly, in C++, you can create objects from the `Customer` class as follows.

```
Customer c1, c2;
```

During program execution, each of your objects (c1 and c2) memory is allocated in a unique space, as shown in Figure 1-5. It means, one object changes are not visible to another object. An object's memory size depends on its class data members' respective data types.

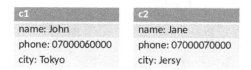

Figure 1-5. *Customer objects: c1 and c2 example memory allocation maps*

Later, during program execution, with the help of a related set and get member functions object's data member can be accessed.

For example, in C++, to retrieve object c1's phone number, you can simply write the following lines of code.

phone_num = c1.getPhone#();

Similarly, you can change object c2's city using the following lines of code.

c2.setCity ("New York");

Only the c2 object's city will be changed in memory, as shown in Figure 1-6.

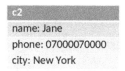

Figure 1-6. *Customer object c2 memory changes after modifying c2 city details*

Next, let's learn how OOP inheritance principles are helpful in the software development process for extending classes with new features to reduce code and development time.

CHAPTER 1   THE IMPORTANCE OF OBJECT-ORIENTED PROGRAMMING

Inheritance

Following OOP inheritance principles greatly simplifies the software development process for extending a software system with new features and reducing time for development by reusing the existing code.

The inheritance feature of OOP allows you to write reusable and extendible classes. For instance, you started developing a cricket players information system. You can start by defining a `Cricket_Player` class as follows for maintaining common details of any cricket player. Later, you can easily extend the `Cricket_Player` class to model `BatsMan`, as shown in Figure 1-7.

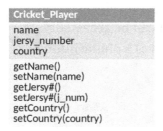 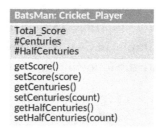

Figure 1-7. *The left side shows the Cricket_Player class. The right side shows the inherited class: BatsMan from Cricket_Player.*

By inheriting the `BatsMan` class from `Cricket_Player`, it gives the following benefits.

- In the `BatsMan` class, you define the details only by extending the `Cricket_Player` class.

  Although you did not include `Cricket_Player` code related to its data members (`name`, `country`, etc.) and member functions (`getName()`, `getCountry()`, etc.), your `BatsMan` gets inherited with `Cricket_Player` data members and member functions code, as shown in Figure 1-8.

CHAPTER 1   THE IMPORTANCE OF OBJECT-ORIENTED PROGRAMMING

Figure 1-8. *Because of inheritance features, the BatsMan class gets inherited with Cricker_Player data members and member functions. It means you need not write the code explicitly while defining the BatsMan object to set the BatsMan name, jersy_number, and country. You can utilize the inherited code from Cricket_Player.*

Inheriting the BatsMan class from the Cricket_Player class means BatsMan objects include Cricket_Player data members, and BatsMan objects can access Cricket_Player member functions code. You can clearly understand it regarding memory allocation for inherited objects and member functions availability to the inherited objects.

- BatsMan object memory allocation includes its fields (Total_Score, #Centuries, #HalfCenturies) and inherited fields (name, jersy_number, and country) of Cricket_Player.

- BatsMan objects are allowed to access its member functions, such as getScore() and setScore(), and inherited member functions, such as getName() and setName(), of Cricket_Player.

Inheritance principles save time in writing and testing code by reusing the existing code. Mainly, inheritance enables easily extending existing classes with new features for implementing a new variety of classes by following all OOP principles. Specifically, you can use private or protected inheritance for the restriction of extending base class features into derived classes.

Usually, OOP languages support many inheritance approaches, such as single-level, multilevel, multiple, and hybrid manners. You can choose a suitable inheritance based on your requirements.

Now that you've discovered the importance of inheritance, let's discuss how to develop a system with common interfaces to simplify access.

Polymorphism

One of the major requirements for making any software successful is offering a minimum number of standard user-accessing interfaces to use the software.

For example, developing a data processing application using the same function name, such as sort(), to arrange data elements of any list simplifies the usage of the application.

Similarly, you developed software for drone control, and you must provide a simple and limited number of standard interfaces for interacting with a drone, such as set_mode(), arm(), load_mission(), simple_goto(), and take_off(). Later, you may need to handle a variety of drones, but you should be able to support these common interfaces for interacting with any drone.

Similarly, to make any gaming software easy to play, it should offer only a minimum number of controls to interact with various game objects. For instance, if a player wants to use a gun, then it must have common interfaces such as aim(), load(), and fire() for interacting with any sophisticated gun.

On the other hand, if you increase many interfaces, you end up offering a long cheat sheet for interactions. Hence, you must minimize the number of interfaces and be able to use common popular interfaces for specialized objects (e.g., advanced drones, sophisticated guns) and normal objects (e.g., simple drones, guns).

To handle these challenges, you need to overload the functions of objects. Using OOP static polymorphism and dynamic polymorphism principles, it is possible to use one name with a variety of function definitions. Hence, polymorphism helps you develop software with a minimal number of interfaces to improve usability. After exploring OOP concepts, let's summarize how OOP concepts and approaches are helpful in software development.

How OOP Approaches Simplify the Software Complexity

You can see the power of OOP approaches in the following major aspects of software development.

- **Simplifies modeling**: Easy to model any real-world problem entities using OOP key constructs such as classes and objects. For instance, you can model simple entities such as customers, users, and students and easily model complex entities such as drones, robots, and IoT devices. You have seen some real-world entity modeling in previous sections.

- **Flexible software development process**: OOP offers greater flexibility and simplicity in terms of the software development process. Key features such as classes, objects, and inheritance allow developers to easily divide the complex problem into independent smaller problems. It enables parallel development and independent testing, making extending and integrating all key software building blocks easier. For example, developing a game application can be done at a rapid speed with multiple teams in parallel by working on modeling and developing various users, enemies, weapons, vehicles, and gaming environment setups.

- **Reusable and extendible software components**: It is easier to produce reusable and extendible software components quickly. OOP inheritance principle enables team members to easily create reusable and extendible software components. Inheritance eliminates the need of writing redundant code, and encourages reuse of the existing code. For instance, to develop employee services applications, developers can eliminate writing a lot of code related to managing personal and professional details, and it also helps in easily extending existing applications for introducing new roles and users in the system.

- **Simplifies integration and connecting software**: OOP association and aggregation principles greatly simplify the integration of software blocks and connecting dots. For example, developing an online shopping application to model customers purchasing an item can be easily modeled by associating the customer and the item objects with a transaction class. On the other hand, modeling a complex IoT device with many sensors can be done easily by aggregating all necessary sensor objects into IoT device classes.

- **Simplifies user interface design**: Fundamentally, interactions with software become complicated when users need to remember a lot of menus, commands, and options. Hence, developers must consider all necessary common interfaces and minimize the number of interfaces in software user interface design. For example, to interact with a document editing application, you use three well-known commands (cut, copy, paste) to alter text, figures, images, tables, and so forth. Similarly, you use minimal keyboard keys such as forward, backward, left, and right arrows to interact with gaming objects and characters. For instance, these options help players interact and control gaming vehicles easily.

By following polymorphism OOP principles, designing software using minimal interfaces for user interactions is possible. Besides, it is possible to define common interfaces for the system to easily remember system interaction options. Knowing the importance of OOP principles, let's start with how to use OOP concepts for modeling real-world entities.

Systematically Modeling Real-World Entities into Software

Let's examine how OOP basic constructs help you deal with the initial ambiguity of modeling real-world problems into a software solution space. Unlike procedural programming approaches (focus on functions), you can systematically model entities of real-world problems into software building blocks using the following high-level procedure.

CHAPTER 1   THE IMPORTANCE OF OBJECT-ORIENTED PROGRAMMING

1. Start by defining the problem scope and context in terms of your software system use cases.

2. Identify users involved with your software system for various tasks and model them as objects for interacting with your proposed software system.

3. Next, list each user's interactions or tasks with the proposed software system. Inspect each user's interactions or tasks with the real-world system in detail to model the basic real-world entities as objects to be considered part of your software system.

   After identifying the basic objects of the proposed software system, you can group similar objects into respective classes.

4 Finally, each class can be modeled as follows by defining the class's data members and member functions.

   a. Identifying class data members

      - The object's data (attributes, fields, characteristics, specifications, and state) needed to carry out transactions or tasks

      - The object's data needed for others (users and objects) from the system to carry out transactions or tasks

   b. Identifying class member functions

      - How others (users or objects) interact with an object to carry out transactions, tasks, or activities

      - Identifying object-specific functions, tasks, roles, and responsibilities

Hands-on Activity: Online Shopping

Let's start by learning how to model various real-world entities of an online shopping application. First, let's define the scope of the hands-on activity.

1. Define the Problem Scope and Context

Any user can browse your shopping application to view a variety of items. However, to buy, cancel, or return items only registered customers can do so. To simplify our discussions, only a cash-on-delivery option is provided for customers.

As part of maintaining shopping items, shopkeepers can only update stock details. All transactions performed in the shop must be registered. After defining the our problem scope and context, identify various users interacting with your online shopping application.

2. Identify and Understand Users

From the problem's description, you can quickly identify the following users interacting with the online shopping application to do transactions or tasks.

- Any user
- Customer
- Shopkeeper

3. List all Users/actors transactions, actions, and tasks

Users will interact with an online shopping application to browse items, and if they are interested, they register with the application to become a customer. Hence, general interactions of a user with an online shopping application are shown in Figure 1-9.

CHAPTER 1   THE IMPORTANCE OF OBJECT-ORIENTED PROGRAMMING

Figure 1-9. *User interactions with the online shopping application*

That means you should model customers as objects in the application. Next, inspect customer's interactions with your online application.

Customers

Customers usually browse items, and place orders for buying items, as shown in Figure 1-10. From the general interactions, you should understand the necessity of modeling items and orders as objects. Then, after placing orders, customers can view their past orders and cancel or return orders. That means you must model canceled and returned order objects, too.

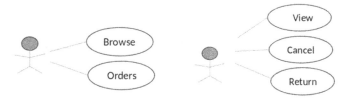

Figure 1-10. *Customer interactions with shopping applications for browsing items, viewing past orders, canceling orders, and returning orders*

Observing user and customer interactions with the application identifies the following objects for modeling the online application.

- Customer
- Item
- Order
- Canceled order

24

> **Note** To simplify the discussion, canceling or returning an order is only modeled as canceled.

Next, let's discuss shopkeeper interactions and check for new objects to be modeled.

Shopkeeper

Usually, the shopkeeper's main role is monitoring and updating item details. Hence, you must model shopkeeper objects in the application. Besides, he/she must check received orders and manage orders for delivery, return, and cancellation. Delivering an order involves modeling a delivery partner. But, to simplify the discussion, let's assume the shopkeeper is a delivery partner. Hence, you do not model delivery partners.

Overall, the shopkeeper interacts with item and order objects.

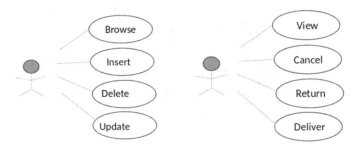

Figure 1-11. *Shopkeepers interact with applications for updating stock details, and managing customer orders*

You can start modeling the following basic objects by inspecting customer and shopkeeper interactions.

- Customer
- Shopkeeper
- Delivery partner

- Item
- Order
- Canceled order
- Delivered order

Next, let's inspect each object and their interaction in detail to model them as classes.

4. Inspect User Interactions for Modeling Classes

Let's start with inspecting customers and shopkeeper tasks or transactions or activities.

Customer Registration

In the online shopping application, customer registration creates a new customer object. The application must maintain a customer profile with all necessary details to deal with a customer transaction. For example, for customer registration, the following minimum details are needed from the customer to authenticate, place, and get orders: name, phone number, city, country, and PIN. After successful customer registration, customers must be assigned a unique identifier.

Customer Class

To focus on modeling basic OOP construct classes, data type details and syntax of member functions are not discussed here. Let's start by identifying a high-level definition of classes to help you easily apply your classes in any OOP language. Now, you can quickly model a customer class (see Figure 1-12) with all the details mentioned earlier. Data members under the data members section define the corresponding set and get member functions for accessing the customer object's data.

CHAPTER 1   THE IMPORTANCE OF OBJECT-ORIENTED PROGRAMMING

Figure 1-12. *Customer class with its data members and member functions*

After defining the Customer class, you can perform programming tasks in an online shopping application using the customer objects' set and get member functions easily. For example, to deliver items to a customer address you can access the specific customer object c1 and get his address details as follows.

```
Customer c1; //Assume c1 is your customer
phone_num = c1.getPhone#();
city = c1.getCity();
pin = c1.getPin();
country = c1.getCountry();
```

Next, let's model the Shopkeeper class.

Shopkeeper Registration

In the online shopping application, shopkeeper registration creates a new shopkeeper object. To deal with shopkeeper transactions, the following minimum details are needed to authenticate and manage stock and orders: name, phone number, city, country, and PIN. After successful shopkeeper registration, he/she must be assigned a unique identifier.

27

CHAPTER 1   THE IMPORTANCE OF OBJECT-ORIENTED PROGRAMMING

Shopkeeper Class

You can model a shopkeeper class (see Figure 1-13) with all the details under the data members section, define the corresponding set, and get member functions for accessing the shopkeeper object's data.

Figure 1-13. *Shopkeeper class with its data members and member functions*

After defining the Shopkeeper class in an online shopping application, you can perform programming tasks using the shopkeeper objects' set and get member functions easily. For example, to allow a shopkeeper to access stock or orders, you need to access a few important details of a shopkeeper as follows.

```
Shopkeeper s1; //Assume s1 is a shopkeeper
phone_num = s1.getPhone#();
sid = s1.getSid();
```

Next, let's model another class called item of your online shopping application.

28

CHAPTER 1   THE IMPORTANCE OF OBJECT-ORIENTED PROGRAMMING

Browsing Items

Customers and shopkeepers usually check item details for accessing item details and order management. That means the application must maintain every item's details for sharing with customers and shopkeepers to manage stock and orders. Usually, customers view item details (name, price, quantity, description) for placing orders, and shopkeepers update item details (quantity, price, description) for managing orders. For example, the following minimum item details must be maintained: Identifier (ID), name, price, quantity, and description.

Item Class

Let's model item class with the item details under the data members section, define the corresponding set and get member functions for accessing item object data in the application (see Figure 1-14).

Figure 1-14. *Item class with its data members and member functions*

After defining the Item class, you can perform programming tasks in an online shopping application using the item objects' set and get member functions. For example, you can easily update an item's quantity to handle order transactions as follows.

CHAPTER 1   THE IMPORTANCE OF OBJECT-ORIENTED PROGRAMMING

```
Item i1; //Assume i1 is needed item object
i1.setQty(2);
```

Next, let's model the order class for recording transactions.

Placing Orders

Customers select items and order from your online shopping application. Your application with the following necessary details, such as order id, customer id, item id, quantity, total cost, and date.

The application must also have an order status to maintain details such as canceled, returned, and delivered.

After defining the Order class (see Figure 1-15), you can perform programming tasks using the order objects' set and get member functions.

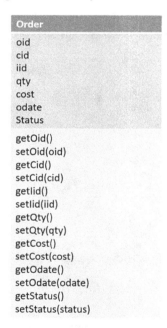

Figure 1-15. *Order class with its data members and member functions*

30

For example, to cancel an order can be done as follows.

```
Order o1; //Assume o1 is your order
o1.setStatus(1); //1 means cancelling the order
```

Next, let's model the canceling order class for the online shopping application development.

Canceling an Order

When a customer changes his mind and cancels an order or returns items, it must be handled by the application to do a refund process. It is modeled as a canceled order and maintains the following details: order id, canceled date, refund amount and refund date.

After defining the `CancelledOrder` class (see Figure 1-16), you can perform programming tasks using its objects' set and get member functions.

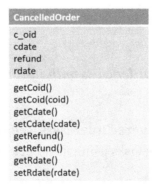

Figure 1-16. *CancelledOrder class with its data members and member functions*

For example, you can set the possible refund amount and expected refund date to process a canceled order.

```
CancelledOrder c1; //Assume o1 is your order
c1.setRefund(10); //10 means dollar
c1.setRdate("12JAN2024"); //Assume date is string
```

Finally, let's model the delivered orders class for the online shopping application development.

Delivering Orders

The shopkeeper checks orders and assigns a delivery partner to deliver customers' successful orders. It must be recorded and modeled as a delivered order as shown in Figure 1-17.

Figure 1-17. *DeliveredOrder class with its data members and member functions*

After defining the `DeliveredOrder` class (see Figure 1-17), you can perform programming tasks using its objects' set and get member functions.

For example, the following provides delivery partner details.

```
DeliveredOrder d1; //Assume o1 is your order
dpid = d1.getDpid();//You can use dpid for further process
```

Well done! You have modeled important classes for an online shopping application. It helps you to quickly start developing your application using any OOP language. To get a little more experience and explore other domains.

Let's model a simple, adventurous game.

CHAPTER 1   THE IMPORTANCE OF OBJECT-ORIENTED PROGRAMMING

Hands-on Activity: Simple Adventurous Game

Let's start by defining the gaming application for this hands-on activity.

1. Define Problem Scope and Context

In the adventurous game world, a player starts from a starting location and explores paths to reach a target location. While the player is moving toward the target location, he faces several challenges from enemies. Moreover, while reaching the game's target, a player or an enemy can grab guns and bombs at various locations and attack each other.

Next, let's quickly identify users or gaming characters involved in our game world and model them as the game objects.

2. Identify and Understand Gaming Characters and 3. Inspect all Users/actors transactions, actions, and tasks

From the problem description, you can easily identify the player and enemy game characters.

In this simple game world, for a player or enemy to reach a target, they must move in various directions, jump over objects, and collect guns and bombs for attack. The only difference between the enemy and the player character is that the game controls the enemy character, and the player character is controlled by whoever plays the game. Hence, you see the following common interactions (see Figure 1-18) for the player or the enemy character.

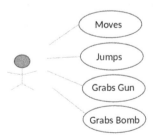

Figure 1-18. *Player or enemy interaction in the gaming application*

33

Two more important objects (guns and bombs) to model for game development have been identified. The player or enemy character can interact with bombs and guns, as shown in Figure 1-19.

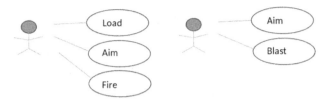

Figure 1-19. *Player or enemy interactions with guns (left) and bombs (right)*

Overall, you need to model the following important objects.

- Player
- Enemy
- Gun
- Bomb

4. Inspect Game Characters and objects Interactions for Modeling Classes

In the game context, a player or enemy character travels through game paths. While traveling, they can find guns, bombs, and vehicles to complete the game. While moving a player or enemy character, their location coordinates, speed, and direction of traveling details needed to be maintained. Besides, as players or enemies can grab guns and bombs, you must maintain their list of guns and bombs collected during the game.

> **Note** To simplify, the game context does not model vehicles.

Hence, you must model the player or enemy character with details such as x, y, speed, direction, guns, and bombs.

Next, let's inspect some player and enemy character actions.

- **Grabs gun**: The player or enemy character can collect and use guns for attack. Hence, you must maintain a list of guns.

- **Grabs bomb**: The player or enemy character can collect and use bombs for attacking. Hence, you must model a list of bombs.

Player and Enemy Classes

After identifying all the interactions of player or enemy characters in the game world, you can model them as classes (see Figure 1-20) with all their transactions needed as data in data members sections and define respective set and get member functions for accessing their data.

CHAPTER 1   THE IMPORTANCE OF OBJECT-ORIENTED PROGRAMMING

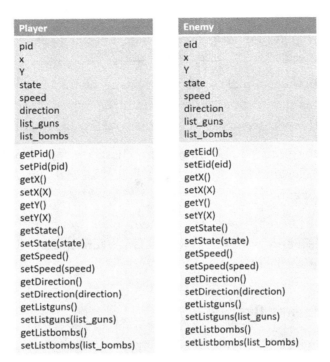

Figure 1-20. *Player and Enemy classes with their data members and member functions*

If you observe the Player class definition, you included a player id to identify a player in the simple game. Similarly, you included an enemy id in the Enemy class. After defining the Player class, you can execute the following task in the game world: moving the player character in a specific direction at a specified speed.

```
Player p1; //Assume p1 is your player
p1.setDirection(1); //1 means North
o1.setSpeed(30); // 30 m/s
```

Similarly, after defining the Enemy class, you can implement the following task: an enemy character grabbing a gun.

```
Enemy e1; //Assume p1 is your player
e1.setListbombs(1); //example: 1 means a new bomb grabbed
```

Well done! You modeled the most important classes of the game world. You may have wondered if there is a lot of redundant code between the Player and Enemy classes. Yes, you are right. You can avoid it using inheritance principles.

Next, let's inspect interactions of players or enemies related to guns and bombs in the game to model gun and bomb classes. Let's start with gun interactions.

- **Load gun**: The player or enemy character can interact with a gun to load bullets. Hence, so you must model the number of bullets.

- **Aim gun**: The player or enemy character can aim at an angle. Hence, you must model the angle.

- **Fire gun**: The player or enemy character can fire a gun. It leads to a reduction in the number of bullets. Hence, you must model the number of bullets.

Now that you've inspected all basic interactions between player and enemy characters with guns, let's model the Gun class in the simple game world.

Gun Class

You can model a gun class as you explore all interactions of player or enemy characters with gun objects and which data is important for respective interaction. In the Gun class, include all details of gun interactions as data members define respective set and get member functions for interacting with gun objects (see Figure 1-21).

CHAPTER 1　THE IMPORTANCE OF OBJECT-ORIENTED PROGRAMMING

Figure 1-21. *Gun class with its data members and member functions*

After defining the Gun class, you can execute the following task: aiming a gun object at a specific angle.

```
Gun g1; //Assume g1 is your gun
g1.setAngle(30); //30 degrees
```

Bomb Class

Let's inspect interactions related to how to use bombs in the game for modeling the Bomb class.

- **Aim bomb**: The player or enemy character can throw a bomb at an angle. Hence, you must model the angle.

- **Blast bomb**: The player or enemy character can blast a bomb. It leads to a change of bomb state from active to inactive. Hence, you must model the state (active or inactive).

As you explore all interactions of player or enemy characters with bomb objects and which data is important for respective interaction, you can model a bomb class. In the Bomb class, you include all details of the bomb's interactions as data members define the respective set and get member functions for interacting with bomb objects (see Figure 1-22).

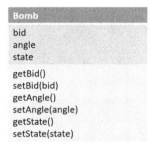

Figure 1-22. *Bomb class with its data members and member functions*

After defining the Bomb class, you can implement the following task: blasting a bomb object at a specific angle.

```
Bomb b1; //Assume g1 is your gun
b1.setAngle(30); //30 degrees
b1.setState(1); //1 means blast
```

Well done! You have completed modeling real-world entities related to simple gaming applications.

Summary

This chapter emphasized the importance of OOP, principles, and concepts of OOP for developing a variety of real-world applications. Specifically, you have learned key programming constructs called classes and objects of the OOP. Then, you saw how to use classes for modeling sample real-world application entities such as customers, players, animals, and IoT sensors. Specifically, by doing hands-on activities related to modeling online shopping and gaming applications, you have systematically modeled the real-world entities of these applications into classes.

Now that you understand the basics of OOP, the next chapter explains it using C++.

CHAPTER 1 THE IMPORTANCE OF OBJECT-ORIENTED PROGRAMMING

Practice: Hands-on Activities

1. Identify users and real-world entities of the following applications.

    a. An online vehicle booking application

    b. An online food-ordering application

    c. An online cinema booking application

2. For each of these applications

    a. Identify each user and real-world entities' interactions.

    b. Identify each user and real-world entity's characteristics/specifications/attributes/fields/state necessary for carrying out tasks.

    c. Draw class diagrams of all users and real-world entities.

3. Identify users and real-world entities of the following gaming applications.

    a. Any racing game

    b. *Super Mario World* game

    c. Any war game

4. For each of these applications

    a. Identify each user and real-world entities' interactions.

    b. Identify each user and real-world entity's characteristics/specifications/attributes/fields/state necessary for carrying out tasks.

    c. Draw class diagrams of all users and real-world entities.

CHAPTER 1   THE IMPORTANCE OF OBJECT-ORIENTED PROGRAMMING

5. Identify users and real-world entities of the following smart applications, which involve smart devices such as drones and IoT sensors.

6. For any smart application

    a. Identify users' and real-world entities' interactions.

    b. Identify each user and real-world entity's characteristics/specifications/attributes/fields/state necessary for carrying out tasks.

    c. Draw class diagrams of all users and real-world entities.

CHAPTER 2

Start Learning OOP Using C++

Chapter 1 discussed OOP principles and concepts for modeling various real-world problem solutions. As part of designing software solutions for online shopping, gaming, and smart applications, you learned how OOP concepts such as classes and objects are helpful to easily map their real-world problems space entities such as customers, items, players, animals, guns, and sensors into software. This chapter teaches C++ programming constructs to easily implement real-world entities and their activities, tasks, transactions, and operations.

C++ is an extension of the C language. It was invented by Bjarne Stroustrup. It supports all C programming features and programming constructs. A variety of popular software is developed using C++, including operating systems, compilers, databases, embedded systems, device drivers, simulation software, and scientific applications. C++ is well known for its simple syntax, performance, and powerful programming constructs for efficiently accessing computing resources such as memory and input-output devices.

This chapter focuses on the necessary C++ programming constructs and how to use them for developing interesting hands-on activities. Hence, before going further in the book, you should have basic C programming

CHAPTER 2 START LEARNING OOP USING C++

knowledge and revisit the necessary programming constructs such as data types, structures, pointers, conditional instructions, loops, and functions. This chapter covers the following topics.

- C++ OOP constructs
- Modeling real-world entities using C++ classes and objects
- Interacting with objects
- Object access control modes

C++ OOP Constructs

As C++ is an extension of C language, it supports all C language features and programming constructs. Before going into C++ details, this book assumes you have basic knowledge of the following C programming constructs.

- C keywords, variables, data types (`int, unsigned, long, char, float, double`), and their ranges
- Comments (`/* */`) and input-output statements (`printf`, and `scanf`)
- Expressions with the following operators: arithmetic (+, -, *, /, %), logical (&&, ||, !), bitwise (&, |, ~), and conditional (? :)
- Conditional instructions (`if, else, switch`) and iterative instructions (`for, while, do-while`)
- Arrays (e.g., `int a[5]`) and structures
- Pointers (`*, ->`) and dynamic memory allocation functions (`malloc()`, and `free()`)

Now, let's start learning C++ specific features and programming constructs.

C++ Specific Programming Constructs

To write any C++ program, you must know the following C++ programming constructs.

- C++ specific keywords and operators
- Input-output statements
- C++ OOP basic constructs
- C++ built-in classes

C++ Specific Keywords

You can quickly understand the vocabulary of C++ programming by knowing the following.

- C++ classes, access specifiers, and inheritance: The following keywords define classes, member functions, and inherited classes in your upcoming programs.

    `class, public, private, protected, friend, virtual, operator`

- C++ dynamic memory and pointers: The following keywords are used for dynamic memory allocation and accessing object fields.

    `new, delete, this`

- C++ specific features: The following keywords utilize special C++ features such as macro functions, generic functions, and handling exceptions.

    `inline, template, try, throw, catch`

Next, let's look at C++ specific operators.

CHAPTER 2   START LEARNING OOP USING C++

C++ Specific Operators

In this section, we will study about important operators related to accessing classes and objects.

- Classes and objects related operators: (:: , . , ->)

    scope resolution operator (::) defines class member functions outside the class.

    To define a getA() function outside of the Sensor class, you can define it as follows.

    ```
    void Sensor :: getA()
    {
    }
    ```

    Object fields or member functions accessing operators: . and ->

    To access a function from the Sensor class using its object s1 and pointer to s1 as follows.

    ```
    Sensor s1;
    Sensor *ptr;
    ptr = &s1;
    S1.getA();
    Ptr->getA();
    ```

- Reference variables related operator: (&)

    A reference variable is defined as an alias of another variable. Once you define a reference variable for a variable, then without passing the address of the original variable, you can simply pass the reference variable to a function for accessing the original variable.

46

CHAPTER 2   START LEARNING OOP USING C++

To define a reference variable in C++, you can do the following.

```
int a=100;
int ref_a = &a;
```

Now you can access a using ref_a.

```
ref_a = ref_a +100; //changes a value to 200.
```

- Dynamic memory allocation and deallocation operators: new and delete

The new operator used for allocating dynamic memory allocation similar to malloc() in C programming. For example, allocate a character buffer of size 100 bytes as follows.

Syntax: datatype pointer_variable = new datatype [size];

```
char *buffer; buffer = new char[100];
```

It allocates 100 bytes of memory block, and the starting address is returned to the buffer pointer.

The delete operator used for releasing dynamically allocated memory similar to free() in C programming.

Syntax: delete pointer_variable;
delete buffer;

- Commenting operators: (// and /* */)

The following are examples.

single line of code commenting:
// c= a+b;

Multiple lines of code commenting:
```
/*
    c = a;
    a = a+1;
*/
```

Input-Output Statements

C++ supports the following programming constructs for handling input and output instructions using C++ built-in input and output stream library (iostream.h).

In C++, input and output instructions are formed using cin object with input operator (>>), and cout object with output operator, respectively.

You can write the following input statements to read inputs into a, b, and c integer variables.

```
int a, float b, char c;
cout<<"Enter values into variables\n";
cin>>a>>b>>c;
```

During program execution, you can observe the following.

```
Enter values into variables
100 10.5 a
```

You can write the following input statements to read inputs into a and b variables.

```
int a, b;
cout<<"Enter values into variable a\n";
cin>>a;
cout<<"Enter values into variable b\n";
cin>>b;
```

During program execution, you can observe the following.

```
Enter values into variable a
100
Enter values into variable b
10.5
```

Similarly, to print values of variables (a, b, and c), you can write the following output statements.

```
cout<<"value of a:"<<a<<" value of b:"<<b<<"value of c:"<<c;
```

During program execution, you can observe the following.

```
value of a:100 value of b: 10.5 value of c: a
```

To output values of variables (a, b, and c) onto a console, you can write the following output statements.

```
cout<<"\nvalue of a:"<<a<<"\nvalue of b:"<<b<<"\nvalue of c:"<<c;
```

During program execution, you can observe the following.

```
value of a:100
value of b: 10.5
value of c: a
```

Next, let's learn C++ basic OOP constructs.

C++ Basic OOP Constructs

This section explains the basic OOP constructs for modeling real-world entities as classes and creating instances (objects) of classes.

- **C++ Classes**
- **C++ Objects**

CHAPTER 2   START LEARNING OOP USING C++

C++ Classes

Let's start with learning the C++ class structure. C++ class declaration contains the following important sections as you see in the syntax of a class:

Syntax of a class.

```
class Class_Name
{
    Access specifier:
        Data members section; (or internal fields)
    Access_specifier:
        Member functions section; (or access functions)
};
```

- **Class**: Class declaration starts with a keyword called class followed by your class name: Class_Name. To apply the OOP principle called *data encapsulation*, C++ classes allow you to define related data members and member functions inside the class.

- **Access specifiers**: Besides OOP principle data encapsulation, C++ classes support data hiding. To implement data hiding, C++ classes support three types of access specifier sections inside the class.

- **Public access specifier**: Class data members and member functions are defined under the public section to allow access from the class member functions and external functions (e.g., main()).

- **Private access specifier**: Class data members and member functions are defined under the private section to only allow access from the class member functions. It means external functions (e.g., `main()`) are not allowed to access the class's `private` members (data members or member functions).

- **Protected access specifier**: Class *data members* and *member functions* are defined under `protected` section to allow access from the class *member functions* and its inherited classes only. It is discussed in more detail in upcoming chapters.

- **Data members section**: Usually, a real-world entity's characteristics, specifications, attributes, and state are modeled as data members (or *internal fields* of a `class`) using necessary data types such as `int`, `char`, `struct`, and so on.

  - Examples include `Customer` (`cid`, `name`, `phone`, etc.), `Gun` (`model`, `bullets`, `range`, etc.).

  - To protect sensitive *data members* of a class, they are defined under the `private` access specifier section.

  - To allow open access to a few class *data members*, they can be defined under the `public` access specifier section.

- **Member functions section**: Under this section, real-world entities' internal fields accessing member functions, real-world entities tasks' related functions, interaction functions, and management or control-related functions are defined. As part of applying abstract data types (ADT) using classes, class member functions play an important role in abstracting class data members. Member functions ensure simple interaction with the class objects from external functions.
  - The following are examples.
    - `Customer` internal fields accessing functions: `getPhone()`, `setPhone()`, etc.
    - Gun interactions/control functions: `load()`, `aim()`, `fire()`, etc.
- To protect secret or sensitive functions, they are defined under the `private` access specifier section. Private functions can be accessed by external functions (e.g., `main()`) only from the `class public` member functions.
- Under the `public` section, open access functions are defined. Public functions are useful for accessing class private members (data members or member functions) from the external functions (e.g., `main()`).
- Member functions can be defined inside or outside of the class.

Let's write an example `Sensor` class by including sample fields and member functions as follows:

Example of a Sensor class declaration.

```
class Sensor
{
    private:
        int sid;
        int sensing_value;
    public:
    //member function defined inside of the class
int getSid()
    {
        return sid;
    }
    //the following functions will be defined outside of
      the class
    int getSenseValue();
    void setSid(int id);
    int setSenseValue(int value);
};
```

After declaring your Sensor class, define its member functions outside the class.

Syntax:
```
Return_type class_name::function_name(arguments)
{
}
int Sensor::getSenseValue()
{
    return sensing_value;
}
void Sensor::setSenseValue(int value)
{
    sensing_value = value;
}
```

```
void Sensor::setSid(int id)
{
    sid = id;
}
```

Let's look at important implementation details related to the Sensor class.

- It combines (encapsulated) sensor objects related data (data members section) and their accessing functions (member functions) inside a `class` called `Sensor`.

- It defines a `Sensor` class with its sensor id (`sid`) and sensing value (`sensing_value`) as data members (or internal fields).

- To protect and hide `sid` and `sensing_value` data members accessing outside the `class`, they are defined under the `private` access specifier section.

- To allow sensor `private` fields access through only the `Sensor` class member functions, it defines `getSid()`, `setSid()`, `getSenseValue()`, `setSenseValue()` access functions. These member functions simplify interaction with `Sensor` class objects.

- Overall, the `Sensor` class follows OOP principles such as data encapsulation, data hiding, and abstracting its data.

Next, let's look at how to create sensor objects and access them in your `main()` code.

C++ Objects

Let's start with creating a sensor object s1 in your main() code, then access it using set functions for setting sensor id and sensing values, and finally output sensor details using get functions as follows.

```
int main()
{
      //Define sensor object s1
      Sensor s1;
      //memory size of objects
      cout<<"Size of object:"<<sizeof(s1)<<"\n";
      //Access s1 object private fields for setting values
         using public set functions
      s1.setSid(100);
      s1.setSenseValue(1);

      //Access s1 object private fields for retrieving values
         using public get functions
      cout<<"Sensor Id"<<s1.getSid()<<"\n";
      cout<<"Sensor Value"<<s1.getSenseValue();
}
```

Before going further, let's review a few important details about your Sensor object s1.

- You define a sensor object like any other data type variable: (Sensor s1).

- When your program execution starts and encounters Sensor s1 instruction, your s1 object is created by allocating necessary memory to provide access to all its internal fields (sid, sensing_value).

- Next, following the OOP principles of data hiding and data abstraction, you accessed s1 internal private fields (data members: sid, sensing_value) using public member functions (set and get functions).

Next, as part of *modeling multiple real-world entities*, let's review how simple it is to create multiple objects and an array of objects.

```
int main()
{
      //Define multiple sensor objects: s1 and s2
      Sensor s1, s2;
      //Define array of sensor objects
      Sensor s[10];
      //To access array of objects, you can follow the simple
        C array accessing rules as follows:
      for( int i=0; i<10; i++)
      {
           s[i].setSid(i+1);
           s[i].setSenseValue(i);
      }
      //To access array of objects, you can follow the simple
        C array accessing rules as follows:
      for( int i=0; i<10; i++)
      {
           cout<<"Sensor Id"<<s[i].getSid()<<"\n";
           cout<<"Sensor Value"<<s[i].getSenseValue();
      }
}
```

Let's look at a few important details related to Sensor objects s1, s2, and s[10].

CHAPTER 2 START LEARNING OOP USING C++

- You defined two sensor objects: `s1` and `s2`.

- When your program execution starts, then for `s1` dedicated memory is allocated for all its internal fields (`sid, sensing_value`).

- Similarly, for `s2` dedicated memory is allocated for all its internal fields (`sid, sensing_value`). However, `s2` memory need not be allocated next to `s1`.

- Whereas array of objects: `s[10]`, dedicated memory blocks are allocated for ten objects. Moreover, all these memory blocks are allocated in a sequential order. Hence, the array of objects can be accessed using their corresponding index.

- Hence, for accessing each object `s[i]` (dedicate memory), a simple loop to set or get their internal fields (`sid, sensing_value`) using `s[i]` object and its member functions are used.

Next, as part of understanding how easy to use C++ classes and their objects for various tasks, let's get to know a few of the built-in classes.

C++ Built-in Classes

Handling text data and dynamic arrays is important in the upcoming hands-on activities. As part of simplifying our programming discussions and focusing on learning OOP principles, let's discuss the two important C++ built-in classes: `string` and `vector`.

C++ String Class

A string is a sequence of characters. Strings are very helpful for processing text data in your applications. In C language, you handle strings-related tasks with the help of character arrays. However, managing and accessing

CHAPTER 2 START LEARNING OOP USING C++

character arrays is difficult when their size is dynamic. In C++, you can use the string class available in the C++ library called string.h to simplify text processing-related operations such as inserting characters, deleting characters, and modifying characters. Let's inspect the following tasks related to the string class and its accessing functions.

Declare and initialize a string object in C++ as follows.

```
string buffer = "hands-on approach for learning stings";
```

Reading string object values using cin.

```
string buffer;
getline(cin,buffer);
```

Concatenate two strings.

```
string buffer1 = "Hello";
string buffer2 = " C++ programmer";
string buffer3 = buffer1+buffer2;
cout<<buffer3;
```

When you test these lines of code in main(), it outputs the following.

```
Hello C++ programmer
```

Insert a character at the end of a string object using its member function push_back().

```
string buffer1 = "hello";
buffer1.push_back('a');
cout<<buffer1;
```

When you test these lines of code in main(), it outputs the following.

```
helloa
```

Delete a character from the end of the string object buffer1 using its member function pop_back().

```
buffer1.pop_back();
cout<<buffer1;
```

When you test these lines of code in main(), it outputs the following.

```
hello
```

Replace a character in a string object buffer1 using its member function replace().

```
Replace the first character with 'H':
buffer1.replace(0,1,'H');
cout<<buffer1;
```

When you test these lines of code in main(), it outputs the following.

```
Hello
```

Swap two strings using a string object swap() member function.

```
string buffer1 = "hello";
string buffer2 = "hai";
buffer1.swap(buffer2);
cout<<"Buffer1:"<<buffer1<<" Buffer2:"<<buffer2;
```

When you test these lines of code in main(), it outputs the following.

```
Buffer1: hai Buffer2: hello
```

To find the length of a string using its length() member function.

```
string buffer1 = "hello";
cout<<buffer1.length();
```

When you test these lines of code in main(), it outputs the following.

```
5
```

There are many useful member functions available with string class. Next, let's quickly check the C++ built-in vector class and its member functions.

C++ Vector Class

The C++ vector class helps create dynamic generic arrays of any data type (int, char, struct, class). The vector class is available in a C++ library called vector.h. Let's inspect the following tasks related to vectors.

Declare a vector object vint to hold an integer element in C++ as follows.

```
vector<int> vint;
```

Then, you can use the vector object vint in your program for inserting and displaying values using array accessing.

```
vector<int> vint;
for (int i=0;i<3;i++)
{
    int input;
    cin >> input;
    vint.push_back(input);
    cin>>vint[i];
}
for (int i=0; i<vint.size(); i++)
{
    cout<<vint[i];
```

When you test these lines of code in main(), entering three values (10, 20, 30) into vector vint outputs the following.

```
10 20 30
```

You can also try to use the following member functions on vint.

CHAPTER 2 START LEARNING OOP USING C++

Insert an element at the end of the vint object using its member function called push_back().

vint.push_back(123);

When you test these lines of code in main(), it inserts 123 at the end of the vector vint. You can observe that the vint object contains the following values: 10 20 30 123.

Insert an element at the beginning of the vint object using its member function called insert().

vint.insert(vint.begin(), 5);

When you test these lines of code in main(), it inserts 123 at the end of the vector object vint. You can observe that the vint object contains the following values: 5 10 20 30 123.

Delete an element from the end of the vint using its member function called push_back().

vint.pop_back();

When you test these lines of code in main(), it deletes 123 from the end of the vector object vint. You can observe that the vint object contains the following values: 5 10 20 30.

Delete an element from the beginning of the vint.

vint.erase(vint.begin());Is this vint here?

When you test these lines of code in main(), it deletes 5 from the beginning of the vector. You can observe that the vint object contains the following values: 10 20 30.

Similarly, you can also declare vector of objects in C++ as follows.

vector<Sensor> vsen;

Insert a sensor object at end of the vsen.

61

```
Sensor s1;
vsen.push_back(s1);
```

Delete an element from the end of vsen.

```
vsen.pop_back();
```

There are many useful member functions available with vector class. As part of a simple discussion, only the basic functions are introduced.

Moreover, there are many C++ built-in classes available for your use. I recommend you explore these after completing the first five chapters of the book. Table 2-1 provides information on the requirements to perform the hands-on activities in this book.

Table 2-1. Minimal Test Environment for Hands-on Activities

Parameter	Details
Hardware configuration	8GB RAM
	64-bit, i5 core
Operating System	Ubuntu 20.04
Compiler	g++
Editor	vim

Next, let's learn how to write a common C++ program and test it.

C++ Program Structure

To write a simple C++ program you usually do the following steps.

- Include all necessary header files
- Declare a namespace for usage
- Declare your classes

CHAPTER 2   START LEARNING OOP USING C++

- Define member functions of the classes
- Write your main() testing code

For example, C++ program please check the following code.

```
//1. Header files
#include <iostream>
#include <string>
//2. namespace declaration
Using namespce std;
//3. Class declration
class Sensor
{
      private:
            int id;
            string name;
      public:
            void setId(int sid);
            void setName(string sname);//is this string here?
            int getId();
};
//4. Define its member functions
void Sensor::setId(int sid)
{
      id = sid;
}
void Sensor::setName(string n)
{
      name = n;
}
```

```
int Sensor::getId()
{
    return id;
}
//5. Define your main() testing code
int main()
{
    Sensor s1;
    s1.setId(100);
    s1.setName("Temprature");
    cout<<"Your sensor id is: "<<s1.getId()<<"\n";
    return 0;
}
```

After writing the code, save it with a program name such as *example.cc*. Then, test it using the following commands.

Compile and link your code using the following command:
`# g++ example.cc -o example`
Execute or run your code using the following command:
```
# ./example
Your sensor id is: 100
```

Next, let's practice OOP by modeling real-world entities using C++.

Model Real-World Entities Using C++ Classes

In this chapter, you practice implementing a variety of real-world entities using C++ classes with data members and member functions. This helps you follow OOP principles such as data encapsulation, hiding, and creating real-world entities as abstract data types. This section covers the following.

CHAPTER 2   START LEARNING OOP USING C++

- Practicing online shopping applications related to real-world entities.

  - Create a `Customer` class with all example registration details as data members with suitable access specifiers. Then, implement customer objects internal fields accessing member functions for online shopping related transactions.

  - Model an `Item` class with all example item specifications for keeping it in an online shopping application. Then, implement item objects' internal fields accessing member functions for online shopping-related transactions.

- Practicing gaming applications–related entities.

  - Create an `Animal` class to model gaming animal characters with necessary characteristics as data members with suitable access specifiers. Then, implement animal objects, such as interactions or access functions for gaming tasks.

  - Create a `Gun` class to model gaming gun objects with necessary specifications as data members with suitable access specifiers. Then, implement gun objects as example interaction functions for gaming tasks.

Let's start with the following hands-on activity to model a customer class related to online shopping applications.

CHAPTER 2   START LEARNING OOP USING C++

MODELING A CUSTOMER CLASS

Model a `Customer` class related to online shopping applications to implement customer objects and their transactions.

1. Using C++ classes, declare your `Customer` class by including necessary `private` data members (or fields, such as id, name, phone number, and address details) for registration activities. Then, in the `public` section, declare customer details accessing functions such as get and set member functions as follows.

```cpp
#include<iostream>
#include<string.h>
using namespace std;
class Customer
{
    string cid;
    string name;
    char phone[11];
    string city;
    string country;
    unsigned int pin;
    public:
        string getCid();
        void setCid(string id);
        string getName();
        void setName(string cname);
        char* getPhone();
        void setPhone(char cphone[11]);
        string getCity();
        void setCity(string ccity);
        string getCountry();
```

CHAPTER 2   START LEARNING OOP USING C++

```
        void setCountry(string ccountry);
        unsigned int getPin();
        void setPin(unsigned int pin);
};
```

2. Outside the `class`, create a suitable set and get `public` member functions for accessing necessary `private` fields of the `Customer` class from the external function such as `main()`. Public set and get member functions help you to access customer objects' `private` fields, such as phone and `city` to execute tasks related to checking and updating customer details from external functions such as `main()`.

```
string Customer::getCid()
{
    return cid;
}
void Customer::setCid(string id)
{
    cid = id;
}
string Customer::getName()
{
    return name;
}
void Customer::setName(string cname)
{
    name = cname;
}
char* Customer::getPhone()
{
    return phone;
}
```

CHAPTER 2　START LEARNING OOP USING C++

```cpp
void Customer::setPhone(char cphone[11])
{
    strcpy(phone, cphone);
}
string Customer::getCity()
{
    return city;
}
void Customer::setCity(string ccity)
{
    city = ccity;
}
string Customer::getCountry()
{
    return country;
}
void Customer::setCountry(string ccountry)
{
    country = ccountry;
}
unsigned int Customer::getPin()
{
    return pin;
}
void Customer::setPin(unsigned int cpin)
{
    pin = cpin;
}
```

Well done. You have successfully defined a `Customer` class for handling customer registration activities in online shopping applications. Next, let's model an item class related to online shopping applications.

MODELING AN ITEM CLASS

Model another interesting `class`: `Item` related to online shopping applications to implement item objects and their related transactions.

1. Declare your `Item` class by including necessary `private` data members (or fields) for handling tasks related to items browsing (id, name, description, price) and stock maintenance (quantity). Then, in the `public` section, declare items internal fields accessing functions such as get and set member functions as follows.

```
#include<iostream>
#include<string.h>
using namespace std;
class Item
{
    string iid;
    string name;
    unsigned int price;
    unsigned int qty;
    string descr;
    public:
        string getIid();
        void setIid(string id);
        string getName();
        void setName(string iname);
        unsigned int getPrice();
        void setPrice(unsigned int iprice);
        unsigned int getQty();
        void setQty(unsigned int iqty);
```

```
            string getDescr();
            void setDescr(string idescr);
    };
```

2. Outside the class, create a suitable set and get public member functions for accessing Item objects' private fields, such as price and qty. It helps implement tasks related to online shopping, such as retrieving item details, checking the availability of items, and updating stock details from external functions such as main().

```
string Item::getIid()
{
    return iid;
}
void Item::setIid(string id)
{
    iid = id;
}
string Item::getName()
{
    return name;
}
void Item::setName(string iname)
{
    name = iname;
}
unsigned int Item::getPrice()
{
    return price;
}
void Item::setPrice(unsigned int iprice)
{
```

```
        price = iprice;
    }
    unsigned int Item::getQty()
    {
        return qty;
    }
    void Item::setQty(unsigned int iqty)
    {
        qty = iqty;
    }
    string Item::getDescr()
    {
        return descr;
    }
    void Item::setDescr(string idescr)
    {
        descr = idescr;
    }
```

Well done. You have created another interesting class of online shopping applications. Similarly, you can revisit Chapter 1 and identify interesting classes. Next, let's model gaming application classes such as animals and guns.

MODELING AN ANIMAL CLASS

Model an interesting class Animal related to a **game application** to model a variety of Animal objects and their related interactions.

1. Declare your Animal class by including necessary private data members (or fields: animal name, location of the animal, and characteristics such as speed) and their gaming interaction functions in the public section as follows.

```
#include<iostream>
#include<string.h>
using namespace std;
class Animal
{
    string name;
    int angle;
    int speed;
    int x,y;
    public:
        string getName();
        void setName(string aname);
        int getAngle();
        void setAngle(int aangle);
        int getSpeed();
        void setSpeed(int aspeed);
        int getX();
        void setX(int ax);
        int getY();
        void setY(int ay);
};
```

2. Outside the `class`, create suitable animal interactions using set and get public member functions for accessing animal locations (x, y), and speed for gaming interactions. For example, you can implement gaming tasks such as checking whether an animal is in a location and interacting with animals to change their speed from external functions such as `main()`.

```
string Animal::getName()
{
    return name;
}
```

```cpp
void Animal::setName(string aname)
{
    name = aname;
}
int Animal::getAngle()
{
    return angle;
}
void Animal::setAngle(int aangle)
{
    angle = aangle;
}

int Animal::getSpeed()
{
    return speed;
}
void Animal::setSpeed(int aspeed)
{
    speed = aspeed;
}
int Animal::getX()
{
    return x;
}
void Animal::setX(int ax)
{
    x = ax;
}
int Animal::getY()
{
    return y;
}
```

CHAPTER 2   START LEARNING OOP USING C++

```
void Animal::setY(int ay)
{
    y = ay;
}
```

Well done. You have created an `Animal` class related to gaming applications. Next, model a gaming application related to weapons such as guns.

MODELING A GUN CLASS

Model a Gun class related to a **game application** to model various Gun objects and their related interactions.

1. Declare your Gun class by including necessary `private` data members (or fields) for keeping guns at specific locations, identifying guns, and describing gun specifications. And declare gun object interaction functions in the `public` section as follows.

```cpp
#include<iostream>
#include<string.h>
using namespace std;
class Gun
{
    string model;
    int angle;
    int bullets;
    int x,y;
    public:
        string getModel();
        void setModel(string model);
        int getAngle();
        void setAngle(int gangle);
```

```
        int getBullets();
        void setBullets(int gbullets);
        int getX();
        void setX(int gx);
        int getY();
        void setY(int gy);
        void fire(int angle, int speed);
};
```

2. Outside the `class`, create suitable Gun object interactions using public member functions: set and get for keeping guns at specific locations, loading bullets, and so on. These functions help carry out gaming application interactions, such as attacking and firing guns from external functions such as `main()`.

```
string Gun::getModel()
{
    return model;
}
void Gun::setModel(string gmodel)
{
    model = model;
}
int Gun::getAngle()
{
    return angle;
}
void Gun::setAngle(int gangle)
{
    angle = gangle;
}
int Gun::getBullets()
```

```
{
    return bullets;
}
void Gun::setBullets(int gbullets)
{
    bullets = gbullets;
}
int Gun::getX()
{
    return x;
}
void Gun::setX(int gx)
{
    x = gx;
}
int Gun::getY()
{
    return y;
}
void Gun::setY(int gy)
{
    y = gy;
}
void Gun::fire (int gangle, int speed)
{
    angle = gangle;
    bullets = bullets-speed;
}
```

Well done. You have developed Animal and Gun classes related to gaming applications. Similarly, you can revisit Chapter 1 and identify interesting gaming classes.

Superb. You have practiced developing real-world entity classes using C++. Next, let's interact with objects of the respective classes to carry out interesting tasks or activities.

Interacting with Objects

This section describes how to interact with objects for the following example activities.

- Registering customer details, then interacting with custom objects for important transactions such as retrieving phone numbers and updating their address.

- Add new items to your shopping application, then interact with item-specific objects to check availability, update prices, and so forth.

- As part of developing a game, model any animal character and interact with them to know its location, change its speed, and so on. Similarly, model gun objects and interact with them for loading bullets, and firing your gun objects.

INTERACT WITH CUSTOMER OBJECTS

1. Let's do the following example tasks to develop an online shopping application.

    a. Copy the `Customer` class and its member functions defined in the previous section, and save it in a `customer.cc` file for implementing and testing the following tasks.

    b. Register a customer.

c. Retrieve specific customer details such as phone number and city.

d. Update customer phone number and address details.

2. To carry out these activities, you interact with `Customer` class objects as follows in your `main()` program.

```
int main()
{
    cout<<"Creating a customer object and setting all its field with suitable values:\n";
    Customer c1;
    c1.setCid("Customer1");
    c1.setName("John");
    char phone[11];
    strcpy(phone,"9000080000");
    c1.setPhone(phone);
    c1.setCity("Delhi");
    c1.setCountry("India");
    c1.setPin(500001);
    cout<<"Customer1 registered successfully and object name: c1\n";

    cout<<"Retrieve Customer1 (c1) Phone number and City details:\n";
    cout<<"Customer Phone Number:"<<c1.getPhone()<<"\n";
    cout<<"Customer City:"<<c1.getCity()<<"\n";

    cout<<"Update Customer1 (c1) Phone number and Address details:\n";

    strcpy(phone,"9089089080");
    c1.setPhone(phone);
```

CHAPTER 2 START LEARNING OOP USING C++

```
       cout<<"Customer Updated Phone Number:"<<c1.
       getPhone()<<"\n";

       cout<<"Customer Pin Number:"<<c1.getPin()<<"\n";
       c1.setPin(500002);
       cout<<"Customer Updated Pin Number:"<<c1.
       getPin()<<"\n";
       return 0;
   }
```

3. Test your code using g++ compiler and observe the following.

   a. Registering customer object name (c1)

   b. Fetching customer (c1) details

   c. Updating customer (c1) details

   ```
   # g++ customer.cc -o customer_obj_interactions
   # ./customer_obj_interactions
   ```

   Creating a customer object and setting all its field with suitable values:
   Customer1 registered successfully and object name: c1
   Retrieve Customer1 (c1) Phone number and City details:
   Customer Phone Number:9000080000
   Customer City:Delhi
   Update Customer1 (c1) Phone number and Address details:
   Customer Updated Phone Number:9089089080
   Customer Pin Number:500001
   Customer Updated Pin Number:500002

Well done. You have successfully tested your `Customer` class by implementing the tasks given in the hands-on activity.

Next, let's interact with your `Item` class to carry out important activities of online shopping applications.

INTERACT WITH ITEM OBJECTS

1. As part of developing an online shopping application, let's do the following example tasks related to **items**.

    a. Copy the Item class and its member functions defined in the previous section and save it in the items.cc file for implementing and testing the following tasks.

    b. Add a new item into stock.

    c. Browse item details.

    d. Check item availability.

    e. Update item price.

2. To carry out these activities, you interact with Item class objects as follows in your main() program.

```
int main()
{
    cout<<"Adding a new item:\n";
    Item i1;
    i1.setIid("Item1");
    i1.setName("Shirt");
    i1.setPrice(1000);
    i1.setQty(10);
    i1.setDescr("Fashion product");
    cout<<"New item added and its object is:i1 \n";

    cout<<"Browsing a specific item (i1) details:\n";
    cout<<"Item Name:"<<i1.getName()<<"\n";
    cout<<"Item Price:"<<i1.getPrice()<<"\n";
    cout<<"Item Qty:"<<i1.getQty()<<"\n";
```

CHAPTER 2   START LEARNING OOP USING C++

```
        cout<<"Checking item availability:\n";
        if (i1.getQty() > 0)
        {
            cout<<"Item (i1) is available\n";
        }

        cout<<"Updating item (i1) price:\n";
        cout<<"Item\'s increased Price:"<<i1.
        getPrice()<<"\n";
        return 0;
    }
```

3. Test your main() code and observe the following.

    a. Newly added item object name

    b. Item details

    c. Item availability

    d. Updating item price

    g++ items.cc -o item_interactions
    ./item_interactions
    Adding a new item:
    New item added and its object is:i1
    Browsing a specific item (i1) details:
    Item Name:Shirt
    Item Price:1000
    Item Qty:10
    Checking item availability:
    Item (i1) is available
    Updating item (i1) price:
    Item's increased Price:1200

Well done. You have successfully tested your Item class by implementing the tasks given in the hands-on activity.

CHAPTER 2   START LEARNING OOP USING C++

Next, let's interact with gaming application classes to develop interesting gaming world-related activities.

INTERACT WITH ANIMAL OBJECTS

1. To develop gaming world characters, let's interact with an animal object for the following activities.

    a. Copy the Animal class and its member functions defined in the previous section, and save it in an animal.cc file for implementing and testing the following tasks.

    b. Create an animal object (a1) for modeling the cheetah character.

    c. Check a particular location to determine whether your cheetah (a1) is there.

    d. Interact with your cheetah object (a1) to check whether it can jump.

    e. Interact with a cheetah object to change its running speed.

2. To carry out these activities, interact with Animal class objects as follows in your main() program.

```
int main()
{
    Animal a1;
    a1.setName("Cheetah");
    a1.setAngle(45);
    a1.setSpeed(50);
    a1.setX(100);
    a1.setY(100);
    cout << "Your cheetah object name a1\n";
```

```cpp
        cout<<"Let's check at 0,0 any animal is there\n";
        int x=a1.getX();
        int y=a1.getY();
        if (x==0 && y==0)
        {
            cout<<"Careful there is an animal\n";
        }
        else
        {
            cout<<"No! But, near far there is an animal\n";
        }

        cout<<"Let's check Animal can jump\n";
        if (a1.getAngle()>0)
        {
            cout<<"Oh! Animal can jump over you!\n";
        }
        else
        {
            cout<<"It cannot jump. But careful!\n";
        }

        cout<<"Change animal running speed\n";
        a1.setSpeed(70);
        cout<<"Animal is running at high speed
        "<<a1.getSpeed()<<"Kmph Careful\n";

        return 0;
    }
```

3. Test your Animal objects and observe the following.

    a. Your cheetah character object name (a1)

    b. Check a particular location to see if your cheetah (a1) is present.

c. Check if the cheetah (a1) can jump or not.

d. Observe the cheetah's (a1) running speed.

```
# g++ animal.cc -o animal_interactions
# ./animal_interactions
```
Your cheetah object name a1
Let's check at 0,0 any animal is there
No! But, near far there is an animal
Let's check Animal can jump
Oh! Animal can jump over you!
Change animal running speed
Animal is running at high speed 70Kmph Careful

Well done. You have completed your gaming application Animal class.

Next, let's interact with another gaming application class Gun for implementing interesting activities related to the gaming world.

INTERACT WITH GUN OBJECTS

1. As part of creating a game world, you need to model various weapons. Let's model and interact with a Gun object.

    a. Copy the Gun class and its member functions defined in the previous section, and save it in a gun.cc file for implementing and testing the following tasks.

    b. Create a Gun object (g1), load it with 100 bullets, and keep it at location (10,10).

    c. Check a particular location. Is there any Gun?

    d. If you find your Gun object g1, fire it until the bullets are there.

    e. While firing, set a specific angle and speed for your Gun object (g1).

CHAPTER 2 START LEARNING OOP USING C++

2. To carry out these activities, you interact with Gun class objects as follows in your main() program.

```
int main()
{
    cout<<"Place a gun at 10,10 location with 100 bullets\n";

    Gun g1;
    g1.setModel("HiFi");
    g1.setX(10);
    g1.setY(10);
    g1.setBullets(100);

    cout<<"check is there any gun at your location then fire it at speed 10 bullets/sec\n";

    int x=g1.getX();
    int y=g1.getY();

    if (x!=0 && y!=0)
    {
        cout<<"There is a gun\n";
        while (1)
        {
            g1.fire(10,10);
            cout<<"Firing at angle 10 ...\n";
            if (g1.getBullets()<=0)
            {
                cout<<"Oh! No bullets\n";
                break;
            }
```

CHAPTER 2 START LEARNING OOP USING C++

```
        }
      }
      return 0;
}
```

3. Test your Gun objects and observe the following.

   a. Observe the Gun object (g1) location.

   b. Check for Gun object (g1) availability.

   c. Firing details.

   d. No more bullets warning message.

```
# g++ gun.cc -o gun_interactions
# ./gun_interactions
```
Place a gun at 10,10 location with 100 bullets
check is there any gun at your location then fire it at
speed 10 bullets/sec
There is a gun
Firing at angle 10 ...
Firing at angle 10 ...
Firing at angle 10 ...
..

Firing at angle 10 ...
Oh! No bullets

Well done. You have successfully developed your gaming application Gun class.

In this section, you learned to implement real-world entities as classes and interact with their objects.

Next, let's learn how to hide the private data of real-world entities and protect their objects' access from external functions.

CHAPTER 2   START LEARNING OOP USING C++

Object Access Control Modes

In the previous section, you learned how to interact with objects to perform application tasks. You observed that it is common to access objects' internal data and access functions from external functions such as `main()`. That means external functions can change objects' data and objects behavior. When you do not control an object's sensitive data access, there are huge chances for corrupting or misusing the application. Hence, you must know how to control objects' internal data and access functions. As part of this, class internal fields are usually defined under the `private` section and accessing functions under the `public` section. Next, let's discuss the importance of `public` and `private` sections for controlling objects' internal details access.

C++ provides three access specifiers to control an object's internal data members (fields) and accessing functions.

- **Public**: Public access specifier offers open access to class data members and member functions using the class objects. Usually, the `public` section defines member functions such as set and get functions such as `getPhone()`, `setPrice()`, and `setBullets()` for providing access to class `private` data members and member functions from external functions.

    - The `public` access functions definition helps you to impose necessary constraints or conditions to check implementation before accessing class private data members.

    - Under this section, you usually define only accessing functions.

87

- In summary, public member functions of a class are the gate pass to access private data members and member functions of the class.

  For example.

  ```
  Class ABC
  {
        public:
        int a;
        int getA()
        {
              return a;
        }
  };
  int main()
  {
        ABC obj;
        obj.a = 10;
        obj.getA();
        return 0;
  }
  ```

  Here, you can observe that the main() function is accessing public field a and getA() using the obj of class ABC directly.

- **Private**: Data hiding is the one important principle of OOP. You attach private access specifiers to class data members or member functions to achieve it at class level. Usually, all sensitive data members are defined under the private section. For example, customers phone number, item price, bullets of guns, animals speed, and sensors sensing values. Private data members or member functions of a `class` cannot be accessed using objects of the class.

- Access to private data members or member functions of a class must be through public member functions only.

- C++ also supports `friend` functions to access a class's private fields or member functions. It is discussed in upcoming chapters.

- Overall, accessing a class's private data or member functions is through only public member or friend functions.

```
Class ABC
{
      private:
            int a;
      public:
            int getA()
            {
                  return a;
            }
};

int main()
{
      ABC obj;
      obj.a = 10; //Not allowed
      obj.getA(); //Allowed
}
```

CHAPTER 2   START LEARNING OOP USING C++

> Here, you can observe that the `main()` function can access the private field using only the public access function `getA()` from the `obj` of `class ABC`. However, `main()` cannot change the private field a using the object `obj`.

- **Protected**: It is a special access specifier for inheritance implementation in OOP. This is discussed in upcoming chapters.

Next, let's discuss the importance of data hiding in C++ by comparing it with the C programming approach.

ACCESS CONTROL WITH C OBJECTS

1. Let's test whether the C `structure` offers access control to its data members by doing the following activities.

    a. Save the following task code in `iot_sensor_def_caccess.cc`.

    b. Define a C `structure` to model `IoTSensor` with the important fields such as `id`, `sense_value`, and `battery_level`.

    c. Define a C function to change the `IoTSensor` structure variables inside an external function called `ChangeSensor`.

    ```cpp
    #include<iostream>
    #include<string>
    #include<vector>
    #include <bits/stdc++.h>
    using namespace std;
    struct cIoTSensor
    {
        int id;
        float sense_value;
    ```

```
        int battery_level;
};
void ChangeSensor(cIoTSensor &cs1)
{
    cs1.id = -1;
    cs1.sense_value = 0.0;
    cs1.battery_level = -1;
}
```

2. Define the `main()` testing code to do the following activities.

    a. Create a `cIoTSensor` structure variable and assign values to its internal fields.

    b. Check configured values by printing `cIoTSensor` structure variable internal fields.

    c. Try to configure invalid values to the `cIoTSensor` variable and print them.

    ```
    int main()
    {
        cIoTSensor c1;
        c1.id = 1;
        c1.sense_value = 0.01;
        c1.battery_level = 90;

        cout<<"From an external function: main()\n";
        cout<<"Configuring valid values for data members
        of IoTSensors  using C structure variable\n ";
        cout<<"Id: "<<c1.id<<" Sense Value "<<c1.
        sense_value<<" Battery Level "<<c1.battery_
        level<<"\n";
    ```

```
            cout<<"From an external function: ChangeSensor\n";
            cout<<"Trying to Configure invalid values for
            data members of IoTSensors using C structure
            variable\n ";
            ChangeSensor(c1);
            cout<<"Id: "<<c1.id<<" Sense Value "<<c1.
            sense_value<<" Battery Level "<<c1.battery_
            level<<"\n";

            return 0;
        }
```

3. Test your code and observe the following.

    a. Your main() code can set suitable values to the cIoTSensor variable.

    b. The external function ChangeSensor successfully sets invalid values to c structure cIoTSensor internal fields.

    ```
    # g++ iot_sensor_def_caccess.cc -o c_access
    # ./c_access
    From an external function: main()
    Configuring valid values for data members of
    IoTSensors  using C structure variable
    Id: 1 Sense Value 0.01 Battery Level 90
    From an external function: ChangeSensor
    Trying to Configure invalid values for data members
    of IoTSensors using C structure variable
    Id: -1 Sense Value 0 Battery Level -1
    ```

The results show that C structure internal fields can be accessed from any external functions without any control.

Next, let's learn how to hide private data of real-world entities and protect their objects' access from external functions.

CHAPTER 2 START LEARNING OOP USING C++

ACCESS CONTROL WITH C++ OBJECTS

1. Let's experiment with C++ access control for protecting its internal data members by doing the following activities.

    a. Save the following task code in iot_sensor_def_cppaccess.cc.

    b. Define a C++ class to model IoTSensor with the important fields (data members) such as id, sense_value, and battery_level. Define all data members under the private access control section.

    c. Declare all necessary set and get functions under the public section for accessing IoTSensor internal private fields.

```
#include<iostream>
#include<string>
#include<vector>
#include <bits/stdc++.h>
using namespace std;

class IoTSensor
{
    private:
        int id;
        float sense_value;
        int battery_level;
        void setSenseValue(float val);
    public:
        void setId(int sen_id);
        int getId();
        float getSenseValue();
        void setBatteryLevel(int level);
        int getBatteryLevel();
};
```

93

d. Define setId public access function for setting private field: id of IoTSensor objects. Hence, any external function to set id of sensor objects must call setId with only a valid range of values between 100 and 200. However, for retrieving the id of IoTSensor objects, any external function must call getId().

```
void IoTSensor::setId(int sen_id)
{
    if (sen_id>=100 && sen_id<=200)
        id = sen_id;
}
int IoTSensor::getId()
{
    return id;
}
```

e. Define setSenseValue public access function for setting private field: sense_value of IoTSensor objects. Hence, any external function to set the sense_value of sensor objects must call setSenseValue with only a valid range of values between 0.0 and 10.0. On the other hand, for retrieving the sense_value of IoTSensor objects, any external function must call getSensevalue().

```
void IoTSensor::setSenseValue(float val)
{
    if (val>=0.0 && val<=10.0)
        sense_value = val;
}
float IoTSensor::getSenseValue()
{
    return sense_value;
}
```

CHAPTER 2   START LEARNING OOP USING C++

f. Define `setBatteryLevel` public access function for setting private field:`battery_level` of `IoTSensor` objects. Hence, any external function to set `battery_level` of sensor objects must call `setBatteryLevel` with only a valid range of values between 1 and 100. However, for retrieving `battery_level` of `IoTSensor` objects, any external function must call `getBatteryLevel()`.

```
void IoTSensor::setBatteryLevel(int level)
{
    if (level>=0 && level<=100)
        battery_level = level;
}
int IoTSensor::getBatteryLevel()
{
    return battery_level;
}
```

2. Define the following two external functions.

   a. `iChangeIoTSensor()` to set invalid values into `IoTSensor` objects using `public` access functions of the `IoTSensor` object.

   b. `vChangeIoTSensor()` to set valid values into `IoTSensor` objects using public access functions of the `IoTSensor` object.

```
void iChangeIoTSensor(IoTSensor &is)
{
    is.setSenseValue(-1);
}
void vChangeIoTSensor(IoTSensor &is)
{
    is.setSenseValue(1.0);
}
```

CHAPTER 2   START LEARNING OOP USING C++

3. Define the **main()** test code for the following activities.

   a. Create an IoTSensor object is1 and, using the public access function of the object, set valid values to its internal fields such as id, sensing values, and battery levels.

   b. Confirm the successful creation of the IoTSensor object by displaying its values using the public access functions of the object.

   c. Change the IoTSensor is1 object internal private field such as sense_value using the object.

   d. Change the IoTSensor is1 object internal private field such as sense_value to invalid value by calling iChangeIoTSensor with is1 object argument.

   e. Change the IoTSensor is1 object internal private field such as sense_value to valid value by calling vChangeIoTSensor with is1 object argument.

```
int main()
{
    IoTSensor is1;
    is1.setId(101);
    is1.setSenseValue(11.0);
    is1.setBatteryLevel(90);

    cout<<"Configuring valid values for data members
    of IoTSensor using its object public access
    functions\n ";
    cout<<"Id: "<<is1.getId()<<" Sense Value
    "<<is1.getSenseValue()<<" Battery Level "<<is1.
    getBatteryLevel()<<"\n";

    cout<<"From an external function: main()\n";
    cout<<"Trying to configure private data members
    of IoTSensor using its object directly \n ";
```

```
is1.sense_value = -1.0;
cout<<"Id: "<<is1.getId()<<" Sense Value
"<<is1.getSenseValue()<<" Battery Level "<<is1.
getBatteryLevel()<<"\n";

cout<<"From an external function:
iChangeIoTSensor\n";
cout<<"Trying to configure invalid values for
private data members of IoTSensor using its
public member functions\n ";
iChangeIoTSensor(is1);
cout<<"Id: "<<is1.getId()<<" Sense Value "<<is1.
getSenseValue()<<" Battery Level "<<is1.
getBatteryLevel()<<"\n";

cout<<"From an external function:
vChangeIoTSensor\n";
cout<<"Trying to configure valid values for
private data members of IoTSensors using its
public member functions\n ";
vChangeIoTSensor(is1);
cout<<"Id: "<<is1.getId()<<" Sense Value "<<is1.
getSenseValue()<<" Battery Level "<<is1.
getBatteryLevel()<<"\n";
return 0;
}
```

4. Let's test your code and observe the following important points.

    a. When `main()` is attempting to change `is1` object internal `private` fields directly without public access functions, you observe the error messages such as **error: 'float IoTSensor::sense_value' is private within this context.**

CHAPTER 2 START LEARNING OOP USING C++

```
# g++ iot_sensor_def_access.cc -o cpp_access
# ./cpp_access
iot_sensor_def_access.cc: In function 'int main()':
iot_sensor_def_access.cc:70:6: error: 'float
IoTSensor::sense_value' is private within
this context
   70 |   is1.sense_value = -1.0;
      |       ^~~~~~~~~~~
iot_sensor_def_access.cc:10:8: note: declared
private here
   10 |   float sense_value;
      |         ^~~~~~~~~~~
iot_sensor_def_access.cc:70:6: note: field 'float
IoTSensor::sense_value' can be accessed via 'float
IoTSensor::getSenseValue()'
   70 |   is1.sense_value = -1.0;
      |       ^~~~~~~~~~~
      |       getSenseValue()
```

5. Comment the is1 object accessing lines of code, execute your code again, and observe the following.

```
//is1.setSenseValue(11.0); //In main
//is1.sense_value = -1.0; //In main
//is.setSenseValue(-1); //In iChangeIoTSensor
//is.setSenseValue(1.0); //In vChangeIoTSensor
```

   a. IoTSensor object is1 is successfully created and main() can set values into its internal private fields using public access functions such as setId().

   b. main() can retrieve is1 object values using public access functions such as getId().

CHAPTER 2   START LEARNING OOP USING C++

c. iChangeIoTSensor cannot set invalid value: -1.0 (out of valid range) for sense_value: private field of is1 object; hence, only past valid changes are displayed.

d. The valid changes made by vChangeIoTSensor to sense_value field of the is1 object are displayed.

```
# ./cpp_access
Configuring valid values for data members of
IoTSensor using its object public access functions
Id: 101 Sense Value 0 Battery Level 90
From an external function: iChangeIoTSensor
Trying to configure invalid values for private
data members of IoTSensor using its public member
functions
Id: 101 Sense Value 0 Battery Level 90
From an external function: vChangeIoTSensor
Trying to configure valid values for private data
members of IoTSensors using its public member
functions
Id: 101 Sense Value 1 Battery Level 90
```

From the results, you can observe that the private fields (sensing value, battery level) of IoTSensor are accessed only using its public member functions. Otherwise, access to private fields is strictly restricted.

Next, let's practice all the OOP concepts learned in this chapter by doing a hands-on activity.

CHAPTER 2   START LEARNING OOP USING C++

Hands-on Activity: Smart Applications

In the previous sections, using C++ you worked with classes and objects, interacting with objects, and controlling access to objects' internal details (fields and member functions). As part of a hands-on activity related to smart applications, let's discuss how to use classes for modeling IoT sensors. In this task, you do the following activities.

- Implement an IoT sensor simulating class for creating IoT sensor objects.

- Create several IoT sensors and deploy them at various locations.

- After deploying your IoT sensor objects, find which IoT sensors are experiencing a low battery.

- Find locations of IoT sensors, which sensed higher temperature values.

- Based on the locations of sensors, find the closest IoT sensor to the given IoT sensor.

MODELING A SMART APPLICATION IOT SENSOR

1. Implement the following in *iot_sensor.cc*.

2. Define the `IoTSensor` class to model your smart application's `IoTSensor` behavior with the basic fields such as identifier, deployment location (x,y), sensing values, and battery level.

   ```
   #include<iostream>
   #include<string>
   #include<vector>
   #include <bits/stdc++.h>
   ```

```
using namespace std;
class IoTSensor
{
    private:
        string id;
        int x,y;
        float sense_value;
        int battery_level;
    public:
        void setId(string sen_id);
        string getId();
        void setX(int sen_x);
        int getX();
        void setY(int sen_y);
        int getY();
        void setSenseValue(float val);
        float getSenseValue();
        void setBatteryLevel(int level);
        int getBatteryLevel();
};
```

3. Implement suitable set and get member functions for accessing IoTSensor objects as follows.

```
void IoTSensor::setId(string sen_id)
{
    id = sen_id;
}
string IoTSensor::getId()
{
    return id;
}
```

```cpp
void IoTSensor::setX(int sen_x)
{
    x = sen_x;
}
int IoTSensor::getX()
{
    return x;
}
void IoTSensor::setY(int sen_y)
{
    y = sen_y;
}
int IoTSensor::getY()
{
    return y;
}
void IoTSensor::setSenseValue(float val)
{
    sense_value = val;
}
float IoTSensor::getSenseValue()
{
    return sense_value;
}
void IoTSensor::setBatteryLevel(int level)
{
    battery_level = level;
}
int IoTSensor::getBatteryLevel()
{
    return battery_level;
}
```

4. Create a function called getLowBatterySensors to get low-battery IoT sensor objects from the list of deployed IoT sensor objects based on the given battery threshold (value). As there may be multiple IoT sensors experiencing low battery, hence collect them as a vector of sensor objects.

    ```
    vector<IoTSensor> getLowBatterySensors(IoTSensor
    isensor[10], int value)
    {
        vector<IoTSensor> vs;
        for (int i=0;i<10;i++)
        {
            if (isensor[i].getBatteryLevel()<value)
                vs.push_back(isensor[i]);
        }
        return vs;
    }
    ```

5. Create a function called getHighTempSensors to get a list of high-temperature observed IoT sensor objects from the list of ten IoT sensors based on the given temperature threshold (value) as follows.

    ```
    vector<IoTSensor> getHighTempSensors(IoTSensor
    isensor[10], float value)
    {
        vector<IoTSensor> vs;
        for (int i=0;i<10;i++)
        {
                if (isensor[i].getSenseValue()>value)
                    vs.push_back(isensor[i]);
        }
        return vs;
    }
    ```

CHAPTER 2 START LEARNING OOP USING C++

6. Implement a function called findNearestSensorTo from ten IoT sensor objects to a given IoT sensor object. The distanceBetween function calculates the distance between two IoT sensors and to get IoTSensor object based on a given sensor id.

```
float distanceBetween(IoTSensor is1, IoTSensor is2)
{
    int xdisp = is1.getX()-is2.getX();
    int ydisp = is1.getY()-is2.getY();
    return sqrt((xdisp*xdisp+ydisp*ydisp));
}
int SensorIndex(IoTSensor isensor[10], string id)
{
    for (int i=0;i<10;i++)
    {
        if(id == isensor[i].getId())
        {
            return i;
        }
    }
    return -1;
}
IoTSensor findNearestSensorTo(IoTSensor isensor[10],
IoTSensor is1)
{
    IoTSensor target;
    float min_dist = 999999.0;//Set a high value
    depending on your deployment locations.
    target=is1;
    for (int i=0;i<10;i++)
    {
```

CHAPTER 2 START LEARNING OOP USING C++

```
            if (distanceBetween(isensor[i], is1)<=min_dist)
            {
                min_dist =
                distanceBetween(isensor[i], is1);
                if (min_dist!=0.0)
                {
                    target = isensor[i];
                }
                if (min_dist==0.0)
                {
                    min_dist = 999999.0;
                }
            }
        }
        return target;
    }
```

7. Implement your testing code in main() for the following activities.

   a. Deploying ten IoT sensor objects by configuring sensor ids (sensorA, sensorB, etc.), deployment locations ((0,0), (10,10), etc.), sensing values such as (0.001, 0.002, etc.), and battery level such as (100/1, 100/2, etc.).

   b. Display the status of your deployed IoT sensor objects.

   c. Interact with a list of ten IoT sensor objects to display low-battery experiencing sensor details such as sensor id and location.

   d. Interact with a list of ten IoT sensor objects to display high-temperature sensing sensor details such as sensor id and location.

   e. Interact with ten IoT sensor objects and find closer IoT sensor objects for each high-temperature sensing IoT sensor.

```cpp
int main()
{
    IoTSensor isensor[10];
    for (int i=0;i<10;i++)
    {
        isensor[i].setId("sensor"+string(1,'A'+i));
        isensor[i].setX(i*10);
        isensor[i].setY(i*10);
        isensor[i].setSenseValue(i*0.001);
        isensor[i].setBatteryLevel(100/(i+1));
    }

    cout<<"IoT Sensors deployment details:\n";

    for (int i=0;i<10;i++)
    {
        cout<<isensor[i].getId()<<" "
            <<isensor[i].getX()<<" "
            <<isensor[i].getY()<<" "
            <<isensor[i].getSenseValue()<<" "
            <<isensor[i].getBatteryLevel()<<"\n";
    }
    vector<IoTSensor> lowb_sensors;
    lowb_sensors=getLowBatterySensors(isensor,20);
    cout<<"Low battery IoT Sensors: "<<lowb_sensors.size()<<"\n";
    for (int i=0;i<lowb_sensors.size();i++)
    {
        cout<<lowb_sensors[i].getId()<<"Location: ("
            <<lowb_sensors[i].getX()
            <<","<<lowb_sensors[i].getY()<<")"<<"\n";
    }
```

CHAPTER 2   START LEARNING OOP USING C++

```cpp
    vector<IoTSensor> high_sensors;
    float temp=0.005;
       high_sensors=getHighTempSensors(isensor,temp);
       cout<<"High Temperature sensing IoT Sensors:
       "<<high_sensors.size()<<"\n";
       for (int i=0;i<high_sensors.size();i++)
       {
           cout<<high_sensors[i].
           getId()<<"Location: ("
               <<high_sensors[i].getX()
               <<","<<high_sensors[i].
               getY()<<")"<<"\n";
       }

    cout<<"High Temperature sensing IoT Sensors:
    "<<high_sensors.size()<<"\n";
      for (int i=0;i<high_sensors.size();i++)
      {
           IoTSensor target_sensor =
           findNearestSensorTo (isensor, high_
           sensors[i]);
           cout<<target_sensor.getId()<<" is the
           closet IoT sensor to high temprature
           "<<high_sensors[i].getSenseValue()<<"
           sensing sensor :"<<high_sensors[i].
           getId()<<"\n";
       }

    return 0;
}
```

CHAPTER 2 START LEARNING OOP USING C++

8. Test your code and observer the following details.

    a. IoT sensor deployment details

    b. Low-battery IoT sensors

    c. High-temperature sensing IoT sensors

    d. IoT sensor objects closer to the high-temperature sensing IoT sensors

```
# g++ iot_sensor.cc -o iot_sensors
# ./iot_sensors
```
IoT Sensors deployment details:
```
sensorA 0 0 0 100
sensorB 10 10 0.001 50
sensorC 20 20 0.002 33
sensorD 30 30 0.003 25
sensorE 40 40 0.004 20
sensorF 50 50 0.005 16
sensorG 60 60 0.006 14
sensorH 70 70 0.007 12
sensorI 80 80 0.008 11
sensorJ 90 90 0.009 10
```
Low battery IoT Sensors: 5
```
sensorF Location: (50,50)
sensorG Location: (60,60)
sensorH Location: (70,70)
sensorI Location: (80,80)
sensorJ Location: (90,90)
```
High Temprature sensing IoT Sensors: 4
```
sensorG Location: (60,60)
sensorH Location: (70,70)
sensorI Location: (80,80)
sensorJ Location: (90,90)
High Temprature sensing IoT Sensors: 4
```

sensorH is the closet IoT sensor to high temprature 0.006 sensing sensor :sensorG
sensorI is the closet IoT sensor to high temprature 0.007 sensing sensor :sensorH
sensorJ is the closet IoT sensor to high temprature 0.008 sensing sensor :sensorI
sensorI is the closet IoT sensor to high temprature 0.009 sensing sensor :sensorJ

That's superb. You have successfully modeled ten `IoTSensor` objects and interacted with them for carrying out activities such as finding low-battery sensors, high-temperature sensing sensors, and the closest sensors to each high-temperature sensing sensor. I suggest you change the number of sensors for this hands-on activity and test your own scenarios for practice.

Summary

This chapter introduced you to C++ programming learning. You learned how to implement real-world entities as C++ classes, and interact with their objects for carrying out interesting tasks, activities, and transactions as part of real-world applications. You also learned to control classes' sensitive data using C++ access specifiers `private` and `public`. Finally, you practiced a hands-on activity related to smart applications by modeling IoT sensors and interacting with them to carry out different activities.

The next chapter explains the importance of constructors and destructors for systematically executing software startup and shutdown activities.

Practice: Hands-On Activities

1. Declare suitable C++ classes for real-world entities and online vehicle booking application users. For each class, include the following.

   a. Declare necessary private fields.

   b. Declare public member functions (set and get) for accessing private fields.

   c. Declare public member functions for carrying out important interactions.

   d. Implement all necessary member functions for online vehicle booking applications outside the class.

2. Using the online vehicle booking application classes, implement the following interactions.

   a. Register online vehicle application supporting locations.

   b. Register a vehicle with driver details.

   c. Register a User.

   d. Check if any vehicle is available at the user's location.

   e. Find the nearest vehicle available from the user's location.

   f. Find the lowest-fare vehicle available for traveling to the user's location.

3. Declare suitable C++ classes for the online food ordering application real-world entities and users. For each class, include the following.

   a. Declare necessary private fields.

b. Declare public member functions (set and get) for accessing private fields.

c. Declare public member functions for carrying out important interactions.

d. Implement all necessary classes with suitable fields and member functions for online food ordering applications.

4. Using the online food ordering application, classes implement the following interactions.

   a. Register online vehicle application supporting restaurants and their food items.

   b. Register Users.

   c. Register delivery partners.

   d. Check a food item is available at a restaurant.

   e. Check if any delivery partner is interested in accepting order delivery.

   f. Find the highest-rating restaurant.

CHAPTER 3

Systematically Starting and Stopping Software Objects

In Chapter 2, you began exploring OOP using C++ language to model a variety of real-world applications and gaming applications related entities. This chapter explains how to handle the important startup and shutdown activities of software in a systematic approach using C++ constructors and destructors. Constructors are special member functions of a class that are executed automatically when objects of the class are created. Developers use constructors for defining and conforming all major startup sequence activities, such as initialization, configuration, resource allocation, and startup sequence-dependent services. On the other hand, destructors are other special member functions of a class, they get executed when class objects get deleted. Developers use destructors for carrying out activities such as gracefully releasing resources, closing files, and closing services. C++ constructors and destructors greatly simplify debugging activities related to pinpointing software startup and shutdown issues.

As part of this chapter, you start with learning the importance of handling software objects startup and shutdown activities, then you carry out these activities using C++ constructors and destructors. Specifically, this chapter covers the following topics.

CHAPTER 3   SYSTEMATICALLY STARTING AND STOPPING SOFTWARE OBJECTS

- Software objects startup and shut down sequences
- Constructors for handling startup sequences
- Destructors for doing graceful shutdowns
- Hands-on activity: Constructors
- Hands-on activity: Destructors

Software Objects Startup and Shutdown Sequences

Starting a software leads to initializing all its necessary components (objects) and executing necessary activities in a sequence. Similarly, closing a software leads to a sequence of shutdown activities for releasing resources and stopping all component interactions. Let's observe the following tasks for starting and stopping software.

- Starting a software application
  - Initializing and configuring software components in a specific order
  - Allocating computational and memory resources in a specific order
  - Starting and connecting with necessary services in a specific order
- Closing a software application
  - Releasing all acquired resources in a specific order
  - Stopping and disconnecting its components and all interactions in a specific order

CHAPTER 3   SYSTEMATICALLY STARTING AND STOPPING SOFTWARE OBJECTS

Starting a Software Application

Software is a collection of components, and all its components are logically connected to start its functioning. Hence, to ensure a graceful startup sequence of software and its components, you must implement the following activities for each object in a specific order.

- Initialization and configuration
- Resources allocation
- Connecting with necessary services

Initialization and Configuration

It is necessary to initialize each software component with default values and configure them. Let's look at various real-world applications initialization and configuration activities.

- Starting a software game, you can observe the initialization of game characters, vehicles, weapons, and animals displayed on your screen. It allows players to easily visualize and interact with game world entities to continue with the game.

- Starting an online shopping application leads to displaying all available items for their customers. It helps customers to browse items and place orders.

- Starting an online vehicle booking application leads to displaying all nearby landmarks and available vehicles. It helps travelers to locate their destinations and choose a suitable vehicle.

- Starting a smart application involves initializing all its devices with suitable configurations such as addresses, operating power, and channels. It helps applications to easily connect with necessary devices and complete user transactions.

During the startup sequence of a software application, besides software components initialization and configuration activity, there is another important activity called acquiring necessary computational and memory resources to ensure the performance of a software application.

Resources Allocation

To run a complex software application, acquiring the following computational and memory resources from the operating system is necessary. The following tasks are usually done as part of resource allocation for a software application.

- Creating a suitable number of processes and threads for carrying out parallel activities.

- Creating necessary synchronization resources such as semaphores and mutex locks to guarantee process execution order synchronization.

- Setting up interprocess communication resources such as message queues and shared memory for exchanging data among processes.

- Setting up timers for handling counting and timing events.

- Allocating necessary dynamic memory for inputs or outputs processing.

- Creating temporary or regular files for permanent storage (IO devices).

CHAPTER 3   SYSTEMATICALLY STARTING AND STOPPING SOFTWARE OBJECTS

Acquiring all necessary resources at the start of software components helps to avoid long or infinite waiting durations, runtime errors, and crashes. Hence, you must identify suitable resources needed for various software objects of your software and allocate them during the respective object's startup sequence.

Besides default software components configuration and acquiring all necessary resources at the start of software, connecting with other software components or services for executing tasks is also very important.

Connecting with Necessary Services

Complex software usually depends on its multiple software components startup, linking of other software components, and external services linking. Failure of any of the subcomponents or external service connectivity could lead to the unsuccessful start of the software. Let's see the following examples.

- Starting a typical online software application depends on web servers, databases, external services, proxies, and load balancers.

- Starting an online game software application involves all characters, such as enemies, vehicles, weapons, and animals. Network services are needed to allow online users to play the game.

- To start a smart application, all its devices and running services must be started and connected logically to handle all transactions.

It means a successful startup sequence of a software application depends on the execution order of its components and external components. Hence, based on the needs of a software application, the following activities need to be handled during a software object startup.

CHAPTER 3   SYSTEMATICALLY STARTING AND STOPPING SOFTWARE OBJECTS

- Creating and starting dependent objects in a logical order
- Connecting with database servers
- Connecting with proxy servers and load balancers
- Connecting with any local running services
- Connecting with any necessary external Internet servers

Moreover, you must carefully plan these activities with respect to each of the objects involved in your complex software.

The importance and complexity of handling software objects' startup activities were covered in startup sequence discussions. Later, you learn to use C++ constructors to systematically carry out software startup sequence activities. Next, let's discuss the important activities during the software shutdown sequence.

Closing a Software Application

After completing your tasks, you must close the software by doing the following important activities.

- Releasing all acquired resources.
- Stopping and disconnecting all components and their interactions.

Hence, as engineers and developers, we must take care of the shutdown activities of our software implementation. To carry out these activities systematically, let's inspect them in detail.

Releasing Resources

As part of the graceful shutdown of a software application, related to every object, you should handle the following activities during the closing of a software.

- Deleting all synchronization-related resources of objects

- Deleting message queues and shared memory of objects

- Deleting all timers of objects

- Freeing or deleting the memory acquired by objects

- Deleting all unused files of objects

After releasing resources acquired by objects of software, you must handle activities related to stopping all its components, services, and interactions.

Disconnect, Stop, and Remove Services

You observed that a successful starting sequence involves creating necessary processes or threads and connecting with other objects' internal and external services. On the other hand, during shutting down of a software application involves handling the following activities.

- Closing database servers' connections

- Closing proxy servers and load balancer connections

- Disconnecting from any local running services

- Disconnecting from any connected Internet servers

- Closing all open network sockets and files

- Stopping and removing all processes and threads created by objects

That means if you do not close your software, it can lead to system resource misusage, leaving ongoing connections open, and system-limited resources getting occupied unnecessarily and blocked for other necessary usage. Forgetting any of these shutdown activities can lead to opening doors for attackers!

Hence, during software shutdown activity implementations, you must check and confirm releasing all resources, and closing all its components and interactions. In C++ programming, you automatically use destructors to carry out these activities during object deletion.

In summary, after inspecting the starting and closing of a software application sequence, you have learned the importance of carrying out startup sequence and shutdown activities.

Next, let's look at how to declare and define C++ constructors and destructors for executing startup and shutdown activities.

Constructors for Handling Startup Sequences

Let's look at how C++ handles startup sequence activities using constructors by reviewing the following topics.

- C++ for constructors
- C++ supporting constructors
- Hands-on activities for practicing constructors

Constructors in C++

In C++, constructors are nothing but other member functions of a `class`. To implement constructors, you must declare it inside a `class` by following rules.

CHAPTER 3   SYSTEMATICALLY STARTING AND STOPPING SOFTWARE OBJECTS

- Constructors must be defined in the public section of a class.

- The constructor of a class must be defined with the same name as the class name.

- Constructors do not return any values.

- Multiple constructors with a variable number of arguments are allowed in a class.

Let's declare a constructor for the following example class in *test_bomb_constructor.cc*.

```
class Bomb
{
    unsigned int id;
    int x,y;
    int state;
    public:
        Bomb();
};
```

Outside of the Bomb class, let's define the Bomb() constructor for initialization activities as follows.

```
Bomb::Bomb()
{
    cout<<"Bomb object internal fields got initialized automatically with random values\n";
    id = rand()%10000;
    x = rand()%100;
    y = rand()%100;
    state = 1;
}
```

CHAPTER 3 SYSTEMATICALLY STARTING AND STOPPING SOFTWARE OBJECTS

Then, test it by creating a Bomb object b1 in your main() code as follows.

```
int main()
{
    Bomb b1;
}
```

Finally, test its execution as follows in your main() code.

```
# g++ test_bomb_constructor.cc  -o bomb
# ./bomb
Bomb object internal fields were initialized automatically with
random values.
```

From the results, you can observe the following interesting and important details.

- When your program started, the only instruction executed was the Bomb object b1 creation.

- You did not call the Bomb() function explicitly. The bomb () constructor is called automatically.

- Your custom code defined in Bomb() was executed for initializing b1 object internal fields.

- You can confirm it by printing b1 object details using get functions.

It means the constructors of a class are executed as soon as its objects are created. Hence, you can use constructors to carry out software object initialization activities, acquire resources for the objects, and connect with necessary services at the startup sequence of a software application. Let's do an interesting hands-on activity to demonstrate using constructors for carrying out all startup sequence activities. First, let's explore some constructors supported by C++.

122

CHAPTER 3   SYSTEMATICALLY STARTING AND STOPPING SOFTWARE OBJECTS

C++ Supporting Constructors

C++ supports the following constructors.

- **Default constructors** have the same name as the `class` name. It does not take any arguments. When you define a default constructor, the following points must be considered.

    - Only one default constructor is allowed in a `class`.

    - To invoke it in your program, you must define an object for the `class` without any arguments.

    - It is executed when `class` objects are created statically or dynamically without any arguments.

    - When you define a default constructor explicitly, the C++ compiler does not provide any default constructor support. However, the C++ compiler provides a default copy constructor available for you.

Refer to *test_bomb_constructor.cc* for an example.

Observe the following output when you execute the code using the following commands.

```
g++ test_bomb_constructor.cc -o test_constructors
```

```
./test_constructors
Bomb object internal fields were initialized automatically with random values
```

This means when a `b1` object is created, your custom default constructor is executed.

Next, let's look at the role of copy constructors.

- **Copy constructors** are useful for initializing new objects' internal fields (or data members) with existing objects' internal field values. Its name is the same as the `class` name, and it takes the source object as an argument to initialize the destination object. When you define a copy constructor, the following points must be considered.

    - Only one copy constructor can be defined in a class. While copying source object fields into destination object fields, avoid copying dynamically allocated buffers and pointers. It helps you to easily debug memory leaks and double freeing runtime errors.

    - To invoke it in your program, you need to define a `class` object by initializing it with another object of the `class`.

    - It is also executed when `class` objects are created statically or dynamically with a source object as an argument. Passing a source object reference as an argument is recommended to avoid large memory copying overhead.

    - When you define a custom copy constructor, the C++ compiler provides no copy and default constructors.

    - Moreover, when you define a copy constructor, you must define a default constructor. Otherwise, you cannot create objects.

Let's copy your *test_bomb_constructor.cc* to *test_copy_constructor.cc* and make the following changes.

CHAPTER 3   SYSTEMATICALLY STARTING AND STOPPING SOFTWARE OBJECTS

Declare the following copy constructor inside the Bomb class.

```
Bomb(const Bomb &b);
```

Define the following copy constructor outside the Bomb class.

```
Bomb::Bomb(const Bomb &b)
{
    cout<<"Copying bomb objects\n";
    id = b.id;
    x = b.x;
    y = b.y;
    state = 0;
}
```

In the main() code, call the copy constructors as follows.

```
int main()
{
    Bomb b1;
    Bomb b2(b1); //It invokes the copy constructor.
    Bomb b3=b2; //It invokes the copy constructor.
    return 0;
}
```

Next, test this code using the following commands.

```
# g++ test_copy_constructor.cc -o test_copy_constructor
# ./test_copy_constructor
Bomb object internal fields got initialized automatically with random values
Copying bomb objects
Copying bomb objects
```

CHAPTER 3   SYSTEMATICALLY STARTING AND STOPPING SOFTWARE OBJECTS

From the results, you can observe that copy constructors are called to copy bomb objects. Later, when you access b1, b2, and b3 objects, you get the same values from their internal fields, such as id, x, y, and state.

Parameterized constructors: Its name is the same as the class name and takes arguments. These are useful for custom configuring objects by passing suitable argument values. You can define multiple parameterized constructors with a variable number of arguments. When you define a parameterized constructor, the following points must be considered.

- Multiple constructors are allowed.

- To invoke it in your program, you must define a class object by passing a suitable number of arguments.

- It is executed when class objects are created statically or dynamically with a suitable number of arguments.

- By default, no parameterized constructors are provided by the C++ compiler. You must define parameterized constructors before using them.

- When you define a parameterized constructor, you must define the default constructor also. Otherwise, you cannot define objects without any arguments.

- However, a default copy constructor is available for you.

Example.

Copy your *test_bomb_constructor.cc* to *test_parameter_constructor.cc* and make the following changes.

Declare the following parameterized constructors inside the class Bomb.

```
Bomb(int bx, int by);
Bomb(int bid);
```

Declare the following functions inside the class Bomb.

```
int getId();
void setId(int bid);
```

Declare the following functions outside the class Bomb.

```
int Bomb::getId()
{
    return id;
}
void Bomb::setId(int bid)
{
    id = bid;
}
```

Define the following parameterized constructors outside of the class Bomb.

```
Bomb::Bomb(int bx, int by)
{
    x = bx;
    y = by;
    cout<<"Constructor1 called\n";
}
Bomb::Bomb(int bid)
{
    id = bid;
    cout<<"Constructor2 called\n";
}
```

In the main() code, call parameterized constructors as follows.

```
int main()
{
    Bomb b1(10,20); //it prints Constructor1 called
```

```
    b1.setId(1000);
    Bomb b2(1000); //it prints Constructor2 called
    Bomb b3=b2; //It invokes the default copy constructor.
    cout<<"b1 Id:"<<b1.getId()<<"\n";
    cout<<"b2 Id:"<<b2.getId()<<"\n";
    cout<<"b3 Id:"<<b3.getId()<<"\n"
    return 0;
}
```

When you execute the code using the following commands, observe the following output.

```
g++ test_parameter_constructor.cc -o parameter_constructors
./parameter_constructors
Constructor1 called
Constructor2 called
b1 Id:1000
b2 Id:1000
b3 Id:1000
```

From the results, you can confirm that the first parameterized constructors were called. Then, you can observe that the default copy constructor is executed by copying the b2 object's internal field values into the b3 object. Hence, the b3 object also gets the same `id` as the b2 object's `id`. Next, let's check the C++ compiler providing constructors.

C++ Compiler Providing Constructors

C++ compiler, by default, provides a no-argument constructor and a copy constructor for creating and copying objects of a class. Hence, you must observe the following while defining your default and copy constructors in your code.

CHAPTER 3   SYSTEMATICALLY STARTING AND STOPPING SOFTWARE OBJECTS

Let's try to better understand it by doing a simple task in *test_c++_constructors.cc*.

```
class Bomb
{
      unsigned int id;
      int x,y;
      int state;
      public:
            int getId()
            {
                 return id;
            }
            void setId(int tid)
            {
                 id = tid;
            }
};
```

In main(), you can call copy constructors as follows.

```
int main()
{
    Bomb b1;
    b1.setId(1000);
    Bomb b2(b1); //default copy constructor called
    cout<<"b1 Id:"<<b1.getId();
    cout<<"b2 Id:"<<b2.getId();
    Bomb b3=b2; //default copy constructor called
    cout<<"b3 Id:"<<b3.getId();
    return 0;
}
```

Test your code as follows.

```
# g++ test_c++_constructors.cc  -o cpp_default
# ./cpp_default
b1 Id:1000
b2 Id:1000
b3 Id:1000
```

The results show that b2 and b3 objects are getting copies of b1 object details. As you did not include any default constructor and copy constructors in your program, C++ compiler providing constructors are executed. Next, let's practice constructors by doing the following hands-on activities.

Hands-on Activities for Practicing Constructors

As part of learning and practicing constructors for handling startup sequence activities of software, let's do the following activities.

1. In a war gaming context, when the game starts, bombs get deployed at random locations. You create this scenario using the default constructor.

2. Next, you do another interesting hands-on activity related to gaming bomb deployment using a secret file and passing custom locations. You create this scenario using parameterized constructors.

3. Finally, you create a copy of gaming bombs from existing bombs. To carry out this activity, you use copy constructors.

CHAPTER 3   SYSTEMATICALLY STARTING AND STOPPING SOFTWARE OBJECTS

DEPLOY GAMING BOMBS AT RANDOM LOCATIONS

1. Implement your gaming code in the *bombs.cc* file.

2. Define the Bomb class for creating gaming Bomb objects by declaring bomb location (x,y) and state as fields under the private section, and under the public section, declare location and state access get member functions. Finally, include the Bomb() constructor declaration inside the class as follows.

```
#include<iostream>
#include<cstdlib>
#include<fstream>
using namespace std;
class Bomb
{
        unsigned int id;
        int x,y;
        int state;
        public:
                int getId();
                int getX();
                int getY();
                int getState();
                Bomb();
};
```

CHAPTER 3   SYSTEMATICALLY STARTING AND STOPPING SOFTWARE OBJECTS

3. Define your Bomb() constructor for assigning random identifiers, random locations, and active states.

```
Bomb::Bomb()
{
    id = rand()%10000;
    x = rand()%100;
    y = rand()%100;
    state = 1;
}
```

4. Define bomb objects (id,x,y, and state) accessing member functions.

```
int Bomb::getId()
{
    return id;
}
int Bomb::getX()
{
    return x;
}
int Bomb::getY()
{
    return y;
}
int Bomb::getState()
{
    return state;
}
```

5. Write your main() for testing Bomb() constructor execution. Let' create ten gaming Bomb objects for testing as follows.

CHAPTER 3 SYSTEMATICALLY STARTING AND STOPPING SOFTWARE OBJECTS

```
int main()
{
    Bomb b[10];
    for (int i=0;i<10;i++)
    {
        cout<<b[i].getId()<<": ("<<b[i].
        getX()<<","<<b[i].getY()<<")"<<"\n";
    }
}
```

6. Test your code using the following commands.

```
g++ bombs.cc -o random_deploy_bomb
./random_deploy_bomb
9383: (86,77)
6915: (93,35)
5386: (92,49)
1421: (62,27)
8690: (59,63)
3926: (40,26)
9172: (36,11)
5368: (67,29)
5782: (30,62)
5123: (67,35)
```

From the results, you can observe that all ten gaming bombs are deployed at random locations. You have not assigned any specific locations using bomb objects. However, every bomb was configured with a random id, location (x,y), and specific state automatically after executing the program.

Well done. You have learned how to do automatic configuration for bomb objects using the Bomb() constructor. Next, let's look at how to configure gaming bomb objects using specific parameters and load configuration parameters from a given input (secret) file using parameterized constructors.

CHAPTER 3   SYSTEMATICALLY STARTING AND STOPPING SOFTWARE OBJECTS

DEPLOY GAMING BOMBS USING A SECRET FILE

1. Copy your gaming bombs.cc code into *bombs_deploy_custominputs.cc*.

2. Extend your Bomb class by declaring and defining your parameterized constructor for configuring Bomb objects with custom values using arguments as follows.

   ```
   Bomb::Bomb(int bid, int bx, int by, int bstate)
   {
       id = bid;
       x = bx;
       y = by;
       state = bstate;
   }
   ```

3. Declare and define another parameterized constructor for configuring Bomb objects by taking configuration values from a given input file.

   ```
   Bomb::Bomb(fstream &ifile)
   {
       ifile>>id>>x>>y>>state;
       p = new int[10];
   }
   ```

4. Let's write your parameterized constructors testing code in main() for the following activities.

   a. Define ten gaming Bomb objects using dynamic memory and configure their ids starting with 1000, locations (0,0), (20,20), and so on, and set every bomb state to active (1). Finally, display all Bomb object details.

CHAPTER 3   SYSTEMATICALLY STARTING AND STOPPING SOFTWARE OBJECTS

b. Define ten gaming Bomb objects using dynamic memory and configure their id, location (x,y), and state from an input file *BombsDeploy.txt*. The file stores ten gaming Bomb object details (id, x, y, state) line by line.

c. Finally, display only active bomb details.

```
int main()
{
    Bomb *pb[10];
    for (int i=0;i<10;i++)
    {
        pb[i] = new Bomb(i+1000,i*20,i*20,1);
    }
    for (int i=0;i<10;i++)
    {
        cout<<pb[i]->getId()<<": ("<<pb[i]->
        getX()<<","<<pb[i]->getY()<<")"
        <<"Active"<<"\n";
    }

    Bomb *fb[10];
        fstream myfile;
        myfile.open("BombsDeploy.txt",ios::in);
        for (int i=0;i<10;i++)
        {
            fb[i] = new Bomb(myfile);
        }
    for (int i=0;i<10;i++)
    {
        if (fb[i]->getState() == 1)
            cout<<fb[i]->getId()<<":
            ("<<fb[i]->getX()<<","<<fb[i]-
            >getY()<<")"<<"Active"<<"\n";
```

```
        }
        myfile.close();
    }
```

5. Let's test your constructors by doing the following activities.

    a. Check for custom gaming bomb details

    b. Check for gaming bomb details configured through file input

    ```
    # g++ bombs_deploy_custominputs.cc -o bombs_deploy_
    custominputs
    # cat BombsDeploy.txt
    # ./bombs_deploy_custominputs
    1000: (0,0)Active
    1001: (20,20)Active
    1002: (40,40)Active
    1003: (60,60)Active
    1004: (80,80)Active
    1005: (100,100)Active
    1006: (120,120)Active
    1007: (140,140)Active
    1008: (160,160)Active
    1009: (180,180)Active
    1: (10,10)Active
    2: (20,10)Active
    11: (11,11)Active
    22: (23,10)Active
    44: (16,16)Active
    55: (20,10)Active
    ```

The results show that all gaming bomb objects (pb[i]) are displayed. However, when gaming bomb objects are configured through the file, only active bomb details are displayed. You can change the code for displaying all bombs while reading it from fb[i] objects.

CHAPTER 3   SYSTEMATICALLY STARTING AND STOPPING SOFTWARE OBJECTS

COPYING BOMBS FROM EXISTING BOMBS

1. Copy your gaming *bombs.cc* code into *bombs_copy.cc*.

2. Extend your first Bomb class (default constructor) by defining your copy constructor for creating Bomb objects from existing ones. While copying, set the copied bomb object `state` to 0 as follows.

   ```
   Bomb::Bomb(const Bomb &b)
   {
       id = b.id;
       x = b.x;
       y = b.y;
       state = 0;
   }
   ```

3. Write testing `main()` code for copying Bomb objects from original objects. Display the original Bomb objects and copied Bomb objects as follows.

   ```
   int main()
   {
       Bomb b[10];
       for (int i=0;i<10;i++)
       {
           cout<<b[i].getId()<<": ("<<b[i].
           getX()<<","<<b[i].getY()<<")"<<b[i].
           getState()<<"\n";
       }
       Bomb *cb[10];
       for (int i=0;i<10;i++)
       {
   ```

137

CHAPTER 3 SYSTEMATICALLY STARTING AND STOPPING SOFTWARE OBJECTS

```
        cb[i] = new Bomb(b[i]);
        cout<<cb[i]->getId()<<": ("<<cb[i]-
        >getX()<<","<<cb[i]->getY()<<")"<<cb[i].
        getState()<<"\n";
    }

    return 0;
}
```

4. Test your code using the following commands.

```
g++ bombs_copy.cc -o bombs_copy
./bombs_copy
9383: (86,77)1
6915: (93,35)1
5386: (92,49)1
1421: (62,27)1
8690: (59,63)1
3926: (40,26)1
9172: (36,11)1
5368: (67,29)1
5782: (30,62)1
5123: (67,35)1
```
9383: (86,77)0
6915: (93,35)0
5386: (92,49)0
1421: (62,27)0
8690: (59,63)0
3926: (40,26)0
9172: (36,11)0
5368: (67,29)0
5782: (30,62)0
5123: (67,35)0

From the results, you can observe that every b[i] object details got copied into the corresponding cb[i] object and cb[i] state set to 0. It means your custom copy constructor copied one object's details into another.

To confirm it's working, let's comment on your custom copy constructor and test it again using the following commands.

```
# g++ bombs_copy.cc -o bombs_copy
# ./bombs_copy
9383: (86,77)1
..
5123: (67,35)1
9383: (86,77)1
..
5123: (67,35)1
```

The results show that every b[i] object details got copied into the corresponding cb[i] objects. It means the compiler-provided copy constructor copied one object's values into another object.

The Importance of Destructors for Doing Graceful Shutdowns

You learned the importance of and how to implement constructors in C++. Constructors help you easily carry out software startup activities. In this section, you learn how to execute shutdown activities using C++ destructors.

Destructors in C++

Destructors are helpful to handle software shutdown activities systematically. This section starts by explaining how to declare and define destructors in C++. Then, you learn about the destructor's execution behavior.

CHAPTER 3   SYSTEMATICALLY STARTING AND STOPPING SOFTWARE OBJECTS

In C++, destructors are nothing but other member functions of a class. To implement destructors, you must declare it inside a class by following rules.

- Destructors must be defined in the `public` section of a class.

- Destructors of a class must be defined with the same name as the class name and prefixed with the ~ operator.

- Destructors do not take any arguments and return any values.

- Only one destructor is allowed in a class.

Let's declare a destructor for the following example class in *test_bomb_destructor.cc*.

```
class Bomb
{
        unsigned int id;
        int x,y;
        int state;
        char *buffer;
        public:
                Bomb();
                ~Bomb();
};
```

Outside of the `Bomb` class, let's define the `Bomb()` constructor for carrying out initialization activities and allocating a processing `buffer` memory using the `new` operator as follows.

CHAPTER 3 SYSTEMATICALLY STARTING AND STOPPING SOFTWARE OBJECTS

```
Bomb::Bomb()
{
    cout<<"Bomb object internal fields got initialized
    automatically with random values\n";
    id = rand()%10000;
    x = rand()%100;
    y = rand()%100;
    state = 1;
    buffer = new char[100];
    printf(buffer,"Id:%d X:%d Y:%d STATE:%d \n",id,x,y,state);
}
char* Bomb::getBuffer()
{
    return buffer;
}
```

Next, define ~Bomb() destructor for deallocating buffer memory using the delete operator as follows.

```
Bomb::~Bomb()
{
    if (buffer!=NULL)
    {
        cout<<"Destructor called and dynamic buffer
        deallocated\n";
        delete buffer;
        buffer = NULL;
    }
    else
    {
        cout<<"Nothing to do\n";
    }
}
```

141

CHAPTER 3   SYSTEMATICALLY STARTING AND STOPPING SOFTWARE OBJECTS

Test it by creating a Bomb object b1 in a block of your main() code.

```
int main()
{
    {
        cout<<"Inside the block\n";
        Bomb b1;
    }
    cout<<"Outside the block\n";
}
```

Finally, test its execution as follows in your main() code.

```
# g++ test_bomb_destructor.cc  -o bomb
# ./bomb
Inside the block
Bomb object internal fields got initialized automatically with random values
Destructor called and dynamic buffer deallocated
Outside the block
```

From the results, you can observe the following interesting and important details.

- When your program starts, after entering inside the block b1 object is created, and the constructor code is executed.

- As the b1 object lifetime ends outside the block, the object gets deleted, and the destructor code is executed automatically.

- Your custom code defined in ~Bomb() got executed for deallocating dynamically allocated buffer memory.

It means destructors of a class are executed as soon as the object's lifetime ends. So, you can use destructors to carry out software object shutdown activities, such as releasing resources for the objects and closing and disconnecting with other components and services. Next, you do an interesting hands-on activity to demonstrate destructors' usage for shutdown activities.

Hands-on Destructors

As part of the graceful software shutdown related to every object-acquired resource deallocation, you should handle the following activities using destructors.

As part of developing a game, you may create many bomb objects and allocate their buffer memory dynamically using new operator for each bomb. At the end of the game, you must deallocate the dynamically allocated memory automatically. You carry out this activity using C++ destructors.

It is also common to dynamically create objects using new operators for various activities. As part of this task, let's discuss the importance of deleting dynamically created objects for invoking destructors.

> **HANDS-ON ACTIVITY: IMPORTANCE OF DESTRUCTORS**
>
> 1. Implement the following in *bomb_destr.cc*.
> 2. Modify the Bomb class to hold a dynamic character buffer. Define Bomb() constructor to initialize id, location (x,y), and state, concatenate all fields, and copy it into a dynamically allocated character buffer.
>
>    ```
>    #include<iostream>
>    #include<cstdlib>
>    #include<fstream>
>    ```

CHAPTER 3 SYSTEMATICALLY STARTING AND STOPPING SOFTWARE OBJECTS

```cpp
using namespace std;
class Bomb
{
        unsigned int id;
        int x,y;
        int state;
        char *buffer;
        public:
                char *getBuffer();
                Bomb();
                ~Bomb();
};
Bomb::Bomb()
{
    id = rand()%10000;
    x = rand()%100;
    y = rand()%100;
    state = 1;
    buffer = new char[100];
    if (state == 1)
    {
        sprintf(buffer,"Id:%d X:%d Y:%d %d
        Active\n",id,x,y,state);
    }
    else
    {
        sprintf(buffer,"Id:%d X:%d Y:%d %d Not
        Active\n",id,x,y,state);
    }
}
```

CHAPTER 3   SYSTEMATICALLY STARTING AND STOPPING SOFTWARE OBJECTS

```
char* Bomb::getBuffer()
{
    return buffer;
}
```

3. Declare and define ~Bomb() destructor to free dynamically allocated buffer as follows.

```
Bomb::~Bomb()
{
    cout<<"Destructor called\n";
    if (buffer!=NULL)
    {
        delete buffer;
        buffer = NULL;
    }
}
```

4. Let's write testing code to learn the importance of destructors.

   a. Define a Bomb object holding pointer *b1 and start a block of code.

   b. Inside the block define ten Bomb objects and print its dynamically allocated buffer contents by accessing getBuffer().

   c. Before exiting the inner block, copy Bomb b[0] object into new object b1. After exiting the block, print b[0] buffer using b1 pointer as follows:

```
int main()
{
    Bomb *b1;
    {
        Bomb b[10];
        for (int i=0;i<10;i++)
        {
```

CHAPTER 3 SYSTEMATICALLY STARTING AND STOPPING SOFTWARE OBJECTS

```
            cout<<b[i].getBuffer();
        }
        b1 = new Bomb(b[0]);
    }
    if(b1->getBuffer()!=NULL) {
        cout<<"\nAccessing deleted buffer using
        b1:"<<b1->getBuffer()<<"\n";
    }
}
```

5. Well done! You have completed the writing Bomb class with destructors and testing code. Next, comment destructors code, and then execute your test code using the following commands.

```
# g++ bomb_destr.cc -o no_destructor
# ./no_destructor
Id:6915 X:93 Y:35 1 Active
Id:5386 X:92 Y:49 1 Active
Id:1421 X:62 Y:27 1 Active
Id:8690 X:59 Y:63 1 Active
Id:3926 X:40 Y:26 1 Active
Id:9172 X:36 Y:11 1 Active
Id:5368 X:67 Y:29 1 Active
Id:5782 X:30 Y:62 1 Active
Id:5123 X:67 Y:35 1 Active
Id:3929 X:2 Y:22 1 Active
```

Accessing deleted buffer using b1:Id:6915 X:93 Y:35 1 Active

Oh! Although local Bomb objects are deleted after their lifetime (after leaving the block), you can still access deleted objects dynamically allocated buffer. Because you did not delete the dynamically allocated buffer. Hence using the buffer address, you are able to access the buffer contents.

CHAPTER 3   SYSTEMATICALLY STARTING AND STOPPING SOFTWARE OBJECTS

Delete the dynamically allocated `buffer` of objects automatically using destructors. Before going to the next step, uncomment destructors code and run the following commands.

6. Test your updated code using the following commands.

```
# g++ bomb_destr.cc -o with_destructor
# ./with_destructor
Id:9383 X:86 Y:77 1 Active
Id:6915 X:93 Y:35 1 Active
Id:5386 X:92 Y:49 1 Active
Id:1421 X:62 Y:27 1 Active
Id:8690 X:59 Y:63 1 Active
Id:3926 X:40 Y:26 1 Active
Id:9172 X:36 Y:11 1 Active
Id:5368 X:67 Y:29 1 Active
Id:5782 X:30 Y:62 1 Active
Id:5123 X:67 Y:35 1 Active
Destructor called
Destructor called
Destructor called
Destructor called
Destructor called
Destructor called
Destructor called
Destructor called
Destructor called
Destructor called
```

CHAPTER 3　SYSTEMATICALLY STARTING AND STOPPING SOFTWARE OBJECTS

Well done! Destructors are in action immediately after Bomb objects' lifetime expires. You can observe from the results destructors are called for all local ten Bomb objects. However, you should observe that the destructor is not called for a b1 object (dynamically created object). Moreover, you may observe program termination on your computer. Next, let's study it by creating objects dynamically using new and working destructors.

IMPORTANCE OF DELETING DYNAMICALLY CREATED OBJECTS

1. Copy bomb_destr.cc into dyn_bomb_destr.cc and do the following.

2. Let's modify your main() testing codes by creating ten Bomb objects dynamically and printing their dynamically allocated buffer contents as follows.

   ```
   int main()
   {
       Bomb *cb[10];
       for (int i=0;i<10;i++)
       {
           cb[i] = new Bomb();
           cout<<cb[i]->getBuffer();
       }
   }
   ```

3. Test your code using the following commands.

   ```
   # g++ dyn_bomb_destr.cc -o dynamic_objects
   # ./dynamic_objects
   Id:9383 X:86 Y:77 1 Active
   Id:6915 X:93 Y:35 1 Active
   Id:5386 X:92 Y:49 1 Active
   ```

CHAPTER 3 SYSTEMATICALLY STARTING AND STOPPING SOFTWARE OBJECTS

```
Id:1421 X:62 Y:27 1 Active
Id:8690 X:59 Y:63 1 Active
Id:3926 X:40 Y:26 1 Active
Id:9172 X:36 Y:11 1 Active
Id:5368 X:67 Y:29 1 Active
Id:5782 X:30 Y:62 1 Active
Id:5123 X:67 Y:35 1 Active
```

From the results, you can observe that destructors were not executed. The reason for this behavior is your dynamically created objects were not deleted. Since Bomb objects are created using new, you must delete them explicitly. Let' delete dynamically created objects as follows.

4. Update your testing main() by including the following code after the object creation code's for loop.

    ```
    for (int i=0;i<10;i++)
    {
        delete cb[i];
        cb[i] = NULL;
    }
    ```

5. Save your code and test it using the following commands.

    ```
    # g++ bomb_destr.cc -o dynamic_objects
    # ./dynamic_objects
    Id:9383 X:86 Y:77 1 Active
    Id:6915 X:93 Y:35 1 Active
    Id:5386 X:92 Y:49 1 Active
    Id:1421 X:62 Y:27 1 Active
    Id:8690 X:59 Y:63 1 Active
    Id:3926 X:40 Y:26 1 Active
    Id:9172 X:36 Y:11 1 Active
    Id:5368 X:67 Y:29 1 Active
    ```

```
Id:5782 X:30 Y:62 1 Active
Id:5123 X:67 Y:35 1 Active
Destructor called
Destructor called
Destructor called
..
Destructor called
Destructor called
Destructor called
Destructor called
```

That's great. Destructors were in action immediately after the Bomb object's memory was deleted.

Hands-on Activity 1: Constructors

You have learned the importance of constructors. In this section, you do an interesting hands-on activity related to smart application development. Specifically, you learn how to use constructors to implement IoT sensors' startup activities. In this task, you do the following.

- Implement an IoT sensor simulating class for creating IoT sensor objects.

- Create several IoT sensors and deploy them at various locations.

- Configure your IoT sensors for storing specific sensed values in a given file.

- Connect your IoT sensors with a network server (IP address, Port number) called `iperf` **TCP** server. Here, you use the `iperf` server to demonstrate connecting your sensor object using a TCP socket.

CHAPTER 3   SYSTEMATICALLY STARTING AND STOPPING SOFTWARE OBJECTS

- Configure your IoT sensors for sending specific sensed values to the connected network server.

- Test your IoT sensors.

Note   As part of the following task, if the **iperf** tool is not installed, you must install it using the **apt-get install iperf** command. The **iperf** is helpful for quickly setting up simple TCP or UDP client-server applications. You use **iperf** TCP server application to connect IoT sensor objects to it and send sample data from objects to the **iperf** TCP server.

HANDS-ON ACTIVITY: IOT SENSORS STARTUP TASKS

1. Let's start with defining IoT sensors simulating class in *iot_sensor_const.cc*.

   a. Besides all necessary fields (id, x, y, sensing_value, battery_level), you also include a dynamically allocated buffer for processing sensor values, a filename for storing sensed values, and network socket descriptors for sending sensed values to connected servers.

   b. After defining all necessary fields, under the public section, include the corresponding set and get member functions for accessing your sensor objects.

   c. Finally, declare a constructor for configuring filename, network server IP and port number, and thresholds for writing specific values into files and sending them to the connected server.

Your class is defined as follows.

```cpp
#include<iostream>
#include<netdb.h>
#include<cstdlib>
#include<arpa/inet.h>
#include<stdlib.h>
#include<sys/socket.h>
#include<unistd.h>
#include<string>
#include<bits/stdc++.h>
using namespace std;
class IoTSensor {
    private:
        string id;
        int x,y;
        int battery_level;
        float sense_value;
        float sense_thr_file;
        float sense_thr_server;

        int sockfd;
        char filename[15];
        fstream myfile;
        char *buffer;
    public:
        void setFilename(char* file);
        char* getFilename();
        void setId(string sen_id);
        string getId();
        void setX(int sen_x);
        int getX();
        void setY(int sen_y);
```

CHAPTER 3   SYSTEMATICALLY STARTING AND STOPPING SOFTWARE OBJECTS

```
        int getY();
        void setSenseValue(float val);
        float getSenseValue();
        void setBatteryLevel(int level);
        int getBatteryLevel();
        IoTSensor(char *file, const char *server_
        ip, unsigned int server_port, float file_
        thr, float serv_thr)//add ; here
};
```

2. After defining your IoTsensor class, implement your IoTsensor constructor for handling the following activities.

    a. Configure threshold values for writing values and sending values to the network server.

    b. Under dynamic memory, allocate a buffer of size 100 bytes.

    c. Create a sensor file for writing sensing values.

    d. Create a TCP socket using `socket()`.

    e. Configure server IP address and port number using `bind()`.

    f. Connect to the `iperf` TCP network server with the help of a TCP socket using `connect()`.

```
IoTSensor::IoTSensor(char *file, const char *server_
ip, unsigned int server_port, float file_thr, float
serv_thr)
{
    sense_thr_file = file_thr;
    sense_thr_server = serv_thr;
    buffer = new char[100];
```

CHAPTER 3   SYSTEMATICALLY STARTING AND STOPPING SOFTWARE OBJECTS

```
        setFilename(file);
        myfile.open(file,ios::app); if (!myfile)
        {
            cout<<"new file created\n";
        }
        else
        {
            cout<<"opening the existing file\n";
        }
        struct sockaddr_in servaddr, cli;
        sockfd = socket(AF_INET, SOCK_STREAM, 0);
            if (sockfd == -1)
        {
                cout<<"socket creation failed...\n";
        }
        else
        {
            cout<<"Socket successfully created..\n";
        }
        bzero(&servaddr, sizeof(servaddr));
        servaddr.sin_family = AF_INET;
        servaddr.sin_addr.s_addr = inet_addr(server_ip);
        servaddr.sin_port = htons(server_port);
        if (connect(sockfd, (struct sockaddr*)&servaddr,
        sizeof(servaddr)) != 0) {
                cout<<"connection with the server
                failed...\n";
        }
        else
                cout<<"connected to the server..\n";
    }
```

CHAPTER 3   SYSTEMATICALLY STARTING AND STOPPING SOFTWARE OBJECTS

3. Define a suitable set and get member functions for configuring sensor identifier, deployment locations (x,y), battery level, and filename for storage as follows.

```
void IoTSensor::setId(string sen_id)
{
    id = sen_id;
}
string IoTSensor::getId()
{
    return id;
}
void IoTSensor::setX(int sen_x)
{
    x = sen_x;
}
int IoTSensor::getX()
{
    return x;
}
void IoTSensor::setY(int sen_y)
{
    y = sen_y;
}
int IoTSensor::getY()
{
    return y;
}
void IoTSensor::setBatteryLevel(int level)
{
    battery_level = level;
}
```

```
int IoTSensor::getBatteryLevel()
{
    return battery_level;
}
void IoTSensor::setFilename(char *file)
{
    strcpy(filename,file);
}

char* IoTSensor::getFilename()
{
    return filename;
}
```

4. Define a set function for storing sensed values into the configured files based on the threshold value (val), and sending sensed values using TCP connected socket (sockfd) to the connected server based on the threshold value (val). Similarly, define a get function for accessing sensed values as follows.

```
void IoTSensor::setSenseValue(float val)
{
    sense_value = val;
    sprintf(buffer,"Value is %f",val);
    if (val>sense_thr_file)
    {
        cout<<"Writing to file..\n";
        myfile<<buffer;
    }

    if (val>sense_thr_server)
    {
        cout<<"Sending to Server..\n";
```

CHAPTER 3   SYSTEMATICALLY STARTING AND STOPPING SOFTWARE OBJECTS

```
        write(sockfd, buffer, strlen(buffer)+1);
    }
}
float IoTSensor::getSenseValue()
{
    return sense_value;
}
```

5. Write your `main()` program for testing your IoT sensor objects as follows.

   a. Create ten sensor objects dynamically.

   b. Configure sensor objects sensed values storing filenames as *Sensor1.txt*, *Sensor2.txt*, and so on.

   c. Configure network server IP and port numbers 127.0.0.1 and 12345 for your `IoTsensor` objects.

   d. Configure sample thresholds for storing into files and sending to servers.

   e. Configure sensor object identifiers as `sensorA`, `sensorB`, and so on.

   f. Configure `IoTsensor` objects deployment locations (x,y).

   g. Configure sample sensing values for `IoTsensor` objects.

   h. Configure sample battery values for `IoTsensor` objects.

   ```
   int main()
   {
       IoTSensor *isensor[10];
       for (int i=0;i<10;i++)
       {
           char filename[15];
   ```

CHAPTER 3   SYSTEMATICALLY STARTING AND STOPPING SOFTWARE OBJECTS

```
            sprintf(filename,"Sensor%d.txt",i+1);
            float fthr = 0.003;
            float nthr = 0.006;
            isensor[i] = new IoTSensor(filename,"127.0.
            0.1",12345,fthr,nthr);
        }
        for (int i=0;i<10;i++)
        {
            isensor[i]->setId("sensor"+string(1,'A'+i));
            isensor[i]->setX(i*10);
            isensor[i]->setY(i*10);
            isensor[i]->setSenseValue(i*0.001);
            isensor[i]->setBatteryLevel(100/(i+1));
        }
        return 0;
    }
```

6. Let's test it as follows.

   a. Start the `IoTSensor` object without running the network server using the following commands on your computer.

   ```
   # g++ iot_sensor_const.cc -o iot_sensors_start
   # ./iot_sensors_start
   Socket successfully created..
   connection with the server failed...
   ..
   ```

   You can observe all `IoTSensor` object connections failed. This error is because no TCP server is running on port number 12345.

CHAPTER 3 SYSTEMATICALLY STARTING AND STOPPING SOFTWARE OBJECTS

b. Check which files are created by `IoTSensor` objects using the following command on your computer.

```
# ls -rt
Sensor1.txt
Sensor2.txt
..
..
```

You can observe that temporary files were created, but no data was written into them by opening files. Next, you test the code after starting the `iperf` server.

c. Run `iperf` TCP server on port number 12345 using the following command in a new terminal.

```
# iperf -s -p 12345
------------------------------------------------------
Server listening on TCP port 12345
TCP window size:  128 KByte (default)
------------------------------------------------------
```

d. Start your `IoTSensor` objects using the following command in another terminal.

```
# ./iot_sensors_start
opening the existing  file
Socket successfully created..
connected to the server..
opening the existing  file
..
Value is 0.000000
Value is 0.001000
Value is 0.002000
Value is 0.003000
```

CHAPTER 3   SYSTEMATICALLY STARTING AND STOPPING SOFTWARE OBJECTS

```
Value is 0.004000
Writing to file..
Value is 0.005000
..
Value is 0.007000
Writing to file..
Sending to Server..
..
Value is 0.009000
Writing to file..
Sending to Server..
```

The results show that *as your application starts,* all `IoTSensor` objects connect to the `iperf` TCP server. You can confirm it by checking the `iperf` **TCP** server running on the terminal.

```
[ 4] local 127.0.0.1 port 12345 connected with 127.0.0.1 port 44194
[ ID] Interval       Transfer     Bandwidth
[ 4]  0.0- 0.0 sec   0.00 Bytes   0.00 bits/sec
[ 7] local 127.0.0.1 port 12345 connected with 127.0.0.1 port 44198
..
[ 5] local 127.0.0.1 port 12345 connected with 127.0.0.1 port 44196
[ 5]  0.0- 0.0 sec   0.00 Bytes   0.00 bits/sec
[ 21] local 127.0.0.1 port 12345 connected with 127.0.0.1 port 44212 (peer 22113.27765.25888)
[ 21]  0.0- 0.0 sec   18.0 Bytes   1.11 Mbits/sec
..
[ 17] local 127.0.0.1 port 12345 connected with 127.0.0.1 port 44208 (peer 22113.27765.25888)
```

CHAPTER 3   SYSTEMATICALLY STARTING AND STOPPING SOFTWARE OBJECTS

```
[ 17]  0.0- 0.0 sec  18.0 Bytes   762 Kbits/sec
[ 19] local 127.0.0.1 port 12345 connected with
127.0.0.1 port 44210 (peer 22113.27765.25888)
[ 19]  0.0- 0.0 sec  18.0 Bytes   727 Kbits/sec
```
[SUM] 0.0- 0.0 sec   54.0 Bytes 2.18 Mbits/sec

The `iperf` TCP results show IoTSensor objects (sensed value>0.6) send their values, and the `iperf` TCP server received them.

Next, let's check the IoTSensor-generated text files.

e. Open another terminal and give the following commands to check *Sensor.txt* files and their contents.

```
# ls -rt
Sensor1.txt
Sensor2.txt
..
Sensor5.txt
Sensor10.txt

# cat Sensor1.txt
```
Nothing will be displayed.
```
cat Sensor5.txt
Value is 0.004000
cat Sensor10.txt
Value is 0.009000
```

From the results, you can observe that as your *application starts* IoTSensor objects (sensed value >0.3) had written their sensed values into respective *Sensor.txt* files. Hence, you won't find any contents from *Sensor1.txt* to *Sensor2.txt* files. From IoTSensor object 4 (*Sensor5.txt*), you can find the sensed values.

161

CHAPTER 3   SYSTEMATICALLY STARTING AND STOPPING SOFTWARE OBJECTS

Well done. You have completed the `IoTSensor` objects startup sequence hands-on activity successfully. Specifically, you learned during the startup of your `IoTSensor` objects how to configure `IoTSensor` objects automatically with default values, acquire dynamic memory for processing, create necessary files for storage, and connect with external services for sending sensed values.

Next, you learn how to automatically handle shutdown activities of your IoTSensor objects.

Hands-on Activity 2: Destructors

During hands-on activity 1, you observed the following.

- When you start your application, once your `IoTSensor` objects are created, they are configured with all necessary configurations, such as filenames, network server addresses, and thresholds.

- Allotted with suitable dynamic memory for buffers.

- For each `IoTSensor` object, a corresponding storage file was created.

- Automatically connected with configured live network servers.

However, you forgot to do the following important tasks as part of closing your smart application.

- Releasing `IoTsensor` objects' buffer memory

- Closing the files after completing the task

- Closing the network connection after sending the sensed values

- Removing unnecessary files

CHAPTER 3   SYSTEMATICALLY STARTING AND STOPPING SOFTWARE OBJECTS

As part of this hands-on activity, do the following tasks to shut down your application.

- Implement C++ destructors for automatically handling the following tasks when `IoTSensor` objects are deleted.

    - Closing the files after completing the task

    - Closing the network connection after sending the sensed values

    - Removing unnecessary files

HANDS-ON ACTIVITY: IOT SENSORS SHUTDOWN TASKS

1. Let's modify your `IoTSensor` class by including the following line in *iot_sensor_const.cc*..

   ~IoTSensor();

2. Define your `IoTSensor` object's destructor for doing the following tasks.

   a. Deleting allocated memory for `IoTSensor` object' buffer

   b. Closing `IoTSensor` objects opened files

   c. Delete the `Sensor.txt` if there is no content

   d. Close the network socket connection with the `iperf` TCP network server

   ```
   IoTSensor::~IoTSensor()
   {
       cout<<"Shutdown activities:\n";
       cout<<"Deleing the buffer memory!\n";
       delete buffer;
   ```

163

```
            unsigned int file_size;
            file_size=myfile.tellg();
            cout<<"Closing all opened files\n";
            myfile.close();

            if (file_size==0)
            {
                cout<<"Removing files which do not have any
                data: "<<getFilename()<<"\n";
                remove(getFilename());
            }

            cout<<"Closing IoTSensor object network
            connection..\n";
            close(sockfd);
    }
```

3. Extend your `main()` code for deleting all dynamically created IoT objects with the following lines of code.

```
for (int i=0;i<10;i++)
{
    delete isensor[i];
}
```

4. Well done. You have updated the `IoTSensor` class and `main()` function for handling shutdown activities. Let's test it.

5. Let's run your updated application using the following commands after starting the `iperf` **TCP** server in a new terminal.

```
# ./iot_sensors_start
opening the existing file
Socket successfully created..
connected to the server..
```

CHAPTER 3 SYSTEMATICALLY STARTING AND STOPPING SOFTWARE OBJECTS

Writing to file..
Sending to Server..
Writing to file..
Sending to Server..
..

Shutdown activities:
Deleting the buffer memory!
Closing all opened files
Removing files which do not have any data: **Sensor1.txt**
Closing IoTSensor object network connection..
Shutdown activities:
Deleting the buffer memory!
Closing all opened files
Removing files which do not have any data: **Sensor2.txt**
Closing IoTSensor object network connection..
Shutdown activities:
Deleting the buffer memory!
Closing all opened files
Removing files which do not have any data: **Sensor3.txt**
Closing IoTSensor object network connection..
Shutdown activities:
Deleting the buffer memory!
Closing all opened files
Removing files which do not have any data: **Sensor4.txt**
Closing IoTSensor object network connection..
..
Shutdown activities:
Deleting the buffer memory!
Closing all opened files
Closing IoTSensor object network connection..
Shutdown activities:

CHAPTER 3 SYSTEMATICALLY STARTING AND STOPPING SOFTWARE OBJECTS

```
Deleting the buffer memory!
Closing all opened files
Closing IoTSensor object network connection..
```

When you run your application without destructors, even after the application closes, you observe no automatic deletion of buffer memory, closing files, removing unnecessary files, and closing network connections.

These results show that the following shutdown activities are done automatically using destructors: *deleting the buffer memory, closing* files, *removing* files that do not have any data, and *closing* network connections.

It means when your objects get deleted, `~IoTSensor()` **destructor** handles all shutdown activities automatically.

After your application closes, it is highly important to release acquired computational resources, closing its opened network connections to prevent attacks from malicious users. Otherwise, attackers can explore open files and half open socket connections for malicious activities.

Using destructors, all critical shutdown activities are defined in one place and executed automatically. It helps you to easily debug and track shutdown activities.

Well done. You have completed the shutdown activities of your smart application `IoTSensor` objects.

Summary

This chapter explained the importance of C++ constructors and destructors for carrying out software startup and shutdown activities. Besides, you have practiced C++ supporting constructors and destructors using interesting hands-on activities. It helps you to systematically implement complex software applications startup and shutdown activities.

CHAPTER 3 SYSTEMATICALLY STARTING AND STOPPING SOFTWARE OBJECTS

In the next chapter, you learn important C++ specific features, such as friend classes, functions, and other important topics.

Practice: Hands-on Activities

1. List all possible initialization activities, configurations, and resource allocations needed for any of your favorite games.

2. To initialize your game characters, weapons, and vehicle locations, use suitable constructors, implement your C++ code, and test it.

3. Initialize your game characters, weapons, and vehicle locations using secret files using constructors and test it in your C++ code.

4. Connect your game vehicle objects during startup with a TCP network server and send their locations to it. Implement it in your C++ code using constructors and test it.

5. Close all secret files and socket connections opened by your game using destructors. Implement your code and test it.

CHAPTER 4

Exploring Important C++ Features

This chapter begins by exploring C++ special features such as `friend` member functions and `friend` classes for accessing objects' private data and member functions. Then, hands-on activities use friend member functions and friend classes to access the object's secret data. Later, you look at some ways to pass arguments to functions to communicate with objects efficiently. As part of practice, you do activities related to passing arguments by copying values, passing pointers, and references. These activities help you choose the right way to pass arguments to functions.

Next, you see how to handle the sharing of data among objects of a class using `static` fields (data members) and `static` member functions. It helps you to handle allocating and accessing common data of objects. You practice `static` fields and `static` member functions for handling situations such as controlling all object's activities and accessing their common data.

Finally, you discover the importance of using constant pointers, a pointer to a constant, and a constant pointer to a constant. As part of practice activities, you learn how to restrict accidental changes to data members of objects.

CHAPTER 4   EXPLORING IMPORTANT C++ FEATURES

This chapter covers the following topics.

- C++ friend classes and functions
- Hands-on activity: When to use C++ friend concepts
- Best practices in passing arguments
- Sharing data of objects using C++ static
- Restricting accidental changes using C++ const

C++ Friend Classes and Functions

You have already learned how to implement objects' data-hiding features in C++ by including the data members of the class under the `private` section and the corresponding data members accessing functions under the `public` section. Data hiding ensures that nonmember functions (or any external functions) defined outside of a class can access `private` data members using only `public` member functions of the class. However, there are the following important scenarios in which you need to enable special approaches for accessing a class's `private` data members by external functions and other classes.

- When no public member functions are available inside the class to access certain private data members of the class.
- When you are not allowed to define any more public member functions inside the class.
- When you need to provide access to the class's private members (fields and member functions) through specific external functions only.

CHAPTER 4   EXPLORING IMPORTANT C++ FEATURES

In C++, you can handle these challenges using the `friend` concept. If you want to enable an external function to access a class's private data members and member functions, you can define the specific external function as a `friend` function to the class. Similarly, if you want to enable an external class to access a class's `private` data members and member functions, then you can define the specific external class as a `friend` `class` to the class. Let's start with understanding `friend` functions.

C++ Friend Functions

For instance, you defined a class called `class Secret` and defined all its data members and member functions as private. Afterward, your `Secret` class private data and member functions were inaccessible to external functions.

But, suppose one of the external functions needs to access `Secret` objects private data members and member functions. To handle these situations, C++ is offering `friend` functions. You can easily handle it by declaring the external function as a `friend` function inside the `Secret` class, as follows.

```
class Secret
{
    private:

    int secret;
    void setSecret(int id)
    {
        secret = id;
    }
    int getSecret()
    {
        return secret;
    }
```

```
    friend void external_fun(Secret s);
};
void external_fun(Secret s)
{
    s.setSecret(100);
    cout<<s.getSecret()<<"\n";
    cout<<s.secret;
}
```

From these code snippets, you should observe the following.

- Your external function: external_fun is declared a friend function inside the Secret class using the friend keyword.

- Your external_fun is defined without the friend keyword and outside the Secret class.

- Your external_fun is taking a Secret class s object as an input argument to access the class's private data and member functions.

- Inside external_fun, Secret class private data members and member functions access is only through the s object.

- Inside external_fun, you can also observe that the private field (secret) is accessible through Secret member functions (getSecret() and setSecret()), and the secret field is directly also accessible using the s object (s.secret).

Next, Let's test it inside the main() function as follows. Let's save your code snippets in secret.cc and execute it.

```
int main()
{
    Secret s;
    cout<<s.getSecret();
    external_fun(s);
}
```

```
# g++ secret.cc -o friend1
# ./friend1
secret.cc: In function 'int main()':
secret.cc:28:20: error: 'int Secret::getSecret()' is private
within this context
   28 |     cout<<s.getSecret()<<"\n";
      |                    ^
secret.cc:12:5: note: declared private here
   12 |     int getSecret()
      |         ^~~~~~~~~
```

Your Secret class data members and member functions are completely hidden from all external member functions except for the external_fun. Hence, main() does not have access to Secret class private data members and member functions.

Let's remove the s.getSecret line of code and execute it again.

```
# g++ secret.cc -o friend1
# ./friend1
100
100
```

From the results, you can observe that external_fun is able to set the private field secret value to 100 and retrieve it. If you observe the code, in the main() function external_fun is called just like any other function. Since it is a friend function, an object of the Secret class is passed to access the class's private data and member functions.

C++ friend functions help offer access to the private data of a class to only specific external functions. However, friend functions are unsuitable for providing private data access only to a specific class and its objects. It means you need to increase the scope of private data members access to a `class` level. Next, let's look at how to offer access to private data members and member functions of a class to specific classes only.

C++ Friend Class

The C++ `friend` class concept helps ensure a `class`'s `private` data members and member functions access to only specific classes, their objects, and member functions. Suppose you have a `Secret` class with only private data members and member functions, and there is another class called `Authenticated` to access the `Secret` class. Then, it is possible to enforce that only the `Authenticated` `class`, its objects, and member functions can access the `Secret` class. Using the C++ friend concept, the `Secret` class private data members and member functions access can only be provided through the `Authenticated` objects. It can be done by declaring the `Authenticated` as a `friend` `class` inside the `Secret` class. Let's do this task by writing the following code snippets.

```cpp
class Authenticated;
class Secret
{
    private:

    int secret;
    void setSecret(int id)
    {
        secret = id;
    }
```

```
        int getSecret()
        {
            return secret;
        }
        friend class Authenticated;
};
class Authenticated
{
        int myId;
        public:
        void accessSecrets(Secret s)
        {
            myId = 100;
            s.setSecret(100);
            cout<<"Secret set to "<<s.secret;
        }
};
```

From these code snippets, you should observe the following.

- Your Authenticated class is declared as a friend class inside the Secret class using the friend keyword. It means the Authenticated class can access private data members and member functions of the Secret class.

- The Authenticated class defines a public member function called accessSecrets to access Secret class private data members and member functions.

- You can define your main() with a Secret class object and an Authenticated class object. Then, using the Authenticated class object, you can access the Secret class object's private data and member functions.

CHAPTER 4   EXPLORING IMPORTANT C++ FEATURES

- No external functions can access Secret class object's private data members and member functions; only the Authenticated class objects can access them.

- Important note: Although the Authenticated class is a friend to the Secret class, the Secret class cannot access the Authenticated class private data members (myId) and member functions.

Let's test it inside the main() function as follows. Let's save your code snippets and the following main() code snippet in authenicated.cc and test it.

```
int main()
{
    Secret s;
    // s.setSecret(100);
    Authenticated aobj;
    a.accessSecrets(s);
}
```

In the main() function, if you try to access the Secret class private data directly, your code execution throws the following errors.

```
# g++ authenticated.cc
#./a.out
authenticated.cc: In function 'int main()':
authenticated.cc:33:17: error: 'void Secret::setSecret(int)' is private within this context
   33 |     s.setSecret(100);
      |                 ^
authenticated.cc:9:6: note: declared private here
    9 | void setSecret(int id)
```

Let's comment s.setSecret() line of code and execute it.

```
# g++ authenticated.cc
# ./a.out
Secret set to 100
```

In the `main()` function, using the `Authenticated` class object `aobj`, you are invoking its public member function called `accessSecrets` to access the `Secret` class private data members and member functions. It means the `Secret` class is accessible through only `Authenticated` class objects. In this example, you saw that if class A is friend to class B, only class A can access the private data of class B.

Next, as part of hands-on activities, you learn how to make two classes friends with each other.

Hands-on Activity: When to Use C++ Friend Concepts

Let's practice using C++ friend concepts in the following important activities.

- Practicing friend function usage in the context of a sample game implementation.

  - Suppose you need to model a Player class with his id, location (x,y), and secret location (sx,sy) as private data members in a game.

  - You can provide access to the player's location (x,y) through public member functions. However, you are not allowed to define any public member function inside the player class to access the players' secret locations (`sx,sy`).

  - You need to offer players secret location (`sx,sy`) access to a specific external function only.

CHAPTER 4 EXPLORING IMPORTANT C++ FEATURES

- Practicing friend class usage in the context of a sample game implementation scenario.

  - In your game application, there are two groups of players called PlayerA and PlayerB.

  - Every player has a location (x,y).

  - Player locations are accessible only through private member functions.

  - PlayerA and PlayerB are friends to each other. It means a player from PlayerA group can access players' locations in the PlayerB group. Similarly, players from PlayerB group can access the locations of players of the PlayerA group.

  - No other external class and functions can access the locations of PlayerA and PlayerB groups.

Let's start with the following hands-on activity for implementing accessing secret locations of players through friend functions.

FRIEND FUNCTION TO ACCESS PLAYER'S SECRET LOCATIONS

1. Do the following.

   a. Define a player objects modeling class called Player1 with private data members such as id, location (x,y), and secret location (sx,sy).

   b. Define a suitable public set and get member functions to access id, x, and y.

   c. Set secret locations (sx,sy) inside the set functions of (x,y).

CHAPTER 4　EXPLORING IMPORTANT C++ FEATURES

d. Do not define any get functions for accessing sx and sy.

e. Declare a friend function called friendToPlayer inside the Player1 class.

2. Let's define your Player1 class code inside the friendfunctions.cc as follows.

```
#include<iostream>
using namespace std;
class Player1
{
        int id;
        int x,y;
        int sx,sy;
        public:
        void setId(int iid)
        {
            id = iid;
        }
        int getId()
        {
            return id;
        }
        void setX(int ix)
        {
            x = ix;
            sx = x*3;
        }
        void setY(int iy)
        {
            y = iy;
```

CHAPTER 4 EXPLORING IMPORTANT C++ FEATURES

```
            sy = y*3;
        }
        int getX()
        {
            return x;
        }
        int getY()
        {
            return y;
        }
        friend void friendToPlayer(Player1 *p);
};
```

3. Define your friend function to access player objects' secret locations through player object pointer.

```
void friendToPlayer(Player1 *p1)
{
    cout<<"Player id:"<<p1->id<<" secret x "<<p1->sx<<" secret y "<<p1->sy;
}
```

4. Define the main() function for testing your code by accessing the Players secret location using the friend function.

```
int main()
{
    Player1 p1;
    cout<<"Secret accessing"<<p1.sx;
    p1.setId(100);
    p1.setX(10);
    p1.setY(10);
    friendToPlayer(&p1);
}
```

5. Test your code using g++ compiler and observe the following.

    a. `main()` is not allowed to access player object secret location `sx` directly.

    b. `main()` is allowed to access player object normal locations (x,y) using set and get functions

    c. `main()` is allowed to access the player object's secret location (sx,sy) through `friendToPlayer`.

    ```
    # g++ friendfunctions.cc -o friend1
    friendfunctions.cc: In function 'int main()':
    friendfunctions.cc:47:30: error: 'int Player1::sx'
    is private within this context
        47 |     cout<<"Secret accesing"<<p1.sx;
           |                              ^~
    friendfunctions.cc:7:6: note: declared private here
         7 |     int sx,sy;
           |         ^~
    ```

There are errors due to `main()` trying to access the players secret location sx directly. Let's comment it and execute it again as follows:

```
# g++ friendfunctions.cc -o friend1
# ./friend1
Player id:100 secret x 30 secret y 30
```

This time, `main()` can successfully access player object p1 secret locations through the friend function.

Well done! You have successfully tested the friend function.

Next, let's learn how to make two classes friends.

CHAPTER 4 EXPLORING IMPORTANT C++ FEATURES

FRIEND CLASSES

1. As part of practicing friend classes, let's do the following activities.

   a. Define two classes called `PlayerA` and `PlayerB` to model two groups of player objects.

   b. Define `PlayerA` and `PlayerB` classes with private data members such as id, location (x,y).

   c. Define all set and get functions as private member functions.

   d. Allow `PlayerA` objects to access `PlayerB` objects' locations.

   e. Allow `PlayerB` objects to access `PlayerA` objects' locations.

   f. Allow the `main()` function to access PlayerA and PlayerB private member functions through a friend function only.

2. To carry out these activities, let's declare the PlayerA class in `friendclasses.cc`.

   a. Define `id, x, y` as private members and related set and get functions. Next, declare a location access function: `myFriendLocation` to access `PlayerB` location.

   b. Declare an external friend function: `friendtoAB` to access `PlayerA` and `PlayerB` objects data from the `main()`.

   c. Declare `PlayerB` as a friend to it. As `PlayerA` needs to access `PlayerB` data members, there is a forward declaration of `PlayerB` class before the `PlayerA` class definition.

   ```
   #include<iostream>
   using namespace std;
   class PlayerB;
   ```

```
class PlayerA
{
    private:
    int id;
    int x,y;
    void setId(int iid);
    int getId();
    void setX(int ix);
    int getX();
    void setY(int iy);
    int getY();
    void myFriendLocation(PlayerB p1);
    friend void friendtoAB(PlayerA *pa,
    PlayerB* pb);
    friend class PlayerB;
};
```

3. Define all set and get functions for accessing PlayerA fields as follows.

```
void PlayerA::setId(int iid)
{
    id = iid;
}
int PlayerA::getId()
{
    return id;
}
void PlayerA::setX(int ix)
{
    x = ix;
}
```

```
void PlayerA::setY(int iy)
{
       y = iy;
}
int PlayerA::getX()
{
       return x;
}
int PlayerA::getY()
{
       return y;
}
```

4. Define the PlayerB class with private data members such as id, x, and y.

    a. Declare a location access function: myFriendLocation to access PlayerA location.

    b. Declare an external friend function: friendtoAB to access PlayerA and PlayerB objects data from the main().

    c. Declare PlayerA as a friend class to the PlayerB.

    ```
    class PlayerB
    {
          private:
          int id;
          int x,y;
          void setId(int iid);
          int getId();
          void setX(int ix);
          int getX();
          void setY(int iy);
          int getY();
    ```

```
            void myFriendLocation(PlayerA p1);
            friend void friendtoAB(PlayerA *pa,
            PlayerB* pb);
            friend class PlayerA;
      };
```

5. Define all set and get functions for accessing PlayerB fields as follows.

```
void PlayerB::setId(int iid)
{
      id = iid;
}
int PlayerB::getId()
{
      return id;
}
void PlayerB::setX(int ix)
{
      x = ix;
}
void PlayerB::setY(int iy)
{
      y = iy;
}
int PlayerB::getX()
{
      return x;
}
int PlayerB::getY()
{
      return y;
}
```

CHAPTER 4 EXPLORING IMPORTANT C++ FEATURES

6. Define the PlayerB function to access the PlayerA location.

    ```
    void PlayerB::myFriendLocation(PlayerA p1)
    {
            cout<<"My Id is "<<getId()<<"and My friend
            "<<p1.getId()<<"is located at secret location
            (x,y):"<<p1.getX()<<","<<p1.getY()<<"\n";
    }
    ```

7. Define the PlayerA function to access the PlayerB location.

    ```
    void PlayerA::myFriendLocation(PlayerB p1)
    {
            cout<<"My Id is "<<getId()<<"and My friend
            "<<p1.getId()<<"is located at secret location
            (x,y):"<<p1.getX()<<","<<p1.getY()<<"\n";
    }
    ```

8. Define an external friend function to access `PlayerA` and `PlayerB` object's private data from the main().

    ```
    void friendtoAB(PlayerA *pa, PlayerB* pb)
    {
            pa->setId(100);
            pa->setX(10);
            pa->setY(10);
            pb->setId(200);
            pb->myFriendLocation(*pa);
            pb->setX(20);
            pb->setY(20);
            pa->myFriendLocation(*pb);
    }
    ```

CHAPTER 4 EXPLORING IMPORTANT C++ FEATURES

9. Test your code as follows in your `main()` program.

    ```
    int main()
    {
        PlayerA pa;
        PlayerB pb;
        friendtoAB(&pa,&pb);
    }
    ```

10. Test your `main()` code using the following commands and observe the following.

    a. PlayerA objects can access the PlayerB object location.

    b. PlayerB objects can access the PlayerA object location.

    c. `main()` is accessing `PlayerA` and `PlayerB` through `friendtoAB` function.

    ```
    # g++ friendclasses.cc -o friendclasses
    # ./friendclasses
    My Id is 200and My friend 100is located at secret location (x,y):10,10
    My Id is 100and My friend 200is located at secret location (x,y):20,20
    ```

Well done. You completed the task and learned how to make two classes friends with each other and how to access their private data.

Next, let's discuss the various ways to pass arguments to functions.

CHAPTER 4   EXPLORING IMPORTANT C++ FEATURES

Best Practices in Passing Arguments

It is common to pass arguments to functions for carrying out processing tasks. You plan to do the following when you pass arguments from a source function to a destination function.

- The destination function should change the values of the original variables. In this scenario, you pass the address of the original variable to the destination function.

    - The destination function is defined with pointer arguments to hold the addresses of the source function variables. (e.g., int *, Player *, etc.).

    - Having the address of the source function variables, the destination function modifies the values of the original variables from the source function variables' address locations only.

    - In C++, to change the object data (data members values), you must pass the object's address to the destination function.

- The destination function changes should not modify the original variables' values. In this scenario, you pass the copy of the original variable to the destination function.

    - The destination function is defined with new variables to copy the values of the source function variables. (e.g., int, Player, etc.). That means the destination function creates new variables at new locations.

CHAPTER 4   EXPLORING IMPORTANT C++ FEATURES

- Since the destination function changes the copied values of the original variables, the source function's original variables are not changed.

- In C++, to avoid changing the object data (data members values), you should not pass the object's address to the destination function. You should pass only the object name to the destination function.

However, a few exceptions exist when passing arrays to functions, such as when you pass the array name from the source function to the destination function. By default, the array starting address is passed to the destination function. Having the starting address of the source array, the destination function can modify the source array location values directly.

The destination function can be defined with array arguments or pointer arguments. For instance, to pass int a[20] to a function, you can define it as follows.

destinationFunction (int a[20]) or destinationFunction (int *a)

Similarly, to pass an array of objects of a class: Player p[20] to a function, you can define it as follows.

destinationFunction (Player p[]) or destinationFunction (Player *p)

In C++, another important way is called passing reference of a variable for passing arguments to functions. Let's first go over reference variables.

- Reference variables are passed to the destination function for referencing the original variables. Hence, the destination function can change the original variable values. A reference variable works like a pointer variable to change the original variable values, but there are a few differences.

- When you define a reference variable, it must be initialized with a referencing variable. For example, `int a; int &ref = a;` here, `ref` is referencing variable a. You can change `ref` to change the variable values of a. For example, `ref = ref+1` changes the variable a value.

- Unlike pointers, to pass a reference of a variable no need to pass the address of the variable. For example, you can just pass the original variable name (`int a`) from the source function to call a function: `func(a);` and the destination function should be defined with the respective reference variable argument as `fun(int &a)`.

- Reference variables need not be dereferenced like pointer variables to access the values.

- Reference variables simplify the syntax compared to pointers usage.

Next, let's practice passing arguments.

Arguments Passing Activities

This section covers the following concepts by doing activities.

- Passing objects by values, addresses, and references
- Passing an array of objects
- Passing dynamically created array of objects

Let's start by looking at various ways to pass objects to functions.

PASSING OBJECTS TO FUNCTIONS

1. To better understand passing objects as arguments to functions, let's define the following example class called `Item`.

    a. Save all the following code snippets in `passingobjects.cc`.

    b. Define `Item` class with private fields id and price.

    c. Define a constructor to initialize Item id and price.

    d. Define id accessing set and get functions.

    ```
    #include<iostream>
    using namespace std;
    class Item
    {
            int id;
            int price;
            public:
            Item()
            {
                    id = rand()/100;
                    price = 100;
            }
            void setId(int i)
            {
                id = i;
            }
            int getId()
            {
                return id;
            }
    };
    ```

CHAPTER 4 EXPLORING IMPORTANT C++ FEATURES

2. Do the following.

   a. Define a function called changeItem, pass the Item object as a value, and set the id to 100.

   b. Define a function called changeItemwPtr, pass the Item object address, and set the id to 100.

   c. Define a function called changeItemwRef, pass the Item object reference, and set the id to 100.

   ```
   void changeItem(Item i)
   {
           i.setId(100);
   }
   void changeItemwPtr(Item *i)
   {
           i->setId(100);
   }
   void changeItemwRef(Item &i)
   {
           i.setId(100);
   }
   ```

3. Implement your main() testing code as follows and observe the following.

   a. To call the changeItem, pass the object name: i1.

   b. To call the changeItemwPtr, pass the address of the object: &i1.

   c. To call the changeItemwRef, pass the object name as i1.

   ```
   int main()
   {
           Item i1;
           changeItem(i1);
           cout<<"Item id"<<i1.getId()<<"\n";
   ```

```
changeItemwPtr(&i1);
cout<<"Item id"<<i1.getId()<<"\n";

changeItemwRef(i1);
cout<<"Item id"<<i1.getId()<<"\n";
}
```

4. Test your code by executing `passingobjects.cc` and observe the following.

   a. Although `changeItem` updated `id` to 100, changes are not reflected in `main()`. It is because you passed the copy of the object only. Hence, you observe a random id in `main()`.

   b. Changes done to `id` by `changeItemwPtr` are reflected in `main()`, it is due to passing the actual address of the item object.

   c. Changes done to `id` by `changeItemwRef` are reflected in `main()`, it is due to passing the reference of the item object.

   ```
   # g++ passingobjects.cc -o argspassing
   # ./argspassing
   Item id18042893
   Item id100
   Item id100
   ```

From the results, passing either object address or reference is only helpful to change objects' data. Moreover, passing a reference or an address eliminates copying the object from the source function memory space to the destination function memory space.

On the other hand, copying an object from the source function memory space to the destination function memory space does not help change the original object data.

Next, let's pass an array of objects to a function and how it works.

CHAPTER 4 EXPLORING IMPORTANT C++ FEATURES

PASSING ARRAY OF OBJECTS TO A FUNCTION

1. Copy `passingobjects.cc` to `arrayobjects.cc` and make the following changes.

    a. Define a function called `processwarray` and pass an array of items to the function for printing objects' address and item id.

    ```
    void processwarray(Item ti[COUNT])
    {
        for (int i=0;i<COUNT;i++)
        {
            cout<<"Address of item "<<&ti[i]<<"\n";
            cout<<"Item processed "<<ti[i].
            getId()<<"\n";
        }
    }
    ```

    b. Define a function called `processwptr` and pass a pointer to the array of items to the function for printing the object's address and item id.

    ```
    void processwptr(Item *p)
    {
        for (int i=0;i<COUNT;i++)
        {
            cout<<"Address of item "<<&p[i]<<"\n";
            cout<<"Item processed "<<p[i].
            getId()<<"\n";
        }
    }
    ```

2. Define the main() testing code for the following activities.

   a. Define an array of item objects.

   b. Print each item's object address.

   c. Call processwarray() by passing the array name to print the array of item objects' addresses and each item's id.

   d. Call processwptr() by passing the array starting address (through array name) to print the array of item objects' addresses and each item's id.

   ```
   int main()
   {
           Item il[COUNT];
           for (int i=0;i<COUNT;i++)
           {
                   cout<<"Address of item "<<&il[i]<<"\n";
           }

           cout<<"\nSame Locations will be accessed\n";
           processwarray(il);
           cout<<"\nSame Locations will be accessed\n";
           processwptr(il);
   }
   ```

3. Test your code using the following commands and observe the following.

   a. main(), processwarray(), and processwptr() print the same addresses of the array of objects.

   b. Passing the array name itself leads to passing the starting address of the array.

   c. Hence, all three functions are processing the same array of item objects.

CHAPTER 4   EXPLORING IMPORTANT C++ FEATURES

```
# g++ arrayobjects.cc -o arrayofobjs
# ./arrayofobjs
```

```
Address of item 0x7ffd46550ec0
Address of item 0x7ffd46550ec8
Address of item 0x7ffd46550ed0
.. few lines skipped
Same Locations will be accessed
Address of item 0x7ffd46550ec0
Item processed 18042893
Address of item 0x7ffd46550ec8
Item processed 8469308
Address of item 0x7ffd46550ed0
Item processed 16816927
```

```
.. few lines skipped
Same Locations will be accessed
Address of item 0x7ffd46550ec0
Item processed 18042893
Address of item 0x7ffd46550ec8
Item processed 8469308
Address of item 0x7ffd46550ed0
Item processed 16816927
.. few lines skipped
```

The results show that the addresses of item objects printed in main() functions are the same as addresses printed through processwarray(il) and processwptr(il) functions. It means instead of copying actual objects to the functions, you can access the objects using their actual addresses. It eliminates unnecessary copying of memory contents from one process space to another. Hence, it is highly efficient for passing an array of objects to any function.

Another important detail note is that both functions print the same item id values.

That means arrays are passed to a function by default with an array starting address. Hence, functions can update array location values.

Next, let's pass a dynamically created array of object memory blocks to a function and how it works.

> **PASSING DYNAMICALLY CREATED OBJECTS MEMORY BLOCK TO A FUNCTION**
>
> 1. Copy `passingobjects.cc` to `dynobjects.cc` and make the following changes.
>
>   a. Define a function called `process` and pass a pointer to an array of items to the function for printing an object's address and item id.
>
>    ```
>    void process(Item *p)
>    {
>        if(p!=NULL)
>          for (int i=0;i<COUNT;i++)
>          {
>              cout<<"Address of item "<<&p[i]<<"\n";
>              cout<<"Item processed "<<p[i].
>              getId()<<"\n";
>          }
>    }
>    ```
>
>   b. Remove other external functions copied from the `passingobjects.cc`.

CHAPTER 4   EXPLORING IMPORTANT C++ FEATURES

2. Define the main() testing code for the following activities.

   a. Declare a pointer to hold the Item objects.

   b. Allocate ten item objects memory block dynamically using the new operator.

   c. Print each item object address and id.

   d. Call process() by passing the pointer of the dynamically created item objects memory blocks to print the addresses of the item objects and to print each item's id.

   e. Deallocate dynamically created memory.

```
int main()
{
        Item *il;
        il = new Item[COUNT];
        cout<<"main item details\n";
        if (il!=NULL)
        for (int i=0;i<COUNT;i++)
        {
                cout<<"Address of item "<<&il[i]<<"\n";
                cout<<"Item processed "<<il[i].
                getId()<<"\n";
        }
        cout<<"inside function item details\n";
        process(il);
        delete il;
}
```

3. Test your code using the following commands and observe the following.

   a. The main() and process functions access the same item object memory blocks.

   b. The main() and process functions print the same item object addresses and id details.

   ```
   # g++ arrayobjects.cc -o arrayofobjs
   # ./arrayofobjs
   ```
   main item details
   ```
   Address of item 0x564b7a533eb0
   Item processed 18042893
   Address of item 0x564b7a533eb8
   Item processed 8469308
   Address of item 0x564b7a533ec0
   Item processed 16816927
   ..
   ```
   inside function item details
   ```
   Address of item 0x564b7a533eb0
   Item processed 18042893
   Address of item 0x564b7a533eb8
   Item processed 8469308
   Address of item 0x564b7a533ec0
   Item processed 16816927
   ```

From the results, you can observe that when you create an array of object memory dynamically using a new operator, the memory block can be passed to other functions by passing the starting address of the memory block so that the destination function can access the original block of the object's memory.

Next, let's learn how to hide the private data of real-world entities and protect their objects' access from external functions.

CHAPTER 4　EXPLORING IMPORTANT C++ FEATURES

Sharing Data of Objects Using C++ Static

Usually, objects have their own copy of data members. However, in some contexts objects need to share data of a class. For instance, in e-commerce applications, to count the number of customers, it is necessary to aggregate customer registration count. Similarly, in multiplayer games, all player objects may share group details. To handle these requirements in specific classes, it is necessary to include sharing data members for all objects. In C++, you can define shared data members in a class using `static` data members declaration, and to access them, you must define `static` member functions. Let's look at how to declare `static` data members in a class and access them.

The following is an example.

```
Class Registration
{
    public:
        static int count;
        static int getCount()
    {
        return count;
    }
    static void setCount(int c)
    {
        count = c;
    }
};
```

After declaring a static data member inside a class, it must be defined (or initialized) outside the class as follows.

```
int Registration::count;
```

CHAPTER 4   EXPLORING IMPORTANT C++ FEATURES

Another important point to notice about `static` data members is they must be accessed through only `static` member functions. For instance, in the Registration class, static member functions such as static int getCount() and static void setCount(int c) are defined to access static data member count.

```
int main()
{
    Registration r1,r2;
    r1.setCount(10);
    cout<<r2.getCount(); //During execution it displays 10.
    cout<<Registration::getCount(); //Another way of //calling
                                    static member functions.
    return 0;
}
```

You should understand the following differences between normal data members and static data members.

- Every object has a separate copy of memory allocation for each normal data member during the program execution.

- For all objects, only one copy of a static data member is allocated in memory during the program execution.

- Normal data members can be accessed using normal member functions.

- Static data members must be accessed through only static member functions.

Next, let's practice using static data members and static member functions.

CHAPTER 4 EXPLORING IMPORTANT C++ FEATURES

STATIC DATA MEMBERS: USAGE 1

1. In this task, you use static data members for allocating shared data members to all objects of a class. Create a registration class and count the number of registrations by doing the following activities.

   a. Save the following task's code in `registrations.cc`.

   b. Define a registration class with a private data member `id`.

   c. Define a static private data member `count`.

   d. Define set and get member functions for accessing `id`.

   e. Define an `update` static member function for updating the `count`.

   f. Define a `getCount` static member function for accessing the count.

   ```
   #include<iostream>
   using namespace std;
   class Registration
   {
           static int count;
           int id;
           public:
           void setId(int rid)
           {
                   id = rid;
           }
           int getId()
           {
                   return id;
           }
   ```

CHAPTER 4   EXPLORING IMPORTANT C++ FEATURES

```
        static void update()
        {
                count = count+1;
        }
        static int getCount()
        {
                return count;
        }
};
```

2. Every static data member must be defined outside of the class as follows.

   `int Registration::count;`

3. Define the `main()` testing code for the following activities.

   a. Create three Registration objects.

   b. Set each registration object `id`, then update the count using static member function update.

   c. Print the registration ids of each object and the total registration count.

   ```
   int main()
   {
           Registration r1,r2,r3;
           r1.setId(100);
           r1.update();
           r2.setId(200);
           r2.update();
           r3.setId(200);
           r3.update();
   ```

```
                cout<<"Registrations list:"<<r1.getId()<<"
                "<<r2.getId()<<" "<<r3.getId()<<"\n";
                cout<<"Total number of registrations "<<
                Registration::getCount();

                return 0;
            }
```

4. Test your code and observe the following.

    a. Since three registration objects were created, the total count is three.

    b. Moreover, you can observe that static member functions can be called using an object or class name and scope resolution operator (::).

    ```
    # g++ registrations.cc -o regcount
    # ./regcount
    Registrations list:100 200 200
    Total number of registrations 3
    ```

The results show that all three objects shared the count data member. Hence, as each object updates the count, it is reflected to other objects, too.

Next, let's learn the importance of static data members for controlling all player objects' states using a single command.

CONTROL OBJECTS STATE USING STATIC DATA MEMBER

1. In a game context, let's learn how to enable or disable power for all player objects by doing the following activities.

    a. Save the following task's code in `playerscontrol.cc`.

    b. Define a player class with an example private data member such as `id`.

c. Define a player's power as a static data member to enable or disable with a single command.

d. Define set and get member functions for accessing player id.

e. Define static member functions for setting and accessing static data member power.

```cpp
#include<iostream>
using namespace std;
class Player
{
        static int power;
        int id;
        public:
        void setId(int rid)
        {
                id = rid;
        }
        int getId()
        {
                return id;
        }
        static void setPower(int ipower)
        {
                power = ipower;
        }
        static int getPower()
        {
                return power;
        }
};
```

2. Every static data member must be defined outside of the class as follows.

   ```
   int Player::power;
   ```

3. Define the main() testing code to do the following activities.

   a. Create three player objects.

   b. Set each player object id.

   c. Enable all players' power together using the static member function setPower().

   d. Print the power status of all player objects.

   e. Disable all players' power together using the static member function setPower().

   f. Print the power status of all player objects.

   ```
   int main()
   {
           enum powerstate {DISABLE,ENABLE};
           Player p1,p2,p3;
           p1.setId(100);
           p2.setId(200);
           p3.setId(300);
           cout<<"Start with enabling power for all players to fly\n";
           Player::setPower(ENABLE);

           if (p1.getPower() == ENABLE)
           {
               cout<<"Player1 can fly\n";
           }
           if (p2.getPower() == ENABLE)
           {
   ```

```
            cout<<"Player2 can fly\n";
        }
        if (p3.getPower() == ENABLE)
        {
            cout<<"Player3 can fly\n";
        }

        cout<<"Disable flying power for all player\n";
        Player::setPower(DISABLE);
        if (p1.getPower() == ENABLE || p2.getPower()
        == ENABLE || p3.getPower() == ENABLE )
        {
            cout<<"All players can fly\n";
        }
        else
        {
            cout<<"No player can fly! Power is
            disabled.\n";
        }

        return 0;
    }
```

4. Test your code and observe the following.

    a. You can observe that all players' power together is enabled when you set power using the static member function.

    b. You can also observe that all players' power together is disabled when you set power using the static member function.

    ```
    # g++ playerscontrol.cc -o controlpower
    # ./controlpower
    Start with enabling power (set to 1) for all
    players to fly
    ```

```
Player1 can fly
Player2 can fly
Player3 can fly
Disable flying power for all player
No player can fly! Power is disabled.
```

The results show that all players have been enabled and disabled successfully using static data members and static member functions.

Restricting Accidental Changes Using C++ const

You have learned how to control accessing of object data members using access specifiers such as `private`, and how to provide special access for the object's `private` data members through `friend` functions and classes.

On the other hand, you have also explored passing objects to external functions or other object functions to carry out important tasks by interacting with the objects. For example, when you need to access an object's data efficiently from a function without copying the object, you are passing the object's address or reference of the object to the function. However, the destination function can modify the object's data when you pass an object reference or address to a function. Suppose you need to pass objects to destination functions efficiently using pointers, but you want to restrict destination functions not to change any data of the objects. Then, you must learn how to use C++ to support a constant pointer, a pointer to a constant, and a constant pointer to a constant. In C++, you can implement these pointers using the `const` keyword.

The following are ways to restrict accidental changes to variables or objects in C++.

CHAPTER 4　EXPLORING IMPORTANT C++ FEATURES

- **Pointer to constant**: When you need to allow a function to read an object's data but cannot change or alter it, then you must use a pointer to constant. Restricting any modification to an object's data through the pointer is highly helpful.

The following is an example.

```
Class ABC
{
      public:
              int a;
              int getA()
              {
                      return a;
              }
};
int main()
{
      ABC obj;
      obj.a = 10;
      const ABC *p;
      p = &obj;
      p->a = 20; //It is not allowed.
      return 0;
}
```

Here, ABC *p is pointing to a constant object. Hence, the pointer cannot alter the obj value.

CHAPTER 4   EXPLORING IMPORTANT C++ FEATURES

- **Constant pointer**: When you want to assign a single object address to a pointer, you must use a constant pointer. A constant pointer is different from a pointer to constant.

    a. A constant pointer must be initialized with a variable address during a declaration of the pointer. However, the pointer to const need not be initialized during the declaration of the pointer.

    b. A constant pointer cannot be assigned with any other address after declaration, whereas a pointer to const can be assigned multiple times.

    c. A constant pointer helps in restricting multiple objects/variables address assignments to a pointer.

    d. A constant pointer's pointing variable or object data can be changed, whereas a pointer to a constant cannot change its pointing variable or object data.

    The following is an example.

    ```
    Class ABC
    {
         public:
              int a;
              int getA()
              {
                   return a;
              }
    };
    ```

```
int main()
{
    ABC obj1,obj2;
    obj1.a = 10; ABC *const cp = &obj1;
    cp->a=100; //It is allowed.
    cp = &obj2; //It is not allowed.
    return 0;
}
```

Here, you can observe that the constant pointer `cp` is initialized with the `obj1` address. Later, `cp` cannot be initialized with the other object (`obj2`) address. However, using `cp`, the `obj1` data can be changed.

1. Constant pointer to a constant: When you want to enforce a strict rule such as a pointer cannot change the values of its pointing variable or object, and once a pointer is initialized with a variable or object address, the pointer cannot be assigned with the addresses of other variables or objects. Then, you must use a constant pointer to a constant for assigning a variable or object address.

   Let's try to understand its usage by looking at the following example.

```
Class ABC
{
    public:
        int a;
        int getA()
        {
            return a;
        }
};
```

CHAPTER 4 EXPLORING IMPORTANT C++ FEATURES

```
int main()
{
    ABC obj1,obj2;
    obj1.a = 10; const ABC *const cpc = &obj1;
    cpc->a=100; //It is not allowed.
    cpc = &obj2; //It is not allowed.
    return 0;
}
```

Here, you can observe that the pointer `cpc` is initialized with the `obj1` address. Later, `cpc` cannot be initialized with the `obj2` address, and when using `cp`, the `obj1` data cannot be changed.

Next, let's practice these constants and pointers through important activities.

C++ Const and Pointer Usage Activities

This section explains three concepts through activities.

- Pointer to constant, constant pointer, constant pointer to constant

- Passing a pointer to a constant of a player object for restricting accidental changes to the player object

- Passing a constant pointer to a function to avoid later changes to the pointing address in the destination functions

Let's start by looking at const and pointer usages.

CHAPTER 4   EXPLORING IMPORTANT C++ FEATURES

C++ CONST AND POINTER USAGE

1. Let's do the following activities.

   a. Write the following code activities in ptr2const.cc.

   b. Define an integer variable and initialize its value, change its value, and print it.

   c. Declare a pointer to constant and assign the address of the integer variable with it.

   d. Print the integer variable value using the pointer.

   e. Try to change the integer variable value using the pointer. During the execution of the code, you must observe an error message related to a read-only location.

   ```
   #include<iostream>
   using namespace std;
   int main()
   {
           int a=100;
           a=a+50;
           cout<<"a value"<<a<<"\n";

           const int *ptr=&a;
           cout<<*ptr;
           *ptr=*ptr+1;

           cout<<"Accessing a through ptr"<<*ptr<<"\n";;
           return 0;
   }
   ```

213

CHAPTER 4   EXPLORING IMPORTANT C++ FEATURES

2. Test your ptr2const.cc using the following commands and observe the results.

```
#g++ ptr2const.cc
#./a.out
ptr2const.cc: In function 'int main()':
ptr2const.cc:11:6: error: assignment of read-only location '* ptr'
   11 |   *ptr=*ptr+1;
      |   ~~~~^~~~~~~
```

The results show that the pointer to constant (ptr) is not allowed to change the integer variable value. You can comment in line 11 and execute the ptr2const.cc to avoid error messages.

3. Let's look at const pointer usage by doing the following activities.

   a. Write the following code activities in constptr.cc.

   b. Define two integer variables (a and b) and initialize their values.

   c. Declare a constant pointer and assign the address of the integer variable a.

   d. Print the integer variable value using the pointer.

   e. Reassign the constant pointer with the address of variable b. During the execution of the code, you must observe an error message related to a read-only location.

```
#include<iostream>
using namespace std;
int main()
{
        int a=100;
```

CHAPTER 4 EXPLORING IMPORTANT C++ FEATURES

```
int b=200;
int *const p=&b;//must initialize
                 constant pointer
cout<<"Accessing b through p"<<*p<<"\n";
p=&a;
cout<<"Accessing a through p"<<*p;

return 0;
```

}

4. Test your constptr.cc using the following commands and observe the results.

```
#g++ constptr.cc
constptr.cc: In function 'int main()':
constptr.cc:10:3: error: assignment of read-only variable 'p'
   10 |   p=&a;
      |   ~^~~
```

From the results, you can observe that the constant pointer (p) is not allowed to change the address pointed by it. You can comment in line 10 and execute the code to avoid error messages.

Next, let's go over constant pointers to constant usage.

5. Define the main() testing code for the following activities.

   a. Learn const pointer usage by doing the following activities.

   b. Write the following code activities in constptr2const.cc.

   c. Define two integer variables (b and c) and initialize their values.

   d. Declare a constant pointer to const (cp2c) and assign with it the address of the integer variable c.

215

CHAPTER 4   EXPLORING IMPORTANT C++ FEATURES

e. Print the integer variable value using the pointer.

f. Reassign the constant pointer with the address of variable b.

g. Try to change the value of c using cp2c. During the execution of the code, you must observe an error message related to a read-only location.

```
#include<iostream>
using namespace std;
int main()
{
    int b=200;
    int c=300;
    const int *const cp2c=&c;//must initialize
    cout<<*cp2c;
    cp2c=&b;
    *cp2c=*cp2c+1;

    return 0;
}
```

```
# g++ constptr2const.cc
# ./a.out
constptr2const.cc: In function 'int main()':
constptr2const.cc:11:6: error: assignment of read-only variable 'cp2c'
   11 |     cp2c=&b;
      |     ~~~~^~~
constptr2const.cc:12:7: error: assignment of read-only location '*(const int*)cp2c'
   12 |     *cp2c=*cp2c+1;
      |     ~~~~~^~~~~~~~
```

CHAPTER 4   EXPLORING IMPORTANT C++ FEATURES

From the results, you can observe that the pointer (cp2c) is not allowed to change the address pointed by it, and cp2c cannot change the value of the integer variable c. You can comment in lines 11 and 12 and execute it to avoid error messages.

Next, let's do an activity related to a constant pointer pointing to player class objects.

CONSTANT POINTER TO OBJECTS

1. Let's practice constant pointer to objects by doing the following activities.

    a. Save the following task's code in constptr2objs.cc.

    b. Define a Player class to model player objects with the example private fields such as id and power.

    c. Define id and power data members accessing the public set and get member functions.

    ```
    #include<iostream>
    using namespace std;
    class Player
    {
        int power;
        int id;
        public:
        void setId(int rid)
        {
            id = rid;
        }
    ```

```
            int getId()
            {
                    return id;
            }
            void setPower(int ipower)
            {
                    power = ipower;
            }
            int getPower()
            {
                    return power;
            }
    };
```

2. Define an external function called whoispowerful to do the following activities.

    a. It takes two player object pointers (*p1,*p2) as arguments to access two player objects.

    b. Write cheating code such as changing the p1 pointer pointing player object address to the p2 pointer pointing player object address. Set the p1 pointing player object id to its original id (e.g.,100).

    c. Since p1 is now pointing to the p2 pointing player object, the p1 pointing player object also has the same power as the p2 pointing player object's power.

    d. Due to cheating code, this function always returns p1 as a powerful object.

    ```
    Player* whoisPowerful(Player *p1, Player *p2)
    {
            p1=p2;
            p1->setId(100);
            if (p1->getPower() >= p2->getPower())
    ```

```
    {
        return p1;
    }
    else
    {
        return p2;
    }
}
```

3. Define another external function called cwhoispowerful to do the following activities.

    a. It takes two constant pointers to player objects (* const p1, * const p2) as arguments.

    b. Write cheating code such as changing the p1 pointer pointing player object address to the p2 pointer pointing player object address. However, during execution, it leads to a read-only-related error.

    c. Since constant pointers were used, this function always returns the correct player object with maximum power.

    ```
    Player* cwhoisPowerful(Player *const p1, Player *const p2)
    {
        // p1=p2;
        if (p1->getPower() > p2->getPower())
        {
            return p1;
        }
        else
        {
            return p2;
        }
    }
    ```

CHAPTER 4   EXPLORING IMPORTANT C++ FEATURES

4. Do the following tasks in main() as follows.

   a. Define two player objects (p1,p2) and set their ids and power using set functions. While setting values, set high power to the p2 object.

   b. Call whoisPowerful to determine who is a powerful player. Although p2 is set to high power, during execution, you can observe that p1 is more powerful because of the cheating code in whoisPowerful.

   c. Call cwhoisPowerful to determine who is a powerful player. During execution, you can observe that cheating code throws errors due to constant pointers.

   ```
   int main()
   {
           Player p1,p2;
           p1.setId(100);
           p1.setPower(1);
           p2.setId(200);
           p2.setPower(2);

           Player *pa = whoisPowerful(&p1,&p2);
           cout<<pa->getId()<<" is powerful\n";

           Player *pb = cwhoisPowerful(&p1,&p2);
           cout<<pb->getId()<<" is powerful\n";

           return 0;
   }
   ```

5. Test your code by executing the following commands and observe the following.

   a. During testing, you can observe whoisPowerful executes without throwing any errors.

   b. cwhoisPowerful throws errors until you comment in cheating code related to changing constant pointers.

CHAPTER 4   EXPLORING IMPORTANT C++ FEATURES

```
g++ constptr2objs.cc -o powerfulplayer
./powefulplayer
constptr2objs.cc: In function 'Player*
cwhoisPowerful(Player*, Player*)':
constptr2objs.cc:44:11: error: assignment of read-
only parameter 'p1'
   44 |        p1=p2;
      |        ~~^~~
```

The results show that cwhoisPowerful is not allowed to change constant pointer addresses. Hence, it throws errors. Comment in line 44 and comment cwhoisPowerful function, execute the code again, and observe the results.

```
# g++ constptr2objs.cc.cc -o powerfulplayer
# ./powerful
100 is powerful
```

The results show that whoisPowerful cheated code executed successfully and returns the malicious results. Comment whoisPowerful and call cwhoisPowerful and observe the results.

```
# g++ constptr2objs.cc.cc -o powerfulplayer
# ./powerful
200 is powerful
```

The results show that cwhoisPowerful code executed successfully without any cheated code and gave the correct results.

Next, let's do an activity related to a pointer pointing to const player class objects.

CHAPTER 4   EXPLORING IMPORTANT C++ FEATURES

POINTER TO CONST OBJECTS

1. Let's practice pointer to constant objects by doing the following activities.

    a. Save the following task's code in `ptr2constobjs.cc`.

    b. Define a `Player` class to model player objects with the example public fields such as id and power.

    c. Define id and power data members accessing the public set and get member functions.

    ```
    #include<iostream>
    using namespace std;
    class Player
    {
            public:
            int power;
            int id;

            void setId(int rid)
            {
                    id = rid;
            }
            int getId()
            {
                    return id;
            }
            void setPower(int ipower)
            {
                    power = ipower;
            }
    ```

```
        int getPower()
        {
                return power;
        }
};
```

2. Define the `main()` testing code for the following activities.

   a. Define a player p1 object and set its id and power directly using the object p1.

   b. Define a pointer (pptr1) to the p1 object and directly set its id and power using the pptr1. During execution, you can observe changes to the p1 object do not throw an error.

   c. Define a player p2 object and set its id and power directly using the object p2.

   d. Define a pointer to constant (pptr2) to the p2 object and set its id and power directly using the pptr2. During execution, pprt2 can only read p2 object data member values, but any changes to p2 object data member values throw errors.

   ```
   int main()
   {
           Player p1;
           p1.id=100;
           p1.power=1;;
           Player *pptr1;
           pptr1=&p1;
           pptr1->id = 0;
           pptr1->power = 0;
           cout<<"Ptr changed the player id"<<pptr1->id<<"\n";
   ```

CHAPTER 4   EXPLORING IMPORTANT C++ FEATURES

```
            Player p2;
            p2.id=200;
            p2.power=1;;
            const Player *pptr2;
            pptr2=&p2;
            cout<<"Player id"<<pptr2->id<<"\n";
            // pptr2->id=100;
               cout<<"player id"<<pptr2->id<<"\n";
               return 0;
       }
```

3. Test your code using the following commands and observe the following.

```
g++ ptr2constobjs.cc -o ptr2constobjs
./ptr2constobjs
ptr2constobjs.cc: In function 'int main()':
ptr2constobjs.cc:30:11: error: assignment of member
'Player::id' in read-only object
   30 |    pptr2->id=100;
      |    ~~~~~~~~~^~~~
```

The results show that `pptr2` cannot change player object p2 details. It is only allowed to read player object p2 details. Comment on `pptr2` changes, execute the code, and observe the following results.

```
# g++ ptr2constobjs.cc -o ptr2constobjs
# ./ptr2constobjs
Ptr changed the player id0
Player id200
player id200
```

The results show that `pptr1` changed the player object p1 id, but `pptr2` can only read player object p2 details.

Summary

This chapter explored important C++ features to handle various software development challenges. Mainly, you experimented with friend features to access private data members of a class through only friend functions and classes. You practiced using static data members and functions for sharing object data and accessing static data. Finally, you learned how to use const and pointers for restricting accidental changes to data passed over functions.

In the next chapter, you practice OOP principles through simple game scenarios and applications using C++.

Practice: Hands-on Activities

1. Handle the following challenges using friend concepts.

    a. Define a class called HiddenBox with private data members such as gold, silver, and bronze coins and member functions for accessing them (under the private section only).

    b. Think of how to access coins from the main() program.

    c. Think of providing access to the HiddenBox class from only the Owner class. (Define a sample Owner class.)

2. Practice the following.

    a. Define a class called Message with secret text messages and normal text messages as data members.

    b. Think of how to set a secret text message to a specific object and access it from the object only.

    c. Think of how to set a normal message by any object, and it should be accessible for all objects of the Message class.

    d. Think of how to restrict accidental changes to messages of the objects.

225

CHAPTER 5

Quickly and Systematically Model Real-World Problems into Software

Chapter 1 covered OOP principles and concepts for modeling real-world problems and solutions. As part of designing software solutions for online shopping, gaming, and smart applications, you learned how OOP concepts such as classes and objects are helpful to easily map their real-world problems space entities such as customers, items, players, animals, guns, and sensors into software.

This chapter explains how to create simple shopping and gaming applications using C++. Specifically, you learn how to coordinate with relevant objects of an application to implement the interactions and transactions of users involved in realizing the application's use cases.

Let's start with a simple, adventurous game application using C++ classes. As part of the game application, you design a few entities of a simple gaming world, such as players, enemies, weapons, opportunities, and challenges. You also test gaming-world entity interactions during the game-playing scenarios.

CHAPTER 5   QUICKLY AND SYSTEMATICALLY MODEL REAL-WORLD PROBLEMS INTO
            SOFTWARE

First, let's practice by creating a general shopping application using C++ classes. It includes real-world entities of the shopping context, such as customers, shopkeepers, items, and orders. You also test shopping world entity interactions and transactions for realizing use case scenarios. This chapter covers the following.

- Model real-world problems into software design
- Model a game world
- Code a simple gaming world in C++
- Model a software application
- Code simple application in C++

Modeling Real-World Problems into Software Design

OOP approaches are highly useful in dealing with the ambiguity involved in designing software. In OOP, to deal with any complex system, you can start by modeling real-world entities of the domain as related classes. The rest of the complexity can easily be handled by carefully implementing classes with necessary data members and member functions for accessing the data members. Once you realize all the basic classes of a system, you simplify most of the complexity of dealing with ambiguity to realize the system.

The basic classes can be used to realize subcomponents of the complex system. Although you have not learned the complete features of OOP, such as inheritance and polymorphism, having the basic knowledge of OOP, such as classes, objects, data hiding, data encapsulation, and constructors and destructors, you can start the simple application by implementing the following.

CHAPTER 5   QUICKLY AND SYSTEMATICALLY MODEL REAL-WORLD PROBLEMS INTO SOFTWARE

- All real-world entities identified in your applications as classes

- Classes with all necessary data members, member functions, constructors, and destructors

Before finalizing a class, consider how objects interact with other objects and the complete system. Include all necessary object tasks, actions, and accessing functions as member functions.

Besides finalizing the member functions declaration of a class, you must decide the object's startup and shutdown sequence as part of implementing constructors and destructors.

Proceeding further related to every real-world application entity, list important interactions and transactions involved in your application.

Execute interactions and transactions of your application as functions with related class objects as arguments.

Finally, test all use cases of your application.

As part of learning and practicing, you create two simple applications.

Let's start with learning how to deal with the ambiguity in realizing any gaming application world.

A Simple Gaming Application

Let's revisit Chapter 1's simple game application and its real-world entities to model into software. The following lists sample gaming application entities.

- Main characters related to the game, such as players and enemies

- Weapons such guns

- Challenges such as bombs

- Opportunities such as valuable coins

CHAPTER 5 QUICKLY AND SYSTEMATICALLY MODEL REAL-WORLD PROBLEMS INTO SOFTWARE

After identifying the real-world entities of the gaming world, you should do the following.

1. Implement the following classes to model your gaming application real-world entities.

    a. Player

    b. Gun

    c. Bomb

    d. Coin

2. Define each class with data members and member functions.

    a. Players and enemies move in the gaming world, collect guns and coins, and defuse bombs.

    b. Guns are spread in random locations in the gaming world. Every gun has a fixed number of bullets. Players or enemies can collect guns.

    c. Bombs are spread in random locations. Players or enemies try to defuse the bombs.

    d. Coins are spread in random locations. Players or enemies try to collect the coins.

    e. Include data members and accessing functions for carrying out players' and enemies' activities.

3. List important actions or interactions in the gaming world to create scenarios.

    a. How a player or an enemy observes the gaming world before doing any action

    b. Player or enemy interactions/actions with the guns

c. Player or enemy interactions/actions with the bombs

d. Player or enemy interactions/actions with the coins

e. How a player or an enemy has to move to target locations by facing challenges

4. Define a game scenario.

   a. Define the number of players, enemies, guns, bombs, and coins objects involved in the gaming world.

   b. Set up the initial gaming world by configuring the necessary data members for the players, enemies, bombs, guns, and coins.

   c. Initiate players and enemy actions in the gaming setup.

   d. Announce the results of the players at the end of the gaming scenario.

In later sections, you follow a similar procedure to create a simple gaming application using C++.

Next, let's learn how to deal with initial ambiguity in realizing a shopping application.

A Simple Shopping Application

To create a simple shopping application, let's start with real-world entities identified as part of shopping application modeling in Chapter 1. Let's start with the following real-world entities related to a shopping application.

- Users such as customers, shopkeepers, and delivery partners interact with shopping applications

- Various products available as part of shopping, such as items

- Transactions to record as part of the shopping application, such as orders, canceled orders, and delivered orders

CHAPTER 5 QUICKLY AND SYSTEMATICALLY MODEL REAL-WORLD PROBLEMS INTO SOFTWARE

After identifying the real-world entities of the shopping application, you should do the following.

1. Create the following classes to model your shopping application entities.

    a. Customers

    b. Shopkeeper

    c. Delivery partners

    d. Items

    e. Orders

    f. Canceled orders

    g. Delivered orders

2. Define basic classes of the shopping application with necessary data members and member functions to implement shopping application usage scenarios.

    a. Customer registration details should be modeled as data members in the customer class. Define necessary accessing functions.

    b. Shopkeeper registration details should be modeled as data members in the shopkeeper class. Define necessary accessing functions.

    c. Delivery partner registration details should be modeled as data members in the delivery partner class. Define necessary accessing functions.

    d. Items specification details should be defined as data members in the item class. Define necessary accessing functions.

CHAPTER 5   QUICKLY AND SYSTEMATICALLY MODEL REAL-WORLD PROBLEMS INTO SOFTWARE

   e. Customer transaction details related to purchasing items should be modeled as data members of the order class. Define necessary accessing functions.

   f. Customer transaction details related to canceling orders should be modeled as data members of the canceled order class. Define necessary accessing functions.

   g. Shopkeeper actions related to assigning delivery partners to orders should be modeled as data members of the delivered order class. Define necessary accessing functions.

3. After defining all basic classes related to the shopping application, you can start defining **the basic tasks related to shopping applications**.

   a. Customer registration activities as a function to interact with the shopping application.

   b. Shopkeeper registration activities as a function to interact with the shopping application.

   c. Items update activities as a function to interact with the shopping application.

   d. Browsing items as a function to check item details of the shopping application.

4. After defining basic interactions with a shopping application, you should **define customer interaction** with a shopping application.

   a. A customer placing ordering items as a function with necessary customer and item objects as arguments

CHAPTER 5   QUICKLY AND SYSTEMATICALLY MODEL REAL-WORLD PROBLEMS INTO SOFTWARE

   b. A customer canceling an order as a function with necessary customer and item objects as arguments

   c. A customer and their order details checking function with necessary customer and item objects as arguments

5. After defining customer interaction with a shopping application, you should **define shopkeeper interactions** with a shopping application.

   a. Processing orders to assign delivery partners

   b. Processing canceled orders to refund canceled orders to customers

   c. Browsing orders, canceled orders, delivered orders, and refunded orders

6. Implement the following shopping applications use cases.

   a. Items, customers, shopkeeper, and delivery partners registrations

   b. Customers browse items, place orders, view orders, and cancel orders

   c. Shopkeeper browses items, orders, and canceled orders

   d. Shopkeeper processes orders for delivery

   e. Shopkeeper processes canceled orders for refund processing

Next, let's start a simple gaming application.

CHAPTER 5 QUICKLY AND SYSTEMATICALLY MODEL REAL-WORLD PROBLEMS INTO SOFTWARE

Modeling Game World Entities Using C++ Classes

To create a simple game application, start with the building blocks of your game application. As the main building blocks of a game application are players, enemies, weapons, and opportunities, let's use them as classes. Use the following classes to implement a simple real-world gaming world entity.

- The Player class is for modeling players as well as enemies.
- The Gun class is for modeling weapons.
- The Bomb class is for modeling challenges.
- The Coin class is for modeling opportunities.

Let's start by defining a Player class.

PLAYER CLASS

Define the Player class in C++ and save it in the player.h file.

1. To model gaming scenarios such as player moves, collected guns, bombs, and coins, and the state of the player, the following data members are defined in the private section of the Player class.

```
class Player
{
    int id;
    int x;
    int y;
    int state;
```

CHAPTER 5   QUICKLY AND SYSTEMATICALLY MODEL REAL-WORLD PROBLEMS INTO SOFTWARE

```
    enum states {DEAD, LIVE};
    vector<Bomb> bv;
    vector<Coin> cv;
    vector<Gun> gv;
```

2. Initialize the players id, starting position (x,y), and state: dead or alive in the `Player` constructor function.

```
public:
Player()
{
    id = rand()%100;
    x = rand()%9;
    y = rand()%9;
    state = LIVE;
}
```

3. Define public member functions to interact with player objects, such as set and get functions for accessing data members for the player objects.

```
void setId(int iid)
{
    id = iid;
}
int getId()
{
    return id;
}
int getX()
{
    return x;
}
```

CHAPTER 5   QUICKLY AND SYSTEMATICALLY MODEL REAL-WORLD PROBLEMS INTO SOFTWARE

```
int getY()
{
    return y;
}
int getState()
{
    return state;
}
void setState(int istate)
{
    state = istate;
}
void setBomb(Bomb *b)
{
    bv.push_back(*b);
}
void setGun(Gun *g)
{
    gv.push_back(*g);
}
void setCoin(Coin *c)
{
    cv.push_back(*c);
}
```

4. Define the player moves function.

```
void walk()
{
    x = x+1;
    y = y+1;
}
```

CHAPTER 5   QUICKLY AND SYSTEMATICALLY MODEL REAL-WORLD PROBLEMS INTO SOFTWARE

5. Define a function to check whether the player has a specific gun at specific location.

```
bool hasGun(Gun *g)
{
    for (Gun g1: gv)
    {
        if (g1.getX() == g->getX() && g1.getY() == g->getY())
        {
            return true;
        }
    }
        return false;
}
```

6. Define the player stats function to display the player's total count of guns, bombs, and coins.

```
void stats()
{
    cout<<"\nPlayer: "<<id<<" Bombs:"<<bv.size()<<" Coins:"<<cv.size()<<" Guns:"<<gv.size()<<"\n";
}
};
```

Next, let's define the Bomb class to model challenges in the gaming world.

CHAPTER 5   QUICKLY AND SYSTEMATICALLY MODEL REAL-WORLD PROBLEMS INTO SOFTWARE

BOMB CLASS

Let's define the Bomb class in C++ and save it in the bomb.h file.

1. To model challenging situations for players in the gaming world, place bombs in various locations. Players can observe bomb locations and they can act accordingly. Specifically, to defuse a bomb, the state of the bomb is set. For the Bomb class, the following private data members are defined.

   ```
   class Bomb
   {
       int x,y,state;
       enum states {DEFUSED, ACTIVE};
   ```

2. In the gaming application, bomb objects should be created and placed at random locations. To do this task, execute these actions in the Bomb constructor function.

   ```
   public:
   Bomb()
   {
       x = rand()%9;
       y = rand()%9;
       state = ACTIVE;
   }
   ```

3. Apply the following set and get functions for each of the bomb data members to determine the bomb location and state and then defuse it.

   ```
   int getX()
   {
       return x;
   }
   ```

239

CHAPTER 5   QUICKLY AND SYSTEMATICALLY MODEL REAL-WORLD PROBLEMS INTO SOFTWARE

```
        int getY()
        {
            return y;
        }
        int getState()
        {
            return state;
        }
        void setState(int istate)
        {
            state = istate;
        }
};
```

Next, let's use the Coin class to model opportunities in the gaming application.

COIN CLASS

Define the Coin class in C++ and save it in `coin.h` file.

1. To offer opportunities for players in the gaming world, let's keep coins in random locations. Players can check for coins and collect them. Specifically, to collect coins, the state of the coins is set. To execute the Coin class, the following private data members are defined.

```
class Coin
{
    int state;
    int x,y,value;
    enum states {COLLECTED, AVAILABLE};
```

CHAPTER 5   QUICKLY AND SYSTEMATICALLY MODEL REAL-WORLD PROBLEMS INTO SOFTWARE

2. Coin objects should be created and placed at random locations. To do this task, execute these actions in the Coin constructor function.

```
public:
    Coin()
    {
        x = rand()%9+8;
        y = rand()%9+8;
        value = rand()%100;
        state = AVAILABLE;
    }
```

3. To check coin availability, collect the following set and get functions defined for each of the coin data members.

```
int getX()
{
    return x;
}
int getY()
{
    return y;
}
int getValue()
{
    return value;
}
void setValue(int ival)
{
    value = ival;
}
```

```
    int getState()
    {
        return state;
    }
    void setState(int istate)
    {
        state = istate;
    }
};
```

Next, let's create a Gun class to model weapons in the gaming application.

MODELING GUN CLASS

Define the Gun class in C++ and save it in the gun.h file.

1. Let's keep guns in random locations to offer weapons for players in the gaming world. Players can check for guns and collect them. Specifically, to grab a gun, the state of the gun is set. To implement the Gun class, the following private data members are defined.

   ```
   #include <iostream>
   using namespace std;
   class Gun
   {
       int state;
       int x,y,bullets;
       enum states {NOT_AVAILABLE, AVAILABLE};
   ```

2. Gun objects should be created and placed at random locations. To do this task, apply these actions in the Gun constructor function.

CHAPTER 5   QUICKLY AND SYSTEMATICALLY MODEL REAL-WORLD PROBLEMS INTO SOFTWARE

```
public:
Gun()
{
    x = rand()%9+5;
    y = rand()%9+5;
    bullets = 10;
    state = AVAILABLE;
}
```

3. To check gun availability, the following set and get functions are defined for each of the gun data members.

```
int getX()
{
    return x;
}
int getY()
{
    return y;
}
int getBullets()
{
    return bullets;
}
void setBullets(int ibullets)
{
    bullets = ibullets;
}
int getState()
{
    return state;
}
```

CHAPTER 5 QUICKLY AND SYSTEMATICALLY MODEL REAL-WORLD PROBLEMS INTO SOFTWARE

```
void setState(int istate)
{
    state = istate;
}
```

4. Define a simple fire() simulation function so players can attack enemies using a gun.

```
void fire()
{
    if (bullets>0)
    {
        bullets=bullets-1;
    }
    else
    cout<<"No bullets\n";
    }
};
```

Next, let's create a simple game with the help of Player, Bomb, Gun, and Coin classes.

Game Implementation Using C++ Classes

This section covers using functions to interact with various game objects. For instance, the player character does the following in a typical game-playing scenario.

- Observes the gaming world
- Acts with gaming objects in a variety of ways
  - A player jumps over a bomb or defuses a bomb.

CHAPTER 5 QUICKLY AND SYSTEMATICALLY MODEL REAL-WORLD PROBLEMS INTO SOFTWARE

- A player collects, loads, and fires guns.
- A player collects and loses coins.
- Moves in various directions—jumps, flies, and so forth.

To keep things simple, let's implement basic interaction and actions of players to realize game scenarios. Let's first start with player observations in a gaming world.

PLAYER OBSERVATIONS

Implement player observation about the gaming world in game.cc.

1. Include all necessary header files, gun.h, bomb.h, coin.h, and player.h files.

   ```
   #include <iostream>
   #include <thread>
   #include <vector>
   #include <unistd.h>
   #include <bits/stdc++.h>
   #include <time.h>
   #include "gun.h"
   #include "bomb.h"
   #include "coin.h"
   #include "player.h"
   #define COUNT 10
   #define MAXSTEPS 15
   using namespace std;
   ```

CHAPTER 5 QUICKLY AND SYSTEMATICALLY MODEL REAL-WORLD PROBLEMS INTO SOFTWARE

2. Define a function for observing a player how far a bomb is to the player.

```
float distanceBetween(Player *p1, Bomb *p2)
{
    int xdisp = p1->getX()-p2->getX();
    int ydisp = p1->getY()-p2->getY();
    return sqrt((xdisp*xdisp+ydisp*ydisp));
}
```

3. Define a function for observing how far a gun is to the player.

```
float distanceBetween(Player *p1, Gun *p2)
{
    int xdisp = p1->getX()-p2->getX();
    int ydisp = p1->getY()-p2->getY();
    return sqrt((xdisp*xdisp+ydisp*ydisp));
}
```

4. Define a function for observing how far a player is from a coin.

```
float distanceBetween(Player *p1, Coin *p2)
{
    int xdisp = p1->getX()-p2->getX();
    int ydisp = p1->getY()-p2->getY();
    return sqrt((xdisp*xdisp+ydisp*ydisp));
}
```

5. A player observes all deployed bombs, guns, and coins in a game world. Let's implement the following function to know how far a gaming object is from the player.

```
void playerobserves(Player *p1, Bomb b[COUNT],
Gun g[COUNT], Coin c[COUNT])
{
```

```
        cout<<"\nPlayer "<<p1->getId()<<"at"<<p1-
        >getX()<<","<<p1->getY()<<"\n";
        for (int i=0;i<COUNT;i++)
        {
                cout<<"Bomb is "<<distanceBetween(p1,&b[i])<<"
                meters away\n";
        }
        for (int i=0;i<COUNT;i++)
        {
                cout<<"Gun is "<<distanceBetween(p1,&g[i])<<
                "meters away\n";
        }
        for (int i=0;i<COUNT;i++)
        {
                cout<<"Coin is "<<distanceBetween(p1,&c[i])<<
                "meters away\n";
        }
}
```

Next, let's create player actions with bombs, guns, and coins.

PLAYER ACTIONS WITH BOMBS, GUNS, AND COINS

Create player actions related to the gaming world in game.cc.

1. To simulate player interaction with a bomb, implement the following player actions.

    a. If a bomb is far from the player, he plans to defuse it.

    b. As soon as the player reaches a safe distance from the bomb, he defuses it.

CHAPTER 5 QUICKLY AND SYSTEMATICALLY MODEL REAL-WORLD PROBLEMS INTO SOFTWARE

c. Unfortunately, a player may suffer from the bomb blast.

d. Implement these actions in the following function.

```
void playeractbombs(Player *p1, Bomb b[COUNT])
{
    enum states {DEFUSED, ACTIVE};
    cout<<"\nPlayer "<<p1->getId()<<"at"<<p1-
    >getX()<<","<<p1->getY()<<"\n";
    float dist = 5.0;

    for (int i=0;i<COUNT;i++)
    {
        if (distanceBetween(p1,&b[i])<9.0)
        {
            cout<<"Player is palnning to defuse the
            bomb \n";
        }
        if (distanceBetween(p1,&b[i])<4.0&&b[i].
        getState()==ACTIVE)
        {
            cout<<"Player Id: "<<p1-
            >getId()<<"defused the bomb \n";
            b[i].setState(DEFUSED);

            p1->setBomb(&b[i]);
        }
        if (distanceBetween(p1,&b[i])==0.0 && b[i].
        getState()==ACTIVE)
        {
            cout<<"Player was blasted with the bomb";
        }
    }
}
```

CHAPTER 5 QUICKLY AND SYSTEMATICALLY MODEL REAL-WORLD PROBLEMS INTO SOFTWARE

2. To simulate player interaction with a gun, apply the following player actions.

    a. If a gun is far from the player, he runs toward it.

    b. As soon as the player reaches the gun, he collects it.

    c. Unfortunately, the player may miss the gun.

    d. The player uses the gun to fire it.

    e. Simulate all these actions in the following function.

    ```
    void playeractguns(Player *p1, Gun g[10])
    {
        enum states {NOT_AVAILABLE, AVAILABLE};
        cout<<"\nPlayer "<<p1->getId()<<"at"<<p1->getX()<<","<<p1->getY()<<"\n";
        float dist = 5.0;
        for (int i=0;i<COUNT;i++)
        {
            if (distanceBetween(p1,&g[i])<8.0)
            {
                cout<<"Player running towards the Guns \n";
            }
            if (distanceBetween(p1,&g[i])<=2.0 && g[i].getState()==AVAILABLE)
            {
                cout<<"Player is collecting the gun \n";
                g[i].setState(NOT_AVAILABLE);
                p1->setGun(&g[i]);
            }
    ```

249

CHAPTER 5 QUICKLY AND SYSTEMATICALLY MODEL REAL-WORLD PROBLEMS INTO SOFTWARE

```
            if (p1->hasGun(&g[i])==true)
            {
                g[i].fire();
                cout<<"\nPlayer Id: "<<p1-
                >getId()<<" is firing ..\n";
            }
        }
    }
```

3. To simulate player interaction with a coin, use the following player actions.

   a. If a coin is far from the player, he runs toward it.

   b. As soon as the player reaches the coin, he collects it.

   c. Unfortunately, the player may miss the coin.

   d. Implement these actions in the following function.

```
   void playeractcoins(Player *p1, Coin c[COUNT])
   {
       enum states {COLLECTED, AVAILABLE};
       cout<<"\nPlayer "<<p1->getId()<<"at"<<p1-
       >getX()<<","<<p1->getY()<<"\n";
           float dist = 5.0;

       for (int i=0;i<10;i++)
       {
           if (distanceBetween(p1,&c[i])<12.0)
           {
               cout<<"Player is running towards
               coins \n";
           }
           if (distanceBetween(p1,&c[i])<=4.0 &&
           c[i].getState()==AVAILABLE)
```

CHAPTER 5 QUICKLY AND SYSTEMATICALLY MODEL REAL-WORLD PROBLEMS INTO SOFTWARE

```
            {
                cout<<"Player Id:"<<p1->getId()
                    <<"collected a coin \n";
                c[i].setState(COLLECTED);
                p1->setCoin(&c[i]);
            }
        }
    }
```

Next, let's concentrate on a sample player's plans of moving in the gaming world to achieve game targets.

PLAYER MOVES

Implement player or enemy actions related to the gaming world using player objects in game.cc.

1. Define the following simple game plan for a player.

    a. The player observes the gaming world.

    b. The player first reacts to bombs.

    c. The player reacts to guns.

    d. The player reacts to coins.

    e. These actions are executed in the following function.

    ```
    void playermoves(Player *p1, Bomb b[COUNT],
    Gun g[COUNT], Coin c[COUNT])
    {
        playerobserves(p1,b,g,c);
        sleep(1);
        for (int i=0;i<MAXSTEPS;i++)
        {
    ```

CHAPTER 5   QUICKLY AND SYSTEMATICALLY MODEL REAL-WORLD PROBLEMS INTO SOFTWARE

```
            playeractbombs(p1,b);
            playeractguns(p1,g);
            playeractcoins(p1,c);
            p1->walk();
        }
        p1->stats();
    }
```

2. Define the following simple game plan for an enemy as follows.

   a. An enemy observes the gaming world.

   b. The enemy first reacts to guns.

3. The enemy reacts to coins.

   a. The enemy reacts to bombs.

   b. These actions are implemented in the following function.

   ```
   void enemymoves(Player *e1, Bomb b[COUNT],
   Gun g[COUNT], Coin c[COUNT])
   {
       playerobserves(e1,b,g,c);
       sleep(1);
       for (int i=0;i<MAXSTEPS;i++)
       {
           playeractguns(e1,g);
           playeractcoins(e1,c);
           playeractbombs(e1,b);
           e1->walk();
       }
       e1->stats();
   }
   ```

Next, let's work on a simple game scenario.

CHAPTER 5 QUICKLY AND SYSTEMATICALLY MODEL REAL-WORLD PROBLEMS INTO SOFTWARE

MAIN GAME SCENARIO

Use the following simple game scenario in game.cc.

1. Create a player and an enemy object from the Player class. Since constructors are used, the player and the enemy are placed at random locations in the gaming world.

2. Deploy a number of guns, bombs, and coins to set up the gaming weapons, challenges, and opportunities.

    a. To do this, create a suitable number of gun objects, bomb objects, and coin objects from the Gun, Bomb, and Coin classes.

    b. Constructors in the Gun, Bomb, and Coin classes ensure guns, bombs, and coins are placed at random locations and their state is initialized.

3. Call the playermoves function with the player object to execute a player's game plan. Similarly, call enemymoves to execute the game plan of an enemy.

```
int main()
{
    Player p; Player e;
    Bomb b[COUNT];
    Gun g[COUNT];
    Coin c[COUNT];
    playermoves(&p,b,g,c);
    enemymoves(&e,b,g,c);
    return 0;
}
```

CHAPTER 5   QUICKLY AND SYSTEMATICALLY MODEL REAL-WORLD PROBLEMS INTO SOFTWARE

4. Well done! You have implemented a simple game scenario. Let's test it and observe the results, such as player moves and actions, enemy moves and actions, and their stats at the end of the game. You can execute the game using the following commands.

```
# g++ game.cc -o scenario1
# ./scenario1 > gamestats
```

5. Check the player's stats using the following command.

```
# cat gamestats | grep 'Player:'
Player: 83 Bombs:3 Coins:1 Guns:2
Player: 15 Bombs:6 Coins:9 Guns:4
```

6. Check number of coins collected by a player using the following command.

```
# cat gamestats | grep 'Player Id: 15 collected' |wc -l 9
# cat gamestats | grep 'Player Id: 83 collected' |wc -l
```

7. Check number of bombs defused by a player using the following command.

```
# cat gamestats | grep 'Player Id: 15 defused' |wc -l
6
# cat gamestats | grep 'Player Id: 83 defused' |wc -l
3
```

Similarly, using the grep command, you can check for other game events, such as firing and running. Next, let's work on a simple shopping application using C++.

CHAPTER 5   QUICKLY AND SYSTEMATICALLY MODEL REAL-WORLD PROBLEMS INTO SOFTWARE

Model Application Entities Using C++ Classes

To implement a simple shopping application, let's start with real-world entities of a shopping context as basic classes. The following lists real-world entities of a sample shopping application.

- Customer class to model registered customers of a shopping application

- Shopkeeper class to model registered managers to process all shopping transactions

- Delivery partner class to model delivering orders through registered delivery partners

- Item class to model shopping products available for customers

- Order class to model customer transactions related to procuring items

- Canceled order to model customer transactions related to canceling orders

- Delivered orders to model shopkeeper transactions related to ensuring orders were delivered to the customers

Let's start with reusing the Customer class and Item class, which are defined in Chapter 2.

CHAPTER 5 QUICKLY AND SYSTEMATICALLY MODEL REAL-WORLD PROBLEMS INTO SOFTWARE

REUSE CUSTOMER AND ITEM CLASS

1. Copy customer.cc (from Chapter 2) to customer.h and remove the main () function from the customer.h file.

2. Use the Customer class to model registering a list of customers with the shopping application design and testing.

3. Copy items.cc (from Chapter 2) to item.h and remove the main () function from the item.h file.

4. Use the Item class to model registering a list of products with the shopping application so that you can simulate customers browsing items, checking item details, and placing order transactions.

Next, define a Shopkeeper class related to model registered shopkeepers for managing shopping application transactions.

SHOPKEEPER CLASS

Define a Shopkeeper class in the shopkeeper.h file.

1. Using C++ classes, declare your Shopkeeper class by including necessary private data members (or fields such as id, name, phone number, and address details) for registration activities. In the public section, declare shopkeeper details accessing functions such as get and set member functions as follows.

   ```
   #include<iostream>
   #include<string.h>
   using namespace std;
   ```

```cpp
class Shopkeeper
{
    string sid;
    string name;
    char phone[11];
    string city;
    string country;
    unsigned int pin;
    public:
        string getSid();
        void setSid(string id);
        string getName();
        void setName(string cname);
        char* getPhone();
        void setPhone(char cphone[11]);
        string getCity();
        void setCity(string ccity);
        string getCountry();
        void setCountry(string ccountry);
        unsigned int getPin();
        void setPin(unsigned int pin);
};
```

2. Outside the class, implement a suitable set and get public member functions for accessing necessary private fields of the Shopkeeper class from the external function such as main().

```cpp
string Shopkeeper::getSid()
{
    return sid;
}
```

CHAPTER 5 QUICKLY AND SYSTEMATICALLY MODEL REAL-WORLD PROBLEMS INTO SOFTWARE

```cpp
void Shopkeeper::setSid(string id)
{
    sid = id;
}
string Shopkeeper::getName()
{
    return name;
}
void Shopkeeper::setName(string cname)
{
    name = cname;
}
char* Shopkeeper::getPhone()
{
    return phone;
}
void Shopkeeper::setPhone(char cphone[11])
{
    strcpy(phone, cphone);
}
string Shopkeeper::getCity()
{
    return city;
}
void Shopkeeper::setCity(string ccity)
{
    city = ccity;
}
string Shopkeeper::getCountry()
{
    return country;
}
```

CHAPTER 5   QUICKLY AND SYSTEMATICALLY MODEL REAL-WORLD PROBLEMS INTO SOFTWARE

```
void Shopkeeper::setCountry(string ccountry)
{
    country = ccountry;
}
unsigned int Shopkeeper::getPin()
{
    return pin;
}
void Shopkeeper::setPin(unsigned int cpin)
{
    pin = cpin;
}
```

Well done. You have defined a Shopkeeper class for handling shopkeeper registration activities in online shopping applications. Next, let's create a DeliveryPartner class for the shopping application.

DELIVERYPARTNER CLASS

Define a DeliveryPartner class in the deliverypartner.h file.

1. Declare your DeliveryPartner class by including necessary private data members (or fields) such as id, name, and phone number for registration activities. In the public section, declare DeliveryPartner details accessing functions such as get and set member functions.

    ```
    #include<iostream>
    #include<string.h>
    using namespace std;
    class DeliveryPartner
    {
    ```

```
        string did;
        string name;
        char phone[11];
    public:
        string getDid();
        void setDid(string id);
        string getName();
        void setName(string dname);
        char* getPhone();
        void setPhone(char dphone[11]);
};
```

2. Outside the class, implement a suitable set and get public member functions for accessing necessary private fields of the DeliveryPartner class from the external function such as main().

```
string DeliveryPartner::getDid()
{
    return did;
}
void DeliveryPartner::setDid(string id)
{
    did = id;
}
string DeliveryPartner::getName()
{
    return name;
}
void DeliveryPartner::setName(string dname)
{
    name = dname;
}
```

```
char* DeliveryPartner::getPhone()
{
    return phone;
}
void DeliveryPartner::setPhone(char dphone[11])
{
    strcpy(phone, dphone);
}
```

Well done. You have implemented the `DeliveryPartner` class to model the registration of delivery partners to process the delivery of orders in your shopping application. Next, let's create the `Order` class to model customer placing order transactions.

ORDER CLASS

Define an `Order` class in order.h file.

1. Declare the `Order` class by including necessary `private` data members to model customer-procured items, date, and quantity.

    a. Declare a `status` field to model order processing states such as canceled, delivered, and refunded.

    b. Model the total number of orders as a `static` field `count` in your shopping application.

    c. Declare all set and get functions for accessing order details in the `public` section.

    ```
    #include<iostream>
    #include<string.h>
    using namespace std;
    ```

CHAPTER 5   QUICKLY AND SYSTEMATICALLY MODEL REAL-WORLD PROBLEMS INTO SOFTWARE

```
class Order
{
    string oid;
    string cid;
    string iid;
    unsigned int qty;
    unsigned int cost;
    string odate;
    string status;
    static int count;
public:
    string getOid();
    void setOid(string id);
    string getCid();
    void setCid(string id);
    string getIid();
    void setIid(string id);
    unsigned int getQty();
    void setQty(unsigned int iqty);
    unsigned int getCost();
    void setCost(unsigned int icost);
    string getOdate();
    void setOdate(string date);
    string getStatus();
    void setStatus(string istatus);
    static void updateCount();
    static int getCount();
};
```

2. Define the static field count outside of the class as follows.

```
int Order::count;
```

3. Outside the `class`, implement static functions for counting the total number of orders and accessing the order count as follows.

```
void Order::updateCount()
{
    count = count+1;
}
int Order::getCount()
{
    return count;
}
```

4. Define the necessary set and get member functions for accessing order details such as order id, customer id, item id, date, and cost.

```
string Order::getOid()
{
    return oid;
}
void Order::setOid(string id)
{
    oid = id;
}

string Order::getCid()
{
    return cid;
}
void Order::setCid(string id)
{
    cid = id;
}
```

CHAPTER 5 QUICKLY AND SYSTEMATICALLY MODEL REAL-WORLD PROBLEMS INTO SOFTWARE

```cpp
string Order::getIid()
{
    return iid;
}
void Order::setIid(string id)
{
    iid = id;
}
unsigned int Order::getQty()
{
    return qty;
}
void Order::setQty(unsigned int iqty)
{
    qty = iqty;
}
unsigned int Order::getCost()
{
    return cost;
}
void Order::setCost(unsigned int icost)
{
    cost = icost;
}
string Order::getOdate()
{
    return odate;
}
void Order::setOdate(string iodate)
{
    odate = iodate;
}
```

CHAPTER 5   QUICKLY AND SYSTEMATICALLY MODEL REAL-WORLD PROBLEMS INTO SOFTWARE

5. Define the order status update and access-related functions for modeling various states of orders such as processing, canceled, delivered, and refunded.

```
string Order::getStatus()
{
    return status;
}
void Order::setStatus(string istatus)
{
    status = istatus;
}
```

Well done. You have implemented the Order class related to model shopping transactions such as placing orders. Next, let's work on another important class to model customer transactions, such as canceling orders.

CANCELED ORDER CLASS

Define a CancelledOrder class in the cancelled.h file.

1. Declare CancelledOrder class by including necessary private data members (or fields) such as canceled order id, date, refund amount, and expected refund date. In the public section, declare set and get member functions for accessing canceled order data members as follows.

```
#include<string.h>
using namespace std;
class CancelledOrder
{
    string coid;
    string cdate;
```

```
            unsigned int refund;
            string rdate;
        public:
            string getCoid();
            void setCoid(string id);
            string getCdate();
            void setCdate(string date);
            unsigned int getRefund();
            void setRefund(unsigned int irefund);
            string getRdate();
            void setRdate(string date);
    };
```

2. Outside the `class`, define all necessary set and get member functions for processing canceled order details such as canceled order id, date, refund amount, and refund date.

```
    string CancelledOrder::getCoid()
    {
        return coid;
    }
    void CancelledOrder::setCoid(string id)
    {
        coid = id;
    }

    string CancelledOrder::getCdate()
    {
        return cdate;
    }
```

CHAPTER 5 QUICKLY AND SYSTEMATICALLY MODEL REAL-WORLD PROBLEMS INTO SOFTWARE

```
void CancelledOrder::setCdate(string date)
{
    cdate = date;
}

unsigned int CancelledOrder::getRefund()
{
    return refund;
}
void CancelledOrder::setRefund(unsigned int irefund)
{
    refund = irefund;
}

string CancelledOrder::getRdate()
{
    return rdate;
}
void CancelledOrder::setRdate(string irdate)
{
    rdate = irdate;
}
```

Well done. You have implemented a `CancelledOrder` class to model shopping application transactions related to processing customer canceled orders. Next, let's define the `DeliveredOrders` class to model confirmed order delivery in the shopping application.

CHAPTER 5 QUICKLY AND SYSTEMATICALLY MODEL REAL-WORLD PROBLEMS INTO SOFTWARE

DELIVERED ORDER CLASS

Define a `DeliveredOrder` class in deliverorder.h file.

1. Declare `DeliveredOrder` class by including necessary `private` data members (or fields) to model assigning a delivery partner to a confirmed order, such as order id, delivery partner id, and delivery date. Under the `public` section, declare the necessary set and get member functions for accessing delivered order details.

    ```
    #include<string.h>
    using namespace std;
    class DeliveredOrder
    {
        string d_oid;
        string dpid;
        string ddate;
        public:
            string getDoid();
            void setDoid(string id);
            string getDpid();
            void setDpid(string pid);
            string getDdate();
            void setDdate(string date);
    };
    ```

2. Outside the `class`, implement all necessary set and get member functions for processing delivered orders, such as assigning delivery partner id and date in your shopping application.

CHAPTER 5   QUICKLY AND SYSTEMATICALLY MODEL REAL-WORLD PROBLEMS INTO SOFTWARE

```
string DeliveredOrder::getDoid()
{
    return d_oid;
}
void DeliveredOrder::setDoid(string id)
{
    d_oid = id;
}
string DeliveredOrder::getDpid()
{
    return dpid;
}
void DeliveredOrder::setDpid(string pid)
{
    dpid = pid;
}
string DeliveredOrder::getDdate()
{
    return ddate;
}
void DeliveredOrder::setDdate(string date)
{
    ddate = date;
}
```

Well done. By implementing classes for all identified shopping application-related real-world entities, you have created all basic building blocks for shopping application transactions. Next, let's discuss important tasks related to simulating use cases of your shopping application, such as registering customers, items, shopkeepers, delivery partners, and all related transactions.

Next, let's interact with objects of the respective classes to carry out interesting tasks or activities.

CHAPTER 5   QUICKLY AND SYSTEMATICALLY MODEL REAL-WORLD PROBLEMS INTO SOFTWARE

Basic Tasks Related to a Shopping Application

After defining all basic classes related to a shopping application, you can start defining the basic tasks related to shopping applications.

- Customer registration activities as a function to interact with the shopping application.
- Shopkeeper registration activities as a function to interact with the shopping application.
- Delivery partner registration activities as a function to interact with the shopping application.
- Items update activities as a function to interact with the shopping application.

BASIC FUNCTIONS FOR SHOPPING APPLICATION

Use the following functions in the application.cc file.

1. To create a shopping application, do the following tasks using the basic classes: `Customer`, `ShopKeeper`, `DeliveryPartner`, and `Item`. Start by including all necessary header files related to these classes.

   ```
   #include<iostream>
   #include<stdlib.h>
   #include<vector>
   #include"customer.h"
   #include"shopkeeper.h"
   #include"item.h"
   #include"deliverypartner.h"
   #include"order.h"
   ```

CHAPTER 5   QUICKLY AND SYSTEMATICALLY MODEL REAL-WORLD PROBLEMS INTO SOFTWARE

```
#include"cancelled.h"
#include"deliverorder.h"
using namespace std;
```

2. Write an example `customers_registration` function to insert sample customer details related to your shopping application as follows.

```
void customers_register(Customer &c1, Customer &c2)
{
    c1.setCid("C001");
    c1.setName("Customer1");
    char phone[11];
    strcpy(phone,"9000000000");
    c1.setPhone(phone);
    c1.setCity("City1");
    c1.setCountry("Country1");
    c1.setPin(100001);
    cout<<"Customer "<<c1.getCid()<<" was registered\n";
    c2.setCid("C002");
    c2.setName("Customer2");
    char phone2[11];
    strcpy(phone2,"9000000001");
    c2.setPhone(phone);
    c2.setCity("City2");
    c2.setCountry("Country2");
    c2.setPin(100002);
    cout<<"Customer "<<c2.getCid()<<" was registered\n";
}
```

3. Write an example shopkeeper_registration function to insert a sample shopkeeper details related to your shopping application as follows.

```
void shopkeeper_register(Shopkeeper &s1)
{
    s1.setSid("S001");
    s1.setName("Shopkeeper1");
    char phone[11];
    strcpy(phone,"8000000000");
    s1.setPhone(phone);
    s1.setCity("SCity1");
    s1.setCountry("SCountry1");
    s1.setPin(200001);
    cout<<"Shopkeeper "<<s1.getSid()<<" was registered\n";
}
```

4. Write an example delpartner_registration function to insert a sample delivery partner details related to your shopping application as follows.

```
void delpartner_register(DeliveryPartner &d1, DeliveryPartner &d2)
{
    d1.setDid("DP001");
    d1.setName("DPartner1");
    char phone[11];
    strcpy(phone,"7000000000");
    d1.setPhone(phone);
    cout<<"Delivery partner "<<d1.getDid()<<" was registered\n";
    d2.setDid("DP002");
```

CHAPTER 5   QUICKLY AND SYSTEMATICALLY MODEL REAL-WORLD PROBLEMS INTO SOFTWARE

```
    d2.setName("DPartner2");
    char phone2[11];
    strcpy(phone2,"7000000001");
    d2.setPhone(phone);
    cout<<"Delivery partner "<<d2.getDid()<<" was
    registered\n";
}
```

5. Write an example item_insert function to insert sample shopping product details related to your shopping application as follows.

```
void items_insert(Item &i1,Item &i2,Item &i3, Item &i4)
{
    i1.setIid("I001");
    i1.setName("Item1");
    i1.setPrice(1000);
    i1.setQty(10);
    i1.setDescr("Fashion product");
    cout<<"Item "<<i1.getIid()<<" was entered\n";

    i2.setIid("I002");
    i2.setName("Item2");
    i2.setPrice(2000);
    i2.setQty(10);
    i2.setDescr("Entertainment product");
    cout<<"Item "<<i2.getIid()<<" was entered\n";

    i3.setIid("I003");
    i3.setName("Item3");
    i3.setPrice(3000);
    i3.setQty(10);
    i3.setDescr("Smart product");
    cout<<"Item "<<i3.getIid()<<" was entered\n";
```

CHAPTER 5   QUICKLY AND SYSTEMATICALLY MODEL REAL-WORLD PROBLEMS INTO SOFTWARE

```
        i4.setIid("I004");
        i4.setName("Item4");
        i4.setPrice(4000);
        i4.setQty(10);
        i4.setDescr("Electronic product");
        cout<<"Item "<<i4.getIid()<<" was entered\n";
}
```

You have completed basic shopping entities registration-related functions.

Next, let's write necessary functions related to customer interactions with the shopping application for browsing items, placing orders, and canceling orders.

Basic Customer Interactions in a Shopping Application

This section discusses basic customer shopping transactions simulation activities as functions.

1. The customer views their profile details.

2. The customer browses items of the shopping application.

3. The customer procures items using a customer places order function with necessary customer and item objects as arguments.

4. The customer cancels the order using a canceling order function with the customer and item objects as arguments.

5. The customer checks the order using an order browsing function with necessary object arguments.

Let's start with customer interactions.

CHAPTER 5   QUICKLY AND SYSTEMATICALLY MODEL REAL-WORLD PROBLEMS INTO SOFTWARE

CUSTOMER AND HIS SHOPPING INTERACTIONS

Implement the following functions in the application.cc file.

1. Start by defining the customer profile view function as follows.

   ```
   void customer_disp (Customer &c)
   {
       cout<<"Customer id:"<<c.getCid()<<" Phone "<<c.getPhone()<<" City "<<c.getCity()<<"\n";
   }
   ```

2. Define shopping application items browsing function as follows.

   ```
   void items_browsing (Item &i)
   {
       cout<<"Item id:"<<i.getIid()<<" Price "<<i.getPrice()<<" Descr "<<i.getDescr()<<"\n";
   }
   ```

3. Define the following function to simulate a customer placing an order using selected items and quantity as follows.

   a. Set the customer and his procuring item id as part of this order.

   b. Update customer procuring items quantity.

   c. Set the total cost of the order and date.

   d. Set the initial status of the order as "Processing".

   e. Update the total number of orders in the shopping application.

   f. Assign a unique order id and set it to a dynamically created order object.

   ```
   Order* placeOrder(Customer &c1, Item &i1, unsigned int qty)
   {
   ```

```
            if (i1.getQty()>=qty)
            {
                Order *o1 = new Order();
                o1->setCid(c1.getCid());
                o1->setIid(i1.getIid());
                unsigned int cost = qty*i1.getPrice();
                i1.setQty(i1.getQty()-qty);
                o1->setCost(cost);
                o1->setOdate("ODate1");
                o1->setStatus("Processing");
                o1->updateCount();
                o1->setOid("O001"+string(1,'A'+o1->getCount()));
                return o1;
            }
            return NULL;
        }
```

4. Define the following function to simulate a customer canceling one of the orders as follows.

    a. Check order status is processing, then only allow the customer to cancel the order.

    b. Set order id and cancellation date.

    c. Set the total refund amount.

    d. Set the expected refund date.

    e. Set order status to Cancelled.

    ```
    CancelledOrder* cancelOrder(Customer &c1, Order *o1)
    {
        if (o1->getStatus()=="Processing")
        {
    ```

```
            CancelledOrder *c1 = new CancelledOrder();
            c1->setCoid(o1->getOid());
            c1->setCdate("Cdate1");
            c1->setRefund(o1->getCost());
            c1->setRdate("Rdate1");
            o1->setStatus("Cancelled");
            return c1;
        }

        return NULL;
    }
```

5. Define the following function to view the customer's orders and status.

```
    void browseCustOrders(Customer &c1, vector<Order*> &ov)
    {
        for (Order *o: ov)
        {
            if (o->getCid() == c1.getCid())
            {
                cout<<"Order Id"<<o->getOid()<<" date: "<<o->getOdate()<<"cost : "<<o->getCost()
                    <<"status:"<<o->getStatus()<<"\n";
            }
        }
    }
```

Well done. You have successfully implemented the customer interactions related to the shopping application as functions.

Next, let's create shopkeeper interaction functions with the shopping application function to simulate processing, canceling, and delivering customer orders.

CHAPTER 5   QUICKLY AND SYSTEMATICALLY MODEL REAL-WORLD PROBLEMS INTO SOFTWARE

Basic Shopkeeper Interactions in a Shopping Application

This section implements basic customer shopping transactions simulation activities as functions, such as the following.

- Viewing and checking orders, canceling orders, delivering orders, and refunding orders
- Processing confirmed orders to assign delivery partners
- Processing canceled order functions to refund customers

Let's start with shopkeeper interactions.

INTERACT WITH SHOPKEEPER OBJECTS

Use the following functions in the application.cc file.

1. Implement the following function to view all orders of the shopping application.

```
void browseOrders(vector<Order*> &ov)
{
    for (Order *o: ov)
    {
        cout<<"Order Id"<<o->getOid()<<" date:"
        <<o->getOdate()<<"cost : "<<o->getCost()
        <<"status:"<<o->getStatus()<<"\n";
    }
}
```

2. Apply the following function to view all canceled orders of the shopping application.

```cpp
void browseCanOrders(vector<CancelledOrder*> &cv)
{
    for (CancelledOrder *c: cv)
    {
        cout<<"Cancelled Order "<<c->getCoid()<<"
        refund date:"<<c->getRdate()<<"total refund:
        "<<c->getRefund()<<"\n";
    }
}
```

3. Execute the following function to view all delivered orders of the shopping application.

```cpp
void browseDelOrders(vector<DeliveredOrder*> &dv)
{
    for (DeliveredOrder *d: dv)
    {
        cout<<"Delivered Order "<<d->getDoid()<<"
        Deliver date:"<<d->getDdate()<<"Delivery
        Partner: "<<d->getDpid()<<"\n";
    }
}
```

4. Execute the following function to view all refunded orders of the shopping application.

```cpp
void browseRefOrders(vector<Order*> &ov,vector<CancelledOrder*> &cv)
{
    for (Order *c: ov)
    {
```

CHAPTER 5   QUICKLY AND SYSTEMATICALLY MODEL REAL-WORLD PROBLEMS INTO SOFTWARE

```
                if (c->getStatus()=="Refunded")
                {
                    for (CancelledOrder *co: cv)
                    {
                        if (co->getCoid()==c->getOid())
                        {
                            cout<<"Order Id"<<co->getCoid()
                            <<" date:"<<co->getRdate()
                            <<"Refund : "<<co->getRefund()
                            <<"status:"<<c->getStatus()
                            <<"\n";
                        }
                    }
                }
            }
        }
```

5. Use the following function to process the confirmed orders by assigning delivery partners and delivery dates.

   a. This function assigns confirmed orders to delivery partners.

   b. For each confirmed order, an expected delivery date is assigned.

   ```
   void processOrders(vector<Order*> &ov,
   vector<DeliveredOrder*> &dv,DeliveryPartner &dp1,
   DeliveryPartner &dp2)
   {
       int count = 0;
       DeliveredOrder *d;
       for (Order *ov1: ov)
       {
           if (ov1->getStatus()=="Processing")
           {   if (count%2 == 0)
   ```

CHAPTER 5 QUICKLY AND SYSTEMATICALLY MODEL REAL-WORLD PROBLEMS INTO SOFTWARE

```
            {
                d = deliverOrder(dp1,ov1);
                count = count+1;
            }
            else
            {
                d = deliverOrder(dp2,ov1);
                count = count+1;
            }
                cout<<"Order "<<d->getDoid()<<"
                will be delivered by:"<<d-
                >getDdate()<<"\n";
                cout<<"Order "<<d->getDoid()<<"
                will be delivered by Delivery
                Partner:"<<d->getDpid()<<"\n";
                dv.push_back(d);
            }
        }
    }
```

6. Apply the following function to simulate processing the refund for canceled orders.

   a. It simulates the refund process by changing the status of the canceled orders.

   b. Since cancelledOrder already assigns the refund amount and expected refund date, using this function shopkeeper sets the canceled order status to Refunded.

   ```
   void processCanOrders(vector<Order*>
   &ov,vector<CancelledOrder*> &cv)
   {
       for (CancelledOrder *c: cv)
   ```

```
            {
                for (Order *o: ov)
                {
                    if(c->getCoid()==o->getOid())
                    {
                        o->setStatus("Refunded");
                    }
                }
            }
        }
```

Well done. You have successfully implemented the shopkeeper interactions related to the shopping application as functions.

Next, simulate complete shopping application interaction in main() and test the functions.

Simulating Shopping Application Tasks

This section simulates the following tasks in a shopping application.

- Items, customers, shopkeeper, and delivery partners registrations
- Customers browsing items, placing orders, viewing their orders, and canceling orders
- Shopkeeper browsing items, orders, and canceled orders
- Shopkeeper processing order for delivery
- Shopkeeper processing canceled orders for refunds

CHAPTER 5   QUICKLY AND SYSTEMATICALLY MODEL REAL-WORLD PROBLEMS INTO SOFTWARE

SIMULATE ALL SHOPPING APPLICATION TASKS

Implement the following tasks in main() in the application.cc file.

1. Start with the registration process.

    a. Register a shopkeeper.

    b. Register two customers.

    c. Register two delivery partners.

    d. Register four shopping products.

    ```
    int main()
    {
        vector<Order*> ov;
        vector<CancelledOrder*> cv;
        vector<DeliveredOrder*> dv;
        Shopkeeper s1;
        shopkeeper_register(s1);
        Customer c1,c2;
        customers_register(c1,c2);
        DeliveryPartner dp1,dp2;
        delpartner_register(dp1,dp2);
        Item i1,i2,i3,i4;
        items_insert(i1,i2,i3,i4);
    ```

2. Check customers and item details by calling the respective functions.

    ```
    customer_disp(c1);
    customer_disp(c2);

    items_browsing(i1);
    items_browsing(i2);
    items_browsing(i3);
    items_browsing(i4);
    ```

CHAPTER 5   QUICKLY AND SYSTEMATICALLY MODEL REAL-WORLD PROBLEMS INTO
            SOFTWARE

3. Create two sample orders for each customer by calling the placeOrder function as follows.

```
Order *o1;
o1 = placeOrder(c1,i1,2);
ov.push_back(o1);
Order *o2;
o2 = placeOrder(c2,i2,2);
ov.push_back(o2);
Order *o3;
o3 = placeOrder(c2,i3,2);
ov.push_back(o3);
Order *o4;
o4 = placeOrder(c1,i4,2);
ov.push_back(o4);
```

4. Simulate canceling an order (o1) from one of the customers (c1) as follows.

```
CancelledOrder *co;
if (o1->getStatus()=="Processing")
{
    co = cancelOrder(c1,o1);
    cout<<"In process\n";
    cout<<"Order "<<co->getCoid()<<" was cancelled successfully\n";
    cout<<"Cancelled Order "<<co->getCoid()<<" will be refunded by:"<<co->getRdate()<<"\n";
    cout<<"Cancelled Order "<<co->getCoid()<<" total refund: "<<co->getRefund()<<"\n";
    cv.push_back(co);
}
```

CHAPTER 5   QUICKLY AND SYSTEMATICALLY MODEL REAL-WORLD PROBLEMS INTO SOFTWARE

5. Check customers and their order details.

    ```
    cout<<"Customer"<<c1.getCid()<<"orders:\n";
    browseCustOrders(c1,ov);
    cout<<"Customer"<<c2.getCid()<<"orders:\n";
    browseCustOrders(c2,ov);
    ```

6. After completing customer transactions, the shopping applications start simulating shopkeeper transactions, such as checking pending and canceled orders.

    ```
    cout<<"List of orders\n";
    browseOrders(ov);
    cout<<"List of Cancelled orders\n";
    browseCanOrders(cv);
    ```

7. Check the delivery partners' details to process pending orders.

    ```
    cout<<"List of Delivery partners\n";
    deliverp_disp (dp1);
    deliverp_disp (dp2); //Did we reference this in
                            deliverorder.h file?
    ```

8. Simulate delivery of pending orders by assigning delivery partners.

    ```
    cout<<"List of Processing orders for delivery\n";
    processOrders(ov,dv,dp1,dp2);
    cout<<"List of Delivered orders\n";
    browseDelOrders(dv);
    ```

9. Process the canceled orders to refund the amount to customers and end the `main()`.

    ```
        processCanOrders(ov,cv);
        cout<<"List of Refunded orders\n";
        browseRefOrders(ov,cv);
    }
    ```

CHAPTER 5   QUICKLY AND SYSTEMATICALLY MODEL REAL-WORLD PROBLEMS INTO SOFTWARE

10. Test the complete shopping application transaction by executing the following commands.

```
# g++ application.cc -o shopapplication
# ./shopapplication

Customer C001 was registered
Customer C002 was registered
Shopkeeper S001 was registered
Delivery partner DP001 was registered
Delivery partner DP002 was registered
Item I001 was entered
Item I002 was entered
Item I003 was entered
Item I004 was entered

Customer id:C001 Phone 9000000000 City City1
Customer id:C002 Phone 9000000000 City City2

Item id:I001 Price 1000 Descr Fashion product
Item id:I002 Price 2000 Descr Entertainment product
Item id:I003 Price 3000 Descr Smart product
Item id:I004 Price 4000 Descr Electronic product

In process
Order O001B was cancelled successfully

Cancelled Order O001B will be refunded by:Rdate1
Cancelled Order O001B total refund: 2000
```

CustomerC001orders:
Order IdO001B date:ODate1cost : 2000status:Cancelled
Order IdO001E date:ODate1cost : 8000status:Processing

CHAPTER 5   QUICKLY AND SYSTEMATICALLY MODEL REAL-WORLD PROBLEMS INTO
            SOFTWARE

CustomerC002orders:

Order Id0001C date:ODate1cost : 4000status:Processing
Order Id0001D date:ODate1cost : 6000status:Processing

List of orders

Order Id0001B date:ODate1cost : 2000status:Cancelled
Order Id0001C date:ODate1cost : 4000status:Processing
Order Id0001D date:ODate1cost : 6000status:Processing
Order Id0001E date:ODate1cost : 8000status:Processing

List of Cancelled orders

Cancelled Order 0001B refund date:Rdate1total refund: 2000

List of Delivery partners
DeliveryPartner id:DP001 Phone 7000000000
DeliveryPartner id:DP002 Phone 7000000000

List of Processing orders for delivery

Order 0001C will be delivered by:Ddate1
Order 0001C will be delivered by Delivery Partner:DP001
Order 0001D will be delivered by:Ddate1
Order 0001D will be delivered by Delivery Partner:DP002
Order 0001E will be delivered by:Ddate1
Order 0001E will be delivered by Delivery Partner:DP001

List of Delivered orders

Delivered Order 0001C Deliver date:Ddate1Delivery Partner: DP001
Delivered Order 0001D Deliver date:Ddate1Delivery Partner: DP002
Delivered Order 0001E Deliver date:Ddate1Delivery Partner: DP001

CHAPTER 5   QUICKLY AND SYSTEMATICALLY MODEL REAL-WORLD PROBLEMS INTO SOFTWARE

List of Refunded orders

```
Order Id0001B date:Rdate1Refund : 2000status:Refunded
```

Well done. You have successfully implemented and tested example activities related to the shopping application. You can observe transactions related to the shopping application. For example, you can observe customer, shopkeeper, and delivery partner registration and order-related details such as canceled orders, delivered orders, and refunded orders.

Summary

In this chapter, you practiced OOP features in real-world applications such as sample games and shopping applications. Mainly, you observed how OOP features simplify mapping real-world entities to software entities and help implement all interactions, transactions, tasks, and functionalities of the software.

In the next chapter, you learn about another important feature of OOP called *inheritance* using C++ for developing reusable and extendible software.

Practice: Hands-on Activities

1. Create any simple game related to animals, birds, and hunters.

    a. Model a variety of animals, birds, and a hunter.

    b. Simulate hunters try to hunt animals and birds.

    c. Simulate making animals and birds friends with each other.

    d. Simulate scenarios such as animals attacking hunters.

CHAPTER 5   QUICKLY AND SYSTEMATICALLY MODEL REAL-WORLD PROBLEMS INTO SOFTWARE

e. Simulate scenarios such as birds watching hunters.

f. Simulate scenarios such as birds helping animals with hunter locations.

2. Design an online vehicle booking application classes to do the following interactions.

   a. Register online vehicle application supporting locations.

   b. Register a vehicle with driver details.

   c. Register a user.

   d. Check if any vehicle is available at the user's location.

   e. Find the nearest vehicle available from the user's location.

   f. Find the lowest-fare vehicle available for traveling to the user's location.

CHAPTER 6

Quick Software Development Using OOP

You have studied OOP basic principles and how to use these concepts to quickly model and implement software solutions for online shopping, gaming, and smart applications. This chapter explores inheritance approaches to reuse code and save development time. Using C++, you learn how to write reusable code to reduce software development time and avoid redundant code to prevent inconsistent code.

Then, you learn the importance of object composition and aggregation concepts for developing complex software systems. You see how to flexibly compose or connect various classes to build new software systems. As part of practicing inheritance, object composition, and object aggregation, you do programming activities using C++.

Learning inheritance concepts helps you quickly handle challenges in upgrading existing software, creating new versions of software, and rapidly developing new software systems from existing multiple software components.

© Anil Kumar Rangisetti 2024
A. K. Rangisetti, *Hands-On Object-Oriented Programming*,
https://doi.org/10.1007/979-8-8688-0524-0_6

CHAPTER 6   QUICK SOFTWARE DEVELOPMENT USING OOP

This chapter covers the following topics.

- The importance of inheritance
- Practicing the reduce and reuse principle
- Building new software building block versions easily
- Combining or connecting objects wisely
- Practicing inheritance and object association

The Importance of Inheritance

Let's discuss inheritance in a programming context. From programming tasks, you observed that developing a large software application involves implementing multiple classes, and there is a chance that a lot of code may be duplicated (repeated) across the classes. Moreover, creating newer versions of classes can lead to more redundant code. It means developers must organize software classes to avoid redundant and inconsistent code across the classes. This section explains how inheritance concepts are helpful to organize multiple classes to avoid redundant code and easier to extend existing classes to develop new version classes.

Inheritance is a concept of designing new classes from existing classes. Usually, you call existing classes a *base class* (or super class or parent class) and new classes a *derived class* (or subclass or child class). This book uses a base class (or superclass) and a derived class (or subclass) terminology to explain the concepts. Next, let's look at inheritance concepts and approaches in C++.

In C++, you should use the following syntax to create a new class (e.g., Derived) from an existing class (e.g., Base).

```
class Base
{
    public:
    base class data members; (e.g., int base;)
    base class member functions;
    (e.g., void setBase(int b); int getBase();)
};

class Derived: public Base
{
    public:
    derived class data members;(e.g., int derived;)
    derived class member functions;
    (e.g., void setDerived(int d); int getDerived();)
};
```

Let's discuss how public access inheritance helps reuse existing class code in new version classes. Later, you see other access specifiers such as private and protected.

Defining a `Derived` class from a `Base` class using inheritance gives the following benefits.

- Base class complete code is inherited into the `Derived` class. It means inside the `Derived` class member functions can access all public `Base` class data members and member functions.

    ```
    void setDerived(int d) {
    setBase(10); int v = getBase();
    }
    ```

CHAPTER 6   QUICK SOFTWARE DEVELOPMENT USING OOP

- Derived class objects can access all public data members of the Base class.

```
int main() {
Derived d1; d1.base = 10; d1.derived = 200;
}
```

- Derived class objects can access all public data member functions of the Base class.

```
int main() {
Derived d1; d1.setBase(10); d1.getBase();
d1.setSerived(20); d1.getDerived();
}
```

From these simple examples, you observed that inheritance helps reuse the base class code by the derived class and its objects. Next, let's look at inheritance approaches.

Inheritance Approaches

To handle challenges in reusing existing classes, inheritance approaches help to combine multiple existing class features flexibly and efficiently for creating new classes. Mainly, inheritance various approaches help in extending existing classes for creating new version classes, and combining existing classes in multiple ways for creating new classes. You can use the following inheritance approaches.

- Single-level inheritance, multilevel inheritance
- Hierarchical inheritance
- Multiple inheritance
- Combining all inheritance approaches

Let's learn how to use inheritance approaches in C++.

CHAPTER 6 QUICK SOFTWARE DEVELOPMENT USING OOP

INHERITANCE APPROACHES IN C++

Let's start with the basic inheritance approach called single-level inheritance.

1. **Single-level inheritance**: For example, you must maintain personal and employee-specific profiles in software. To do this task without inheritance, you must create the following two classes.

    a. The Person class maintains personal profiles.

    ```
    #include<iostream>
    using namespace std;
    class Person
    {
        string name;
        unsigned int adhar_id;
        public:
        void setName(string n);
        void setAdhar(unsigned int aid);
        string getName();
        unsigned int getAdhar();
    };
    ```

    b. The Employee class maintains employee profiles.

    ```
    class Employee
    {
        string name;
        unsigned int adhar_id;
        int eid;
        unsigned int salary;
    ```

295

CHAPTER 6 QUICK SOFTWARE DEVELOPMENT USING OOP

```
    public:
    void setName(string n);
    void setAdhar(unsigned int aid);
    string getName();
    unsigned int getAdhar();
    void setEid(int e);
    void setSalary(unsigned int s);
    int getEid();
    unsigned int getSalary();
};
```

   c. In the `Employee` class, observe that there is a lot of code related to personal profile maintenance. It is duplicate code and it can lead to inconsistency and performance issues. Let's refine the `Employee` class by inheriting it from the `Person` class.

```
class Employee: public Person
{
    int eid;
    unsigned int salary;

    public:
    void setEid(int e);
    void setSalary(unsigned int s);
    int getEid();
    unsigned int getSalary();
};
```

   d. There is no redundant code among the `Person` and `Employee` classes.

CHAPTER 6   QUICK SOFTWARE DEVELOPMENT USING OOP

e. Moreover, you can access the Person class code from the Employee object as follows.

```
void main()
{
    Employee e1;
    // You can use the Person class code through e1
    object as follows:
    e1.setName("name1");
    e1.setAdhar(12345);
    e1.getName();
    e1.getAdhar();
}
```

2. **Multilevel Inheritance**: Helps you to create new version classes from existing classes.

   a. For example, using multilevel inheritance approaches, you can create new versions of smart device codes easily as follows.

   ```
   class SmartDevice
   {
   };
   class SmartDevicev2:public SmartDevice
   {
   };
   class SmartDevicev3:public SmartDevicev2
   {
   };
   ```

   b. Similarly, you can extend SmartDevicev3 and create newer versions of smart devices.

297

CHAPTER 6 QUICK SOFTWARE DEVELOPMENT USING OOP

3. **Hierarchical Inheritance**: Helps you to create a variety of new classes from a single class.

    a. Using an inheritance hierarchical approach, for example, you can create various cricket players (BatsMan, Bowler) profile maintenance classes from a Player class.

    ```
    class Player
    {
    };
    class Bowler: public Player
    {
    };
    class BatsMan: public Player
    {
    };
    ```

    b. Similarly, you can extend Player and create new player classes (e.g., Keeper).

4. **Multiple inheritance**: Helps you to bring multiple class features and code into new classes.

    a. Using a multiple inheritance approach, for example, you can create a cricket player profile maintenance class from BatsMan and Bowler classes as follows.

    ```
    class BatsMan: public Player
    {
    };
    class Bowler: public Player
    {
    };
    ```

```
class AllRounder:public Batman,Bowler
{
};
```

b. To create the `AllRounder` class, you combine multiple and hierarchical inheritance approaches.

You have learned how to use various inheritance approaches. Next, let's look at handling challenges in combining multiple inheritance approaches.

Issues in Combining Inheritance Approaches

When you combine hierarchical and multiple inheritance approaches, the following details about inherited code from the Base classes must be checked.

- Does a derived class (e.g., `AllRounder`) get inherited with multiple copies of any base class code (e.g., `Player`)?

- Does a derived class get inherited from intermediate base classes (such as `BatsMan`, `Bowler,` etc.) and the intermediate base classes are inherited from the same base class (e.g., `Player`)?

- If the answers are yes to these questions, then there is an **issue of duplicate code of base class** (e.g., `Player`) **in derived classes** (e.g., `AllRounder`). Let's look at how to handle this challenge in the following section.

CHAPTER 6   QUICK SOFTWARE DEVELOPMENT USING OOP

HANDLING CHALLENGES IN THE USAGE OF COMBINED INHERITANCE APPROACHES
---

1. Combining multiple inheritance approaches for implementing various classes to develop software is necessary. Let's check AllRounder class issues.

    a. As per inheritance rules, the Player class code is inherited into the BatsMan and Bowler classes.

    b. Then, AllRounder inherits code from both BatsMan and Bowler classes, which means the Player class code is inherited into AllRounder class twice.

    c. It leads to duplicate code of Player class existence in the AllRounder class.

    d. To avoid duplicate copies from intermediate classes, C++ language supports a virtual way of inheritance.

2. In this problem, intermediate classes (BatsMan and Bowler) should inherit from the base class (Player) using the virtual keyword as follows.

```cpp
class Bowler: public virtual Player
{
};
class Batsman: public virtual Player
{
};
class AllRounder:public Batman,Bowler
{
};
```

CHAPTER 6 QUICK SOFTWARE DEVELOPMENT USING OOP

Because of using `virtual Player` in intermediate classes, the ultimate derived class (`AllRounder`) is inherited with only one copy of `Player` code. It avoids duplicate code and ambiguity issues for linking `Player` member functions in `AllRounder` classes.

From all these inheritance approaches, you can see how inheritance helps reuse existing classes and create new version classes. You learn how to use public, private, and protected access specifiers to define rules for accessing inherited code from derived classes.

You have learned how to handle challenges in combining multiple inheritance approaches. Base classes' complete code is inherited into derived classes. Next, you learn how to use access specifiers for inheriting base class code into derived classes for restricting base class feature access.

Access Controls and Inheritance

You have learned using inheritance approaches. It is possible to inherit the code of base classes into derived classes. Now you learn how to use access specifiers for controlling base class code (`public`, `private`, and `protected` section) access in the derived classes.

- Public inheritance mode: Base class `public` section code is inherited into the derived class `public` section. Hence, the derived class and its objects can access it without any `public` member functions.
  - The base class `private` section code is inherited into the derived class `private` section. Hence, the derived class and its objects should access the base class code with `public` member functions of the base class only.

301

- Base class protected section code is inherited into the derived class protected section. Derived class and its objects can access the base class code without any public member functions.

- Private inheritance mode: Base class every section (public, private, or protected) code becomes private in the derived class. Hence, you must provide public member functions in derived classes to access them outside the derived class.

- Protected inheritance mode: Base class private section code is inherited into the derived class private section.

  - Base class (public and protected) becomes protected in the derived class.

  - Derived class and its objects can access the **base class code (public and protected)** without any public member functions.

PUBLIC, PRIVATE, AND PROTECTED RULES

1. Let's define a Base class with sample code in each access specifier section as follows.

   ```
   class Base
   {
       private:
           int f1;
           int getF1();
       public:
   ```

```
        int f2;
        int getF2();
    protected:
        int f3;
        int getF3();
};
```

2. Inherit the Base class code into the Derived class using the public inheritance mode.

```
class Derived:public Base
{
    public:
    void accessProtectedBase()
    {
        f3=300;
    }
};
```

   a. The Base class private section code is inherited into the private section of the Derived class. To access private members of the Base class, you must define public access functions related to them in the Base class.

   b. The Base class protected section code is inherited into the protected section of the Derived class. To access protected section code of the Base class, Derived class member functions can access it (e.g., f3=100) directly, as shown in the class.

c. However, nonmember functions (e.g., `main()`) cannot access `protected` members of a class without `public` access functions.

```
int main()
{
    Derived d1;
    d1.accessProtectedBase();
    d1.f2=100; //public members can be accessed
    d1.getF2();//public members can be accessed
    d1.getF3() or d1.f3=300;//not allowed.
}
```

3. Inherit the `Base` class from the `Derived` class using `private` inheritance mode as follows.

```
class Derived:private Base
{
    public:
    void accessPublicProtectedBase()
    {
        f2=300;
        cout<<f2;
        f3=300;
        cout<<f3;
    }
};
```

a. The `Base` class **all** sections (`private`, `public`, `protected`) code is inherited into the `private` section of the `Derived` class.

b. Hence, in `main()`, you cannot access `public` or `protected` section codes of the `Base` class using a `Derived` object. You should define a `public` access function in the `Derived` class as shown in the class (e.g., `accessPublicProtectedBase()`) to access the `Base` class `public` section or `protected` section code from `main()`.

CHAPTER 6   QUICK SOFTWARE DEVELOPMENT USING OOP

```
int main()
{
    Derived d1;
    d1.f2=100; //not allowed
    d1.getF2();//not allowed
    d1.getF3() or d1.f3=300;//not allowed.
    d1.accessPublicProtectedBase();
}
```

4. let's inherit Base class from Derived class using protected inheritance mode as follows.

```
class Derived:protected Base
{
    public:
    void accessPublicProtectedBase()
    {
        f2=300;
        cout<<f2;
        f3=300;
        cout<<f3;
    }
};
```

a. The Base class private section code is inherited into the private section of the Derived class. Base class public and protected sections code are inherited into the Derived class protected section.

b. To access inherited public and protected section codes of the Base class from a Derived class object, you must call accessPublicProtectedBase().

305

CHAPTER 6   QUICK SOFTWARE DEVELOPMENT USING OOP

```
int main()
{
    Derived d1;
    d1.accessPublicProtectedBase();
    d1.f2=100; //not allowed
    d1.getF2();//not allowed
    d1.getF3() or d1.f3=300;//not allowed.
}
```

These examples show how to restrict access to a base class inherited code from derived classes. It helps you to choose the right access specifiers for deriving new classes from base classes. Next, you learn how special functions, constructors, and destructors behave in the context of inheritance.

Constructors and Destructors Working Order in Inheritance Context

You have learned using inheritance approaches. It is possible to inherit the code of base classes into derived classes. In this section, you learn how constructors and destructors are executed in the context of inheritance, including the following.

- The order of the base class and derived classes' constructor execution

- The order of the base class and derived classes' destructors execution

- The importance of defining base classes order in multiple inheritance approach

306

ORDER OF CONSTRUCTORS AND DESTRUCTORS EXECUTION

1. Define a `Basic` class with sample constructor and destructor codes and save it in the `iconstdestr.cc` file.

    ```
    #include<iostream>
    using namespace std;
    class Basic
    {
        public:
        Basic()
        {
            cout<<"Basic initialization\n";
        }
        ~Basic()
        {
            cout<<"Basic class shutdown activities\n";
        }
    };
    ```

2. Define a `Special` class by inheriting from the `Basic` class with sample constructor and destructor codes as follows.

    ```
    class Special:public Basic
    {
        public:
        Special()
        {
            cout<<"Special initialization\n";
        }
        ~Special()
        {
    ```

```
            cout<<"Special class shutdown activities\n";
        }
};
```

3. Test the code in main() by creating a Special class object.

```
int main()
{
    Special s1;
}
```

4. Observe the following while executing the testing code.

   a. The base class's object constructor code is executed, then the derived class's object constructor code is executed. It means after carrying out base class objects initialization and startup activities then only derived class objects initialization and activities are started.

   b. The derived class's object destructor code is executed, then the base class's object destructor code is executed. It means that only derived class objects clean up and shutdown activities are started after carrying out destructor class objects clean up and shutdown activities.

   ```
   # g++ iconstdestr.cc -o iconstdest
   # ./iconstdestr
   Basic initialization
   Special initialization
   Special class shutdown activities
   Basic class shutdown activities
   ```

IMPORTANCE OF BASE CLASSES ORDER IN MULTIPLE INHERITANCE APPROACH

1. Define the following in baseclassorder.cc file.
2. Copy the Basic class code into baseclassorder.cc.
3. Define a New sample class as follows.

   ```
   class New
   {
       public:
       New()
       {
           cout<<"New features initialization\n";
       }
       ~New()
       {
           cout<<"New class shutdown activities\n";
       }
   };
   ```

4. Define a Sample class by inheriting from New and Basic classes as follows.

   ```
   class Special:public New, Basic
   {
       public:
       Special()
       {
           cout<<"Special initialization\n";
       }
       ~Special()
       {
   ```

CHAPTER 6   QUICK SOFTWARE DEVELOPMENT USING OOP

```
            cout<<"Special class shutdown activities\n";
        }
};
```

5. Test the code in main() by creating a Special class object.

```
int main()
{
    Special s1;
}
```

6. Observe the following while executing the testing code.

   a. Constructors are executed in the order of base classes (New followed by Basic) inherited into the Special class

   b. Destructors are executed in the reverse order of base classes (Basic followed by New) inherited into the Special class

   ```
   # g++ baseclassorder.cc -o baseclassorder
   # ./baseclassorder
   New features initialization
   Basic initialization
   Special initialization
   Special class shutdown activities
   Basic class shutdown activities
   New class shutdown activities
   ```

7. Change the Special class inheriting base classes order as follows.

   ```
   class Special:public Basic,New
   ```

CHAPTER 6   QUICK SOFTWARE DEVELOPMENT USING OOP

8. While executing the testing code, you should observe the following.

   a. Constructors are executed in the order of base classes (Basic followed by New) inherited into the Special class

   b. Destructors are executed in the reverse order of base classes (New followed by Basic) inherited into the Special class.

   ```
   # g++ baseclassorder.cc -o baseclassorder
   # ./baseclassorder
   Basic initialization
   New features initialization
   Special initialization
   Special class shutdown activities
   New class shutdown activities
   Basic class shutdown activities
   ```

From this simple activity, you observe the importance of the order of base classes inherited into derived classes. As you know, object-oriented software startup and shutdown activities depend on constructors and destructors. It is necessary to define base class order per requirements while inheriting into derived classes.

Next, let's practice inheritance principles by doing relevant programming activities.

Practicing the Reduce and Reuse Principle

Two primary benefits of Inheritance concepts are eliminating redundant code among classes and reusing the existing classes. These benefits are highly important to speed up a software code development process. As part of practicing the inheritance concepts, you do the following activities related to developing application software.

CHAPTER 6 QUICK SOFTWARE DEVELOPMENT USING OOP

- For example, related to software, you need to maintain personal profiles of employees and trainees.

- Avoid redundant code related to maintaining common details of employees and trainees.

- Reuse the existing code related to personal profiles to maintain employee and trainee profiles.

- Clearly define classes to develop consistent code and easily extend the existing classes.

Let's start with defining a personal profiles maintenance class.

PERSONAL PROFILE

Define the personal profile maintenance class in C++ and save it in the `personal.h` file.

1. To maintain personal profiles of employees and trainees consistently, define a `Person` class with common details of employees and trainees.

    a. Include name, contact, and address details.

    b. To access these personal details, declare necessary interfaces such as set and get member functions inside the `Person` class.

    ```
    #include<string.h>
    using namespace std;
    class Person
    {
        string name;
        char phone[11];
        string city;
        string country;
    ```

```
            unsigned int pin;
        public:
            string getName();
            void setName(string cname);
            char* getPhone();
            void setPhone(char cphone[11]);
            string getCity();
            void setCity(string ccity);
            string getCountry();
            void setCountry(string ccountry);
            unsigned int getPin();
            void setPin(unsigned int pin);
    };
```

2. Define the member functions related to personal details such as name and phone number of the Person class as follows.

```
string Person::getName()
{
    return name;
}
void Person::setName(string cname)
{
    name = cname;
}
char* Person::getPhone()
{
    return phone;
}
void Person::setPhone(char cphone[11])
{
    strcpy(phone, cphone);
}
```

CHAPTER 6   QUICK SOFTWARE DEVELOPMENT USING OOP

3. Define the member functions related to personal address details such as city, country, and PIN of the Person class as follows.

```
string Person::getCity()
{
    return city;
}
void Person::setCity(string ccity)
{
    city = ccity;
}
string Person::getCountry()
{
    return country;
}
void Person::setCountry(string ccountry)
{
    country = ccountry;
}
unsigned int Person::getPin()
{
    return pin;
}
void Person::setPin(unsigned int cpin)
{
    pin = cpin;
}
```

After saving this file with the code, let's reuse the Person class to define the employee profile maintenance class.

CHAPTER 6 QUICK SOFTWARE DEVELOPMENT USING OOP

EMPLOYEE PROFILE

Define the employee profile maintenance class in C++ and save it in the employee.h file.

1. Define an Employee class by inheriting from the Person class to reuse the Personal profile maintenance code.

    a. setName, setPhone, setCity, setCountry, and setPin to save or update employees' personal profiles.

    b. getName, getPhone, getCity, getCountry, and getPin to retrieve employees' profiles.

2. To maintain specific details of employees, define the Employee class with common details.

    a. Include the employee identifier, department, hire date, and salary.

    b. To access these employee details, declare necessary interfaces such as set and get member functions inside the Employee class.

    ```cpp
    #include<string.h>
    using namespace std;
    class Employee:public Person
    {
        string eid;
        string did;
        string jdate;
        unsigned int salary;
        public:
            string getEid();
            void setEid(string ieid);
            string getDid();
            void setDid(string idid);
    ```

315

```
            string getJdate();
            void setJdate(string date);
            unsigned int getSalary();
            void setSalary(unsigned int sal);
    };
```

3. Define all member functions of the Employee class as follows to maintain employee-specific details.

```
string Employee::getEid()
{
    return eid;
}
void Employee::setEid(string ieid)
{
    eid = ieid ;
}
string Employee::getDid()
{
    return did;
}
void Employee::setDid(string idid)
{
    did = idid;
}
string Employee::getJdate()
{
    return jdate;
}
void Employee::setJdate(string date)
{
    jdate = date;
```

```
}
unsigned int Employee::getSalary()
{
    return salary;
}
void Employee::setSalary(unsigned int sal)
{
    salary = sal;
}
```

4. Observe that no code related to personal profile maintenance code was defined in the Employee class.

After saving this file with the code, let's test it in the main() code.

EMPLOYEE PROFILE ACCESS TESTING CODE

1. To test the Person and Employee classes, define the following code in emp_proile.cc.

    a. You create a person object (p1) from the Person class and save an example personal profile. Then, print the p1 details.

    b. Next, you create an employee (e1) object from the Employee class and save an example employee profile by including personal and employee-specific details. Then, print the e1 details.

    ```
    #include<iostream>
    #include"personal.h"
    #include"employee.h"
    using namespace std;
    int main()
    ```

CHAPTER 6   QUICK SOFTWARE DEVELOPMENT USING OOP

```cpp
{
    Person p1;
    p1.setName("Person");
    char phone[11];
    strcpy(phone,"9000080000");
    p1.setPhone(phone);
    p1.setCity("City1");
    p1.setCountry("Country1");
    p1.setPin(100001);

    cout<<"Person details:\n";
    cout<<"Name:"<<p1.getName()<<":\n";
    cout<<"Phone Number:"<<p1.getPhone()<<"\n";

    Employee e1;
    e1.setName("Employee");
    char phone1[11];
    strcpy(phone1,"9000080001");
    e1.setPhone(phone1);
    e1.setCity("City2");
    e1.setCountry("Country1");
    e1.setPin(100001);

    e1.setEid("E001");
    e1.setDid("D001");
    e1.setSalary(90000);
    cout<<"Employee details:\n";
    cout<<"EID:"<<e1.getEid()<<"\n";
    cout<<"Name:"<<e1.getName()<<"\n";
    cout<<"DID:"<<e1.getDid()<<"\n";
    cout<<"Salary:"<<e1.getSalary()<<"\n";
}
```

CHAPTER 6 QUICK SOFTWARE DEVELOPMENT USING OOP

2. After saving the code, test emp_profile.cc code using the following command and observe the results.

   a. You can observe that employee object personal details can be accessed using `Person` class interfaces (e.g., `setName`, `getName`, etc.).

   b. The `Person` class code is inherited into the `Employee` class and accessible from `Employee` objects.

   ```
   # gcc emp_profile.cc -o emp
   # ./emp
   Person details:
   Name:Person:
   Phone Number:9000080000
   Employee details:
   EID:E001
   Name:Employee
   DID:D001
   Salary:90000
   ```

After testing the employee profile maintenance code, let's extend the employee profile code to develop and maintain trainees profile.

CHAPTER 6   QUICK SOFTWARE DEVELOPMENT USING OOP

DEFINE TRAINEE PROFILE BY REUSING EMPLOYEE PROFILE CODE

Define a trainee profile maintenance class in C++ and save it in the trainee.h file.

1. Define a `Trainee` class by inheriting from the `Employee` class to reuse the personal and employee profile maintenance code such as

    a. `setName, setPhone, setCity, setCountry, setPin, getName, getPhone, getCity, getCountry,` and `getPin` to maintain personal profiles of trainees.

    b. `setEid, setDid, setSalary, getEid, getDid,` and `getSalary` to maintain employee profiles of trainees.

2. Define the `Trainee` class with common trainee details.

    a. Include the training end date and grade.

    b. Declare necessary interfaces such as set and get member functions inside the `Trainee` class.

    ```
    #include<string.h>
    using namespace std;
    class Trainee:public Employee
    {
        string edate;
        string grade;
        public:
            string getEdate();
            void setEdate(string date);
            string getGrade();
            void setGrade(string igrade);
    };
    ```

CHAPTER 6 QUICK SOFTWARE DEVELOPMENT USING OOP

3. Define all member functions of the Trainee class as follows to maintain trainee-specific details.

```
string Trainee::getEdate()
{
    return edate;
}
void Trainee::setEdate(string date)
{
    edate = date;
}
string Trainee::getGrade()
{
    return grade;
}
void Trainee::setGrade(string igrade)
{
    grade = igrade;
}
```

4. Save the file with the preceding code, and hen test it in the main() code.

5. Define the following code in trainee_proile.cc.

   a. Create a trainee object (t1) from the Trainee class and save an example trainee profile. Then, print the t1 details.

```
#include<iostream>
#include"personal.h"
#include"employee.h"
#include"trainee.h"
using namespace std;
int main()
```

321

```
{
    Trainee t1;
    t1.setName("Trainee");
    char phone1[11];
    strcpy(phone1,"9000080001");
    t1.setPhone(phone1);
    t1.setCity("City2");
    t1.setCountry("Country1");
    t1.setPin(100001);

    t1.setEid("T001");
    t1.setDid("D001");
    t1.setJdate("JDATE1");
    t1.setSalary(10000);
    cout<<"Trainee details:\n";
    cout<<"TID:"<<t1.getEid()<<"\n";
    cout<<"Name:"<<t1.getName()<<"\n";
    cout<<"DID:"<<t1.getDid()<<"\n";
    cout<<"Stipend:"<<t1.getSalary()<<"\n";

    t1.setEdate("EDATE1");
    t1.setGrade("Grade-1");

    cout<<"Training End date:"<<t1.getEdate()<<"\n";
    cout<<"Grade:"<<t1.getGrade()<<"\n";
}
```

6. Save the code. Test trainee_profile.cc code using the following command and observe the results.

   a. Observe that trainee object personal details can be accessed using Person class interfaces (e.g., setName, getName).

CHAPTER 6   QUICK SOFTWARE DEVELOPMENT USING OOP

b. Trainee object employee details can be accessed using `Employee` class interfaces (e.g., `setEid`, `getEid`).

c. The `Person` class and `Employee` code are inherited into the `Trainee` class and accessible from `Trainee` objects.

```
# gcc trainee_profile.cc -o trainee
#./trainee
Trainee details:
TID:T001
Name:Trainee
DID:D001
Stipend:10000
Training End date:EDATE1
Grade:Grade-1
```

Next, let's extend the existing game entities for creating new versions of game entities using inheritance.

Building New Software Building Blocks Versions Easily

In this section, you practice inheritance concepts to implement newer software versions, for instance, newer versions of weapons, bombs, and players, by extending the game entities defined in Chapter 5. Specifically, you do the following activities to extend the game entities.

- Introduce a new version of guns called automatic guns
- Introduce a new version of bombs called time bombs
- Introduce a new version of players with new actions

CHAPTER 6   QUICK SOFTWARE DEVELOPMENT USING OOP

- Set up game scenarios using older and new versions of game entities.
  - For instance, you should be able to deploy automatic and older guns to set up game scenarios.
  - For instance, you should be able to deploy normal bombs and time bombs to set up game scenarios.
  - For instance, you should be able to introduce new version players as well as older version players.

Let's start with automatic guns in the gaming world.

AUTOMATIC GUN VERSION

Define an AutoGun class by extending and reusing the Gun class and saving it in the autogun.h file.

1. To model automatic guns, define the following sample features by extending default Gun class features.

   ```
   #include <iostream>
   using namespace std;
   class AutoGun:public Gun
   {
       unsigned int range;
       unsigned int timer;
       public:
   ```

a. Initialize automatic guns with a higher number of bullets and a default timer.

```
AutoGun()
{
    setBullets(100);
    timer = 10;
}
```

b. Provide special interfaces to enable or disable the automatic mode working of guns.

```
void setAutomode(unsigned int time)
{
    range = rand()%100;
    timer = time;
}
bool isAutoEnabled()
{
    if (timer>0)
    {
        return true;
    }
    else
    {
        return false;
    }
}
```

c. Define a new firing procedure when automatic mode is enabled. To do this, override the `fire()` member function of the Gun class.

```
void fire()
{
    int bullets = getBullets();
```

```
            if (timer > 0)
            {
                cout<<"Auto mode enabled\n";
                if (bullets>0)
                {
                    bullets=bullets-5;
                    setBullets(bullets);
                }
                else
                    cout<<"No bullets\n";
            }
            else
            {
                if (bullets>0)
                {
                    bullets=bullets-1;
                    setBullets(bullets);
                }
                else
                    cout<<"No bullets\n";
            }
        }
    };
```

2. Observe that due to inheritance features, in the AutoGun class you can reuse Gun class member functions such as setBullets and getBullets interfaces.

3. Save this code.

Next, let's define time bombs by extending the existing Bomb class.

CHAPTER 6 QUICK SOFTWARE DEVELOPMENT USING OOP

TIME BOMB VERSION

Define a TimeBomb class by extending and reusing the Bomb class, and save it in the timebomb.h file.

1. To model time bombs, define the following sample features by extending default Bomb class features.

   ```
   #include <iostream>
   using namespace std;
   class TimeBomb:public Bomb
   {
       int id;
       unsigned int timer;
       public:
   ```

   a. Override the setState member function to enable time bombs in game scenarios.

      ```
      void setState(int istate)
      {
          Bomb::setState(istate);
          timer = 10;
      }
      ```

   b. Define time bombs with specific identifiers and access them using setId and getId interfaces.

      ```
      void setId(int iid)
      {
          id = iid;
      }
      int getId()
      {
          return id;
      }
      ```

CHAPTER 6 QUICK SOFTWARE DEVELOPMENT USING OOP

   c. Define the `setTimer` function to set a timer for time bombs.

      i. Based on the timer, activate or disable the bomb using the Bomb class interface called `setState`.

```
void setTimer(unsigned int time)
{
    enum state {DIFFUSED,ACTIVE};
    timer = time;
    if (timer > 0)
    {
        Bomb::setState(ACTIVE);
    }
    else
    {
        Bomb::setState(DIFFUSED);
    }
}
```

   d. Define the `getTimer` function to get timer values of time bombs.

```
unsigned int getTimer()
{
    return timer;
}
};
```

2. Due to inheritance features, in the `TimeBomb` class, you can reuse Bomb class member functions such as `setState` and `getState` interfaces.

3. Save this code.

Next, let's define newer version players by extending the existing `Player` class.

CHAPTER 6   QUICK SOFTWARE DEVELOPMENT USING OOP

NEW VERSION PLAYER

Define a `Playerv2` class by extending and reusing the `Player` class and saving it in `playerv2.h` file.

1. Please note that before defining Playerv2, change the Player class private data members into protected ones. It helps in accessing Player data members directly by Playerv2 member functions.

2. As part of modeling newer version players, define the following sample features by extending default `Player` class features.

    ```
    #include <iostream>
    #include <vector>
    #include <unistd.h>
    #include <bits/stdc++.h>
    using namespace std;

    class Playerv2:public Player
    {
    ```

3. Define new vectors called tbv and agv to collect new versions of guns and bombs.

    ```
    vector<TimeBomb> tbv;
    vector<AutoGun> agv;
    public:
    ```

4. Define a new player action called fly.

    ```
    void fly()
    {
        cout<<"He can fly\n";
        x = x*10;        y = y*10;      }
    ```

329

5. Define another new player action called swim.

    ```
    void swim()
    {
        cout<<"He can swim\n";
        x = x+3;              y = y+3;
    }
    ```

6. Define a new action to set a time bomb called setTimerBomb.

    ```
    void setTimerBomb(TimeBomb *b)
    {
        tbv.push_back(*b);
    }
    ```

7. Define a new action to activate an automatic gun called setAutoGun.

    ```
    void setAutoGun(AutoGun *g)
    {
        agv.push_back(*g);
    }
    ```

8. Override the stats member function of Player to display new weapons and other stats of players.

    ```
    void stats()
    {
        cout<<"\nPlayer: "<<getId()<<" Time Bombs: "<<tbv.size()<<" Auto Guns:"<<agv.size()<<"\n";
    }
    };
    ```

Next, let's set up a sample game context using new version players, weapons, and bombs.

CHAPTER 6   QUICK SOFTWARE DEVELOPMENT USING OOP

SET UP A NEW VERSION GAME CONTEXT

Let's do the following activities to set up a new version game setup in the game.cc file.

1. Include the following files to deploy the older and new game entities.

   ```
   #include<iostream>
   #include<vector>
   #include"bomb.h"
   #include"gun.h"
   #include"player.h"
   #include"timebomb.h"
   #include"autogun.h"
   #include"playerv2.h"
   using namespace std;
   ```

2. Start main() with deploying two older version bombs and guns and an older version player.

   ```
   int main()
   {
       Bomb b1,b2;
       Gun g1,g2;
       Player p1;
   ```

3. Define the older version of player actions.

   a. Activating bombs and guns

   b. Moving forward

   c. Firing older guns

   ```
   p1.setBomb(&b1);
   p1.setGun(&g1);
   ```

CHAPTER 6 QUICK SOFTWARE DEVELOPMENT USING OOP

```
p1.walk();
cout<<"After walking Player1 position:
"<<p1.getX()<<" "<<p1.getY()<<"\n";
cout<<"Player1 gun state: "<<g1.getState()<<"\n";
cout<<"Player1 gun's bullets:
"<<g1.getBullets()<<"\n";
g1.fire();
cout<<"After firing Player1 gun's bullets:
"<<g1.getBullets()<<"\n";
if (b1.getState() == 1)
{
    cout<<"Player1 bomb is active\n";
}
```

4. Define a new version player, a time bomb, and an automatic gun.

```
Playerv2 p2;
TimeBomb tb;
AutoGun ag;
```

5. Give the new version player the following actions.

   a. Activating newer version bombs and guns

   ```
   p2.setAutoGun(&ag);
   p2.setTimerBomb(&tb);
   ```

   b. Activating older version bombs and guns

   ```
   p2.setBomb(&b2);
   p2.setGun(&g2);
   ```

   c. Moving forward and firing guns

   ```
   p2.walk();
   cout<<"After walking Player2 position: "<<p2.getX()<<" "<<p2.getY()<<"\n";
   ```

```
cout<<"Player2 gun state: "<<g2.getState()<<"\n";
g2.fire();
cout<<"After firing Player2 gun's bullets: "<<g2.
getBullets()<<"\n";
cout<<"Player2 gun state: "<<ag.getState()<<"\n";
cout<<"Player2 Autho gun's bullets: "<<ag.
getBullets()<<"\n";
ag.fire();
cout<<"After firing Player2 Autho gun's bullets:
"<<ag.getBullets()<<"\n";
if (b2.getState() == 1)
{
    cout<<"Player2 bomb is active\n";
}
cout<<"Player2 time bomb timer: "<<tb.
getTimer()<<"\n";
```

6. Call the player2 new actions, such as flying and swimming.

```
p2.fly();
cout<<"After flying Player2 position:
"<<p2.getX()<<" "<<p2.getY()<<"\n";
p2.swim();
cout<<"After swimming Player2 position:
"<<p2.getX()<<" "<<p2.getY()<<"\n";
}
```

7. Save the game.cc with the preceding code, execute it, and observe the following.

   a. Older version player objects interact with older guns and bombs.

   b. Older version player objects can walk only.

c. Newer version player objects can interact with both normal guns and automatic guns.

d. Newer version player objects can interact with both normal bombs and time bombs.

e. Newer version player objects can do new actions such as flying and swimming.

```
# g++ game.cc -o game
# ./game
After walking Player1 position: 2 6
Player1 gun state: 1
Player1 gun's bullets: 10
After firing Player1 gun's bullets: 9
Player1 bomb is active
After walking Player2 position: 6 8
Player2 gun state: 1
After firing Player2 gun's bullets: 9
Player2 gun state: 1
Player2 Autho gun's bullets: 100
Auto mode enabled
After firing Player2 Autho gun's bullets: 95
Player2 bomb is active
Player2 time bomb timer: 42
He can fly
After flying Player2 position: 60 80
He can swim
After swimming Player2 position: 63 83
```

From this activity, you observed that inheritance helps easily create new version classes. It helps us to build new versions of software from existing software easily. Next, you learn the importance of combining objects for producing software.

CHAPTER 6   QUICK SOFTWARE DEVELOPMENT USING OOP

Combine or Connect Objects Wisely

An association of classes and integration of objects are necessary to develop complex applications. Inheritance concepts help define classes wisely to avoid redundant code and write reusable and extendible classes. You have practiced inheritance approaches for writing reusable and extendible software. This section explains how to combine or connect objects to classes. Programmers can use objects inside a class using the following two main approaches.

- Composition: Composition of objects inside a class (external class) means tightly coupling internal objects (defined inside the class) with the external class objects. It results in internal object creation or deletion depending on the class objects.
  - You should use object composition only if it is necessary to combine an external object with internal objects. Otherwise, it increases object size unnecessarily and results in performance issues for the software.
  - For example, in a game context, you can create a special weapon by composing it with various weapons.

    ```
    class SpecialWeapon
    {
        Gun g;
        AutoGun ag;
        Bomb b[10];
        public:
          ..
    };
    ```

335

- Aggregation: Aggregation of objects inside a class (external) means loosely coupling internal objects with the class (external) objects. It means external objects are connected with internal objects by including references or pointers of internal objects.

  - You should use object aggregation to connect objects dynamically. Hence, it eliminates the increased size of objects and results in improved software performance.
  - For example, you need to dynamically connect with smart devices or IoT objects to implement smart applications.

    ```
    class SmartApplication
    {
        SmartDevicev2 *s1;
        SmartDevicev3 *s2;
        IoTSensor s1;
        public:
        ..
    };
    ```

Let's start by discussing object composition and an activity related to a gaming application.

Object Composition: Special Gaming Weapon

Let's revisit Chapter 5's simple game application. You created a variety of guns and bombs to be used in gaming scenarios. For instance, special automatic guns from the normal Gun class were implemented using inheritance concepts. Similarly, you have time bombs from the normal Bomb class. You also observed that older and newer weapons can be used in gaming scenarios. In this section, you create special weapons by combining gun objects and bomb objects. Since players interacting with a special weapon should access all its features, you want to use object composition. Moreover, you want to ensure that deleting the special weapon must delete all its internal weapons. Let's work on the following activities.

- Include an automatic gun object configured through only special weapon object interfaces.

- Include multiple time bomb objects inside a special weapon object, which must be configured only with special weapon interfaces.

- Include normal bomb objects inside a special weapon object, which must be configured only with special weapon interfaces.

- Include a normal gun object inside a special weapon object and must be configured through only special weapon object interfaces.

- All internal weapons and bomb configurations should be done through only special weapon objects.

GAMING APPLICATION SPECIAL WEAPONS

Define a `SpecialWeapon` class in `specialweapon.cc` file to test it.

1. To compose existing game weapons objects inside the `SpecialWeapon` class, include the following gaming header files.

    ```
    #include<iostream>
    #include<vector>
    #include"bomb.h"
    ```

CHAPTER 6   QUICK SOFTWARE DEVELOPMENT USING OOP

```
#include"gun.h"
#include"timebomb.h"
#include"autogun.h"
using namespace std;
```

2. Define SpecialWeapon class to compose a suitable number of AutoGun, Gun, TimeBomb, and Bomb objects.

```
class SpecialWeapon
{
    AutoGun ag;
    TimeBomb tb[10];
    Bomb b[10];
    Gun g;
```

3. Define SpecialWeapon interfaces to access the internal bomb and time bomb objects.

```
public:
void setTimeBomb()
{
    for(int i=0;i<10;i++)
    {
        tb[i].setState(1);
    }
    cout<<"Special Weapon's Ten timer bombs set\n";
}
void setBomb()
{
    for(int i=0;i<10;i++)
    {
        b[i].setState(1);
    }
```

```
        cout<<"Special Weapon's Ten bombs set\n";
    }
    void resetTimeBomb()
    {
        for(int i=0;i<10;i++)
        {
            tb[i].setState(0);
        }
    }
    void resetBomb()
    {
        for(int i=0;i<10;i++)
        {
            b[i].setState(0);
        }
    }
```

4. Define SpecialWeapon interfaces to access the internal gun and automatic gun objects.

```
    void gunFire()
    {
        g.fire();
    }
    void autoGunFire()
    {
        ag.fire();
    }
    void setGunBullets(int bullets)
    {
        g.setBullets(bullets);
    }
```

```
            void setAutoGunBullets(int bullets)
            {
                ag.setBullets(bullets);
            }
            int getGunBullets()
            {
                return g.getBullets();
            }
            int getAutoGunBullets()
            {
                return ag.getBullets();
            }
    };
```

5. Define main() to test special weapon objects.

    a. Create a special weapon object.

    b. Configure the special weapon object's internal bombs and time bombs.

    c. Configure the special weapon object's internal gun modes.

    d. Test special weapon object's internal guns by invoking fire functions.

    ```
    int main()
    {
        SpecialWeapon spw;
        spw.setTimeBomb();
        spw.setBomb();
        cout<<"Special Weapon's Gun Bullets:"<<spw.getGunBullets()<<"\n";
        cout<<"Special Weapon's Auto Gun Bullets:"<<spw.getAutoGunBullets()<<"\n";
    ```

```
spw.gunFire();
spw.autoGunFire();
cout<<"After firing Special Weapon's Gun
Bullets:"<<spw.getGunBullets()<<"\n";
cout<<"After firing Special Weapon's Auto Gun
Bullets:"<<spw.getAutoGunBullets()<<"\n";
}
```

6. Save the specialweapon.cc file. Test it using the following.

    a. The special weapon is setting its internal time bombs.

    b. The special weapon is setting its internal bombs.

    c. The special weapon is loading its internal normal gun with bullets.

    d. The special weapon loads its internal automatic gun with bullets.

    e. The special weapon enables automatic gun mode and firing guns.

    ```
    # g++ specialweapon.cc -o specialweapon
    # ./specialweapon
    Special Weapon's Ten timer bombs set
    Special Weapon's Ten bombs set
    Special Weapon's Gun Bullets:10
    Special Weapon's Auto Gun Bullets:100
    Auto mode enabled
    After firing Special Weapon's Gun Bullets:9
    After firing Special Weapon's Auto Gun Bullets:95
    ```

Well done. You have successfully created a special weapon by composing it with weapons and bombs. Next, let's check the importance of multiple objects aggregation.

CHAPTER 6   QUICK SOFTWARE DEVELOPMENT USING OOP

Object Composition and Aggregation

In the last section, you practiced the importance of multiple object composition to create special objects. Composing objects leads to increasing object size and performance issues. Let's do a simple activity to better understand when to compose objects or aggregate objects. For example, implementing sample smart applications for smart devices and IoT sensors.

- Smart applications need access to suitable smart devices.
- Smart devices should have a variety of IoT sensors. If a smart device is unavailable, all its internal IoT sensors also should be unavailable. It means you must use object (IoT sensor) composition to create smart devices.
- Multiple smart applications should be able to access available smart devices.
- Deleting or removing a smart application should not lead to the unavailability of any of its accessing smart devices. It means you must use objects (smart devices) aggregation to create smart applications.

Let's start with smart devices combined with suitable IoT sensors.

SMART DEVICE USING OBJECT COMPOSITION

Implement a `SmartDevice` class in the smart_device.h file.

1. Define a `SmartDevice` class by composing it with three `IoTSensor` objects. Here, let's reuse the `iot_sesnor.h` file from previous source codes.

CHAPTER 6   QUICK SOFTWARE DEVELOPMENT USING OOP

```cpp
#include"iot_sensor.h"
using namespace std;
class SmartDevice
{
    IoTSensor ios1;
    IoTSensor ios2;
    IoTSensor ios3;
```

2. Initialize all three IoT sensor objects with example configurations as part of `SmartDevice` constructor.

```cpp
public:
SmartDevice()
{
    ios1.setId("Sensor1");
    ios1.setX(0);
    ios1.setY(0);
    ios1.setBatteryLevel(100);

    ios2.setId("Sensor2");
    ios2.setX(10);
    ios2.setY(10);
    ios2.setBatteryLevel(100);

    ios3.setId("Sensor3");
    ios3.setX(5);
    ios3.setY(5);
    ios3.setBatteryLevel(100);
}
```

CHAPTER 6   QUICK SOFTWARE DEVELOPMENT USING OOP

3. Define example interfaces for accessing each of these IoT sensor objects.

```
        void configureSensor1(float value)
        {
            ios1.setSenseValue(value);
        }
        float getSensor1Value()
        {
            return ios1.getSenseValue();
        }
        void configureSensor2(float value)
        {
            ios2.setSenseValue(value);
        }
        float getSensor2Value()
        {
            return ios2.getSenseValue();
        }
        void configureSensor3(float value)
        {
            ios3.setSenseValue(value);
        }
        float getSensor3Value()
        {
            return ios3.getSenseValue();
        }
    };
```

Next, let's use SmartDevice objects to design a SmartApplications example.

CHAPTER 6   QUICK SOFTWARE DEVELOPMENT USING OOP

SMART APPLICATION USING OBJECT AGGREGATION

Implement the SmartApplication class in the smartapplication.h file.

1. To create a smart application over smart devices, let's include the SmartDevice header file.

   ```
   #include"smart_device.h"
   using namespace std;
   ```

2. Define a SmartApplication initialization activities in its constructor.

   a. To start a smart application, it must be initialized with two SmartDevice objects. Here, use the aggregation concept to link SmartDevice objects with SmartApplication.

   b. Then, it checks smart devices' sensor values and generates respective events.

   ```
   class SmartApplication
   {
       public:
       SmartApplication(SmartDevice tsd1,
       SmartDevice tsd2)
       {
           SmartDevice &sd1 = tsd1;
           SmartDevice &sd2 = tsd2;
           if (sd1.getSensor1Value()>sd2.getSensor1Value())
           {
               cout<<"Alert1\n";
           }
   ```

345

```
            if (sd1.getSensor2Value()<sd2.getSensor2Value())
            {
                cout<<"Alert2\n";
            }
            if (sd1.getSensor3Value()<sd2.getSensor3Value())
            {
                cout<<"Emergency Alert\n";
            }
        }
```

3. Define a sample interface to determine the status of the smart application.

```
        void SmartApplicationStatus()
        {
            cout<<"Smart Application is running";
        }
    };
```

4. Save smartapplication.h and test it in `main()`.

TEST THE SMART APPLICATION

Define a testing code in the `smartapp.cc` file.

1. To test the smart application, create two smart device objects and configure their internal IoT sensors.

2. Create a smart application object called `s1` by initializing it with the two smart device objects.

CHAPTER 6   QUICK SOFTWARE DEVELOPMENT USING OOP

3. Access smart devices and their internal IoT sensors by printing their sensed values.

```
#include"smart_application.h"
using namespace std;
int main()
{
    SmartDevice *sd1,*sd2;
    sd1 = new SmartDevice();
    sd2 = new SmartDevice();
    sd1->configureSensor1(10.2);
    sd1->configureSensor2(20.2);
    sd1->configureSensor3(30.2);
    sd2->configureSensor1(10.1);
    sd2->configureSensor2(10.2);
    sd2->configureSensor3(30.3);
    SmartApplication *s1 = new SmartApplication
    (*sd1,*sd2);
    s1->SmartApplicationStatus();
    cout<<"SmartDevice1 access"<<sd1->getSensor1
    Value()<<"\n";
    cout<<"SmartDevice2 access"<<sd2->getSensor1
    Value()<<"\n";
```

4. Delete smart application object s1.

    delete s1;

5. Create another smart application object called s2 by initializing it with two existing smart device objects.

6. Check its running status.

CHAPTER 6   QUICK SOFTWARE DEVELOPMENT USING OOP

7. Access smart devices and their internal IoT sensors by printing their sensed values.

```
SmartApplication *s2 = new SmartApplication(*sd1,*sd2);
s1->SmartApplicationStatus();
cout<<"SmartDevice1 access"<<sd1->getSensor1Value()<<"\n";
cout<<"SmartDevice2 access"<<sd2->getSensor1Value()<<"\n";
}
```

8. Save the smartapp.cc file and test it using the following command and observe the following.

   a. SmartApplication s1 starts successfully and it generates sample events.

   b. While the smart application (s1) is active, you can access the smart devices and their internal IoT sensor values.

   c. Although smart application (s1) was destroyed, deploying another smart application (s2) over the existing smart devices is possible. It is due to object aggregation concepts.

   d. Observe the sample smart application (s2) is successfully running and accessing smart devices is possible.

   ```
   # g++ smartapp.cc -o smartapp
   # ./smartapp
   Alert1
   Emergency Alert
   Smart Application is running
   SmartDevice1 access10.2
   SmartDevice2 access10.1

   Alert1
   ```

```
Emergency Alert
Smart Application is running
SmartDevice1 access10.2
SmartDevice2 access10.1
```

Object composition helps create special bulky objects. Similarly, object aggregation helps create software applications by connecting objects using pointers or references.

Next, let's practice using inheritance and object composition in developing smart devices.

Hands-on Activity: Inheritance and Object Association

This hands-on activity uses inheritance and object association methods to develop smart devices. For example, you create the following example smart devices.

- Develop a new smart device called `SmartDevicev2` with special features by reusing `SmartDevice` features and including special `IoTSensor` features. You must use inheritance and object composition concepts for this task.

- Develop a new smart device called `SmartDevicev3` with special features by reusing `SmartDevice` features and including two special `IoTSensor` features. You must use inheritance and object composition concepts for this task.

CHAPTER 6 QUICK SOFTWARE DEVELOPMENT USING OOP

- Develop a new smart device called SmartDevicev4 by reusing features of SmartDevicev2 and SmartDevicev3. Here, you need to handle issues of combining inheritance approaches using virtual to avoid duplicate code.

NEW VERSIONS OF SMART DEVICES

Let's create the SmartDevicev2 class by extending the SmartDevice class for the special smart devices, which should support the following..

- Using objects of SmartDevicev2, all basic sensors of SmartDevice should be accessible for implementing various smart applications.

- Besides basic sensors, objects of SmartDevicev2 should also support the usage of precision IoTSensor for implementing smart applications.

- To implement the new version of smart devices, define the SmartDevicev2 class in smartdevicev2v.h file.

    - Include smart_device.h to reuse SmartDevice class features. Observe that to avoid duplicated code, you are using the virtual inheritance approach.

      ```
      #include"smart_device.h"
      using namespace std;
      class SmartDevicev2: public virtual SmartDevice
      {
      ```

CHAPTER 6 QUICK SOFTWARE DEVELOPMENT USING OOP

- To include precision IoT sensor behavior, you define an IoTSensor object. It means you are **composing** the new IoT sensor object with the SmartDevicev2 objects.

    IoTSensor sps;
    public:

- To initialize SmartDevicev2 objects, configure the precision IoTSensor object by setting its id, location (x,y), and battery.

    ```
    SmartDevicev2()
    {
        sps.setId("HighPrecisionSensor");
        sps.setX(20);
        sps.setY(20);
        sps.setBatteryLevel(100);
    }
    ```

- Provide precision IoT sensor accessing interfaces to configure and retrieve its values for implementing application-specific activities.

    ```
            void configurePrecision(float value)
            {
                sps.setSenseValue(value);
            }
            float getPrecisionSenseVal()
            {
                return sps.getSenseValue();
            }
    };
    ```

351

CHAPTER 6   QUICK SOFTWARE DEVELOPMENT USING OOP

Let's create another `SmartDevicev3` class by extending the `SmartDevice` class for implementing the special smart device, which should support the following.

- Use `SmartDevicev3` objects; all basic sensors of `SmartDevice` should be accessible for implementing various smart applications.
- Besides basic sensors, objects of `SmartDevicev3` should also support the usage of two precision `IoTSensor` for implementing smart applications.

1. To implement the new version of smart devices, let's start defining the `SmartDevicev3` class in smartdevicev3v.h file.

    a. You must include smart_device.h to reuse `SmartDevice` class features. Observe that to avoid duplicated code, let's use the `virtual` inheritance approach.

    ```
    using namespace std;
    class SmartDevicev3: public  virtual SmartDevice
    {
    ```

    b. To include two precision IoT sensors' behavior define two IoTSensor objects. This means **compose** two new sensor objects with the `SmartDevicev3` objects.

    ```
    IoTSensor sps1;
    IoTSensor sps2;
    ```

    c. To initialize `SmartDevicev3` objects, configure the two precision `IoTSensor` objects by setting their id, location (x,y), and battery.

    ```
    public:
    SmartDevicev3()
    {
    ```

```
            sps1.setId("HighPrecisionSensor1");
            sps1.setX(22);
            sps1.setY(22);
            sps1.setBatteryLevel(100);
            sps2.setId("HighPrecisionSensor2");
            sps2.setX(30);
            sps2.setY(30);
            sps2.setBatteryLevel(100);
        }
```

   d. Define each precision IoT sensor accessing interfaces to configure and retrieve their values for implementing application-specific activities.

```
            void configurePrecision1(float value)
            {
                sps1.setSenseValue(value);
            }
            float getPrecision1SenseVal()
            {
                return sps1.getSenseValue();
            }
            void configurePrecision2(float value)
            {
                sps2.setSenseValue(value);
            }
            float getPrecision2SenseVal()
            {
                return sps2.getSenseValue();
            }
        };
```

Next, let's create another smart device called `SmartDevicev4`, which inherits both `SmartDevicev2` and `SmartDevicev3` features.

CHAPTER 6   QUICK SOFTWARE DEVELOPMENT USING OOP

NEW VERSIONS OF SMART DEVICES

Let's create the `SmartDevicev4` class by inheriting features of both `SmartDevicev2` and `SmartDevicev3` classes for implementing the special smart devices, which should support the following.

- Using objects of `SmartDevicev4`, all basic sensors of `SmartDevice` should be accessible to various smart applications.

  - To customize configurations related to basic sensors inherited from `SmartDevice`, override `ConfigureSensor1` and `getSensor1Value`.

  - Configuring sensor1 should result in automatically configuring all basic sensors: sensor1, sensor2, and sensor3 of smart devices.

  - Accessing Sensor1 should result in getting aggregate values of basic sensors of smart devices.

- Besides basic sensors, the precision sensors of `SmartDevicev2` and `SmartDevicev3` are also accessible for smart applications.

1. To implement the new version of smart devices, let's start defining the `SmartDevicev4` class in the `smartdevices.cc` file.

    a. You must include `smartdevicev2.h` and `smartdevicev3.h` to reuse SmartDevice class features.

    ```
    #include"smart_devicev2v.h"
    #include"smart_devicev3v.h"
    using namespace std;
    ```

CHAPTER 6   QUICK SOFTWARE DEVELOPMENT USING OOP

```
class SmartDevicev4: public SmartDevicev2, public
SmartDevicev3
{
    public:
```

b. To customize all basic sensor configuration activities of SmartDevice, define ConfigureSesnor1() by overriding its definition.

```
void configureSensor1(float value)
{
    configureSensor2(value);
    configureSensor3(value);
}
```

c. To retrieve basic sensors, aggregate values override getSensor1Value()

```
        float getSensor1Value()
        {
            return getSensor2Value()+getSensor3Value();
        }
};
```

2. Test all newly created smart devices in main().

```
int main()
{
```

a. Create and test SmartDevicev2 objects.

   i. Configure and access all basic sensors of SmartDevice.

   ii. Configure and access its precision sensor.

```
SmartDevicev2 sd1;
sd1.configureSensor1(10.2);
sd1.configureSensor2(20.2);
```

CHAPTER 6 QUICK SOFTWARE DEVELOPMENT USING OOP

```
sd1.configureSensor3(30.2);
cout<<"SmartDevicev2 sensor1 access"
<<sd1.getSensor1Value()<<"\n";
cout<<"SmartDevicev2 sensor2 access"
<<sd1.getSensor2Value()<<"\n";
cout<<"SmartDevicev2 sensor3 access"
<<sd1.getSensor3Value()<<"\n";
sd1.configurePrecision(10.999);
cout<<"SmartDevice2 precision sensor
access:"<<sd1.getPrecisionSenseVal()<<"\n";
```

b. Create and test SmartDevicev3 objects.

   i. Configure and access all basic sensors of SmartDevice.

   ii. Configure and access both precision sensors.

```
SmartDevicev3 sd2;
sd2.configureSensor1(10.2);
sd2.configureSensor2(20.2);
sd2.configureSensor3(30.2);
cout<<"SmartDevicev3 sensor1 access"<<sd2.
getSensor1Value()<<"\n";
cout<<"SmartDevicev3 sensor2 access"<<sd2.
getSensor2Value()<<"\n";
cout<<"SmartDevicev3 sensor3 access"<<sd2.
getSensor3Value()<<"\n";
sd2.configurePrecision1(40.999);
cout<<"SmartDevice1 precision:"<<sd2.
getPrecision1SenseVal()<<"\n";
```

CHAPTER 6　QUICK SOFTWARE DEVELOPMENT USING OOP

c. Create and test SmartDevicev4 objects.

  i. Configure and access all basic sensors of SmartDevice using newly overridden member functions.

   ```
   SmartDevicev4 sd3;
   sd3.configureSensor1(50.2);
   sd3.configureSensor2(60.2);
   sd3.configureSensor3(70.2);
   cout<<"SmartDevicev4 access"<<sd3.getSensor1
   Value()<<"\n";
   cout<<"SmartDevicev4 access"<<sd3.getSensor2
   Value()<<"\n";
   cout<<"SmartDevicev4 access"<<sd3.getSensor3
   Value()<<"\n";
   ```

  ii. Configure and access all basic sensors of SmartDevice using newly overridden member functions.

   ```
   sd3.configureSensor1(100.99999);
   cout<<"SmartDevicev4 access"<<sd3.
   getSensor1Value()<<"\n";
   cout<<"SmartDevicev4 access"<<sd3.
   getSensor2Value()<<"\n";
   cout<<"SmartDevicev4 access"<<sd3.
   getSensor3Value()<<"\n";
   cout<<"SmartDevicev4 access"<<sd3.
   getSensor1Value()<<"\n";
   }
   ```

CHAPTER 6   QUICK SOFTWARE DEVELOPMENT USING OOP

3. Save smartdevices.cc with the preceding code, execute it, and observe the following.

   a. SmartDevicev2 objects can access basic SmartDevice sensor features and its precision sensor features to any new smart application.

   b. SmartDevicev3 objects can access basic SmartDevice sensor features and its two precision sensor features.

   c. The SmartDevicev4 object implements special behavior by inheriting SmartDevice sensor features and overriding default behaviors.

      i. Although you configured only sensor1 using the SmartDevicev4 object, the remaining sensors are configured based on sensor1.

      ii. Accessing the sensor1 values from SmartDevicev4 objects results in collecting aggregate values of sensors.

      ```
      # g++ smartdevices.cc -o smartdevs
      # ./smartdevs

      SmartDevicev2 sensor1 access10.2
      SmartDevicev2 sensor2 access20.2
      SmartDevicev2 sensor3 access30.2
      SmartDevice2 precision sensor access:10.999
      SmartDevicev3 sensor1 access10.2
      SmartDevicev3 sensor2 access20.2
      SmartDevicev3 sensor3 access30.2
      SmartDevice1 precision:40.999
      SmartDevicev4 access130.4
      SmartDevicev4 access60.2
      SmartDevicev4 access70.2
      SmartDevicev4 access202
      ```

CHAPTER 6   QUICK SOFTWARE DEVELOPMENT USING OOP

```
SmartDevicev4 access101
SmartDevicev4 access101
SmartDevicev4 access202
```

Well done. You learned and practiced using inheritance, object aggregation, and composition features to implement complex software classes. You also observed when to use inheritance and objects combining features in smart devices and applications.

Summary

In this chapter, you learned various inheritance approaches using C++. It helps you design software classes by eliminating redundant and inconsistent code. From hands-on activities, you observed that combining inheritance approaches and handling related issues is necessary for dealing with complex software. You have also discovered the importance of object composition and aggregation to connect existing software code to new software. You also practiced using inheritance, object composition, and object aggregation together.

The next chapter discusses an important OOP feature called *polymorphism* to implement easy-to-use software.

Practice: Hands-on Activities

1. Practice inheritance approaches for the following scenarios.

    a. Create sports information maintenance software classes to maintain various sports and players. Focus on eliminating redundant code among classes.

b. Design online vehicle reservation application-related classes to maintain details about vehicles, employees, and customers details. Focus on eliminating redundant code among classes.

c. Develop online food ordering application-related classes to maintain details about restaurants, food items, staff, and customers. Focus on eliminating redundant code among classes.

2. Practice inheritance, object aggregation, and composition approaches for handling the following challenges.

   a. Implement example game entities of adventurous games to set up interesting game scenarios. Start with including basic vehicles, weapons, and players. Then, introduce new version game entities. Focus on eliminating redundant code among classes and do not compose objects unnecessarily.

   b. Create files and folder maintenance software with basic features such as creating, copying, and deleting files and folders. Focus on eliminating redundant code among classes and do not compose objects unnecessarily.

   c. Design sample smart application software from smart device–simulating classes. Focus on eliminating redundant code among classes and do not compose objects unnecessarily.

CHAPTER 7

Easy-to-Use Software Development Using OOP

Chapter 6 used OOP inheritance concepts to quickly handle challenges in upgrading existing software, creating new versions, and rapidly developing new software systems from existing ones. In this chapter, you learn OOP polymorphism concepts to implement easily accessible software with standard interfaces. Usually, it is difficult to use software with many interfaces; for example, to play any game, the number of controls should be minimal, then only players can enjoy the game. Similarly, accessing any software application should offer only minimal standard user-accessing interfaces. To use any document software, you observe only a few interfaces, such as cut, copy, paste, and delete. From these sample applications, you can observe that instead of creating multiple interfaces to interact with software, defining minimal standard interfaces simplifies usage.

This chapter describes an important concept called *polymorphism* in C++ to develop minimal and standard interfaces for interacting with similar classes and their objects. You learn different ways to apply polymorphism concepts to handle various contexts of software usage, including function overloading and overriding, operator overloading, generic functions, and dynamic polymorphism approaches to handle different scenarios of software usage.

This chapter covers the following topics.

- The importance of polymorphism
- Overloading operators to deal with complex object computations
- Implementing generic functions and data structures
- Using dynamic polymorphism for offering common interfaces

The Importance of Polymorphism

To minimize the number of interfaces to interact with software, it is necessary to use one interface for carrying out similar tasks or functions, actions, or activities of the software. Programmers use the same function name for various tasks or operations. In C++, programmers use the following polymorphism concepts to handle the issues of reusing the same interfaces for various operations, tasks, or actions.

- Function overloading: Use one function name for implementing multiple similar tasks, actions, operations, or activities related to a software application.
    - Example: Use **search** as a function name for searching integers or real numbers or strings: bool search(int l[10]); bool search(float f[10]); bool search(string s[10]);
- Operator overloading: Use standard operators (+, -, *, etc.) for processing standard data and class objects.

CHAPTER 7   EASY-TO-USE SOFTWARE DEVELOPMENT USING OOP

- Example: Overload + operator to perform matrix objects addition.

  `Matrix m1,m2,m3; m3 = m1+m2;`

- Function overriding: Use the same member function prototype in a base class and its derived classes for interacting with related objects.

  - Example: Use the fire() member function for interacting with Gun objects. `class Gun { public: void fire() }; class AutoGun: public Gun { public: void fire() }`

- Dynamic polymorphism: Define standard interfaces and use them for accessing all related Classes objects. Here, programmers use pure virtual functions to declare standard interfaces in a Base class. Later, all inherited classes from the Base class can implement the actual code for virtual functions.

  - Example: `class Phone { void call()=0;}`

    `class Phonev2: public Phone { void call() { printf("calling");};`

The section starts by exploring how to use function overloading in C++.

Function Overloading

Function overloading is known as the usage of static or compile-time polymorphism. Static polymorphism means a function call is linked with the corresponding function code at compile time, which speeds up the program execution. For function overloading, you use the same function name to define multiple functions.

- Function declarations should differ in the number of arguments they take.
  - Example: void max(int a, int b, int c) and void max(int a, int b)
- Function declarations should differ in the type of arguments they take.
  - Example: void max(int a, int b, int c) and void max(float a, float b, float c)
- Function declarations differ because only return types are not valid for function overloading.
  - Not allowed: int max(int a, int b) and void max(int a, int b)

Let's practice the following tasks for learning about function overloading usage.

FUNCTION OVERLOADING

Let's define a `DataAlgorithms` class in a datalgos.cc file to implement a maximum element finding function from a given data elements list.

1. Define `DataAlgorithms` with the following three overloaded functions.

   a. `int maximum(int *d, int len)` returns a maximum element from the list of integer data elements.

   b. `float maximum(float *d, int len)` returns a maximum element from the list of float data elements.

   c. `string maximum(string *d, int len)` returns a maximum length string from the list of strings.

```cpp
#include<iostream>
using namespace std;
class DataAlgorithms
{
    public:
    int maximum(int *d,int len)
    {
        int max;
        max = d[0];
        for (int i=0;i<len;i++)
        {
            if (d[i]>=max)
            {
                max = d[i];
            }
        }
        return max;
    }
    float maximum(float *d,int len)
    {
        float max;
        max = d[0];
        for (int i=0;i<len;i++)
        {
            if (d[i]>=max)
            {
                max = d[i];
            }
        }
        return max;
    }
```

CHAPTER 7   EASY-TO-USE SOFTWARE DEVELOPMENT USING OOP

```
        string maximum(string *d,int len)
        {
            string max;
            max = d[0];
            for (int i=0;i<len;i++)
            {
                if (d[i].length()>=max.length())
                {
                    max = d[i];
                }
            }
            return max;
        }
    };
```

2. From the DataAlgorithms class, observe that all three maximum element finding functions are defined with the same function name called maximum().

3. Test DataAlgorithms overloaded member functions in main():

```
int main()
{
    int d1[10] = {10,20,40,50,90,70,60,80,30,0};
    float d2[10] = {10.9,20.9,40.9,50.9,90.9,70.9,60.9,80.9,30.9,0.9};
    string d3[10] = {"abc", "abcd", "ab", "abcdefghijk", "a","abcdefg","c","d","e","f"};
    DataAlgorithms d;
    int m1 = d.maximum(d1,10);
    cout<<"Max "<<m1<<"\n";
    float m2 = d.maximum(d2,10);
```

```
        cout<<"Max "<<m2<<"\n";
        string m3 = d.maximum(d3,10);
        cout<<"Max "<<m3<<"\n";
```

}

4. After saving all changes in the datalagos.cc file, execute it, and observe the following details.

   a. Observe that the `DataAlgorithms` object invokes the same member function with elements of different data types.

   b. Based on the data type elements, the correct `maximum` function is invoked.

   ```
   g++ datalgos.cc -o datalgos
   ./datalgos
   Max 90
   Max 90.9
   Max abcdefghijk
   ```

Next, let's discuss using the same member function signature in Base and its derived classes.

Function Overriding

Function overriding is an important way of defining the same interfaces for interacting with the base class and its derived class objects. It is different from function overloading. In this case, you should define the same member function signature (function name, return type, and arguments) in both the base and derived classes. Function overriding in inheritance redefines the member function in derived classes. Due to the inheritance feature of reusing the base class code, in derived classes duplicate code exists. Hence, this problem is handled by postponing member function code linkage with a function call based on the object type during runtime. Function overriding is achieved in C++ as follows.

```
class Base
{
    public:
    void sample()
    {
        cout<<"base code..\n";
    }
};
class Derived: public Base
{
    public:
    void sample()
    {
        cout<<"derived code..\n";
    }
};
```

You should observe the following.

- The Derived class is inherited from the Base class.

- In Base and Derived classes, you defined a member function: void sample() with the same function signature. It is known as redefining a member function in function overriding.

- It helps to reuse the same interface sample () to access Base and Derived class objects.

- Due to inheritance, the Derived class gets Base class sample () code also inherited into it. To invoke the Base class sample() in the Derived class it needs to call it as follows: `Base::sample()`.

Let's practice function overriding by doing the following task.

FUNCTION OVERRIDING

1. Define a base class called Phone with a sample member function `call()` to access its objects.

2. Define two new version classes: Phonev2 and Phonev3 from Phone class. But, use the same interface `call()` to access all Phone objects.

3. Redefine the call in the respective classes using the same interface `call()` in Phonev2 and Phonev3.

```
#include<iostream>
using namespace std;
class Phone
{
    public:
    void call()
    {
        cout<<"Normal calling..\n";
    }
};
class Phonev2:public Phone
{
    public:
    void call()
```

CHAPTER 7　EASY-TO-USE SOFTWARE DEVELOPMENT USING OOP

```
    {
        cout<<"Internet calling ..\n";
    }
};

class Phonev3:public Phone
{
    public:
    void call()
    {
        cout<<"Video callig ..\n";
    }
};
```

4. Test access for Phone objects in main() as follows.

```
int main()
{
    Phone p1;
    Phonev2 p2;
    Phonev3 p3;
    p1.call();
    p2.call();
    p3.call();
}
```

5. Save your code in phone.cc and run it.

   a. Observe from the results, based on Phone objects the correct code for call() is getting executed.

   ```
   # g++ phone.cc -o phone
   # ./phone
   Normal calling..
   ```

Internet calling ..
Video callig ..

From this activity, you observe that using function overriding concepts, it is possible to use the same interface in base and derived classes to simplify accessing the related classes' objects.

Next, let's discuss operator overloading to implement polymorphism concepts.

Overloading Operators to Deal with Complex Objects Computations

Operator overloading means giving special power and additional responsibilities to operators. For instance, by overloading standard arithmetic operators (+, -, *), programming can use them for performing standard arithmetic operations and matrix addition, subtraction and multiplication operations. In C++ programming, a few standard operators (<<, >>) are overloaded for standard input output operations using `cin` and `cout` objects.

In C++ most all standard operators can be overloaded except the following operators.

- Ternary operator (?:) and size operator (`sizeof`)
- Class member access operator (., .*)
- Scope resolution operator(::)

The following are the benefits of operator overloading.

- It helps in writing easily understandable code.
- It gives more power to standard operators for doing customized operations over objects.

- It helps simplify access to interfaces when dealing with complex software.
- It helps with developing generic functions and data structures.

Next, let's learn how to overload operators.

How to Overload Operators

To overload operators in C++, programmers define public `operator` member functions or `friend operator` functions using the `operator` keyword and a specific operator symbol.

For example, you do the following to overload binary operators in a class. If both operands of the operator are belongs to same class, the operator function can be member functions of the class.

```
Sample operator+(Sample &c2)
{
    Sample c3;
    c3.value = value + c2.value;
    return c3;
}
```

In main you can test it as follows.

```
Sample c1,c2,c3;
c3=c1+c2;
or
c3 = c1.operator+(c2);
```

You should observe the following.

- You use `operator+` as a member function name.
- You can also observe that the LHS operand of the operator is passed as a default argument to the `operator` function.

CHAPTER 7 EASY-TO-USE SOFTWARE DEVELOPMENT USING OOP

- To overload the binary operator, you should pass the RHS operand of the operator as another argument to the operator member function. In the case of c3= c1+c2; c2 is the other argument for the operator function.

- Arguments can be passed as call-by-value or call-by-reference.

On the other hand, If both operands of the operator are not belongs to the same class or left operand type is not same as class type, then operator function must be friend function as follows:

Declare friend function in the respective class.

```
class Sample
{
..
    friend Sample operator+(Sample1 &c1,Sample &c2);
};
```

Define friend function as follows.

```
Sample operator+(Sample1 &c1, Sample &c2)
{
    Sample c3;
    c3.value = c1.value + c2.value;
    return c3;
}
```

You should observe the following.

- You declared a friend function operator+ inside the Sample class to perform operations over two different Sample objects.

- To overload the binary operator, both were passed arguments.

373

Similarly to overload unary operators in a class, you need not define any arguments with the `operator` function because the object invoking the operator is passed as an argument to the operator function.

The following is an example.

```
Sample operator-()
{
    Sample c3;
    c3.value = -value;
    return c3;
}
```

On the other hand, to overload unary operators using the friend operator function, you need to pass the corresponding object as an argument.

The following is an example.

```
Sample operator-(Sample &s1)
{
    Sample c3;
    c3.value = -s1.value;
    return c3;
}
```

Next, let's do a hands-on activity to overload operators in a class.

Practice Operator Overloading Usage

Let's overload a few operators for Coin class objects.

- Overload +: Aggregating list of coin objects for creating a high valued coin object.
    - For example, it is helpful to create an interesting game scenario where players can turn their collected coins into a magical coin with high value.

- Overload comparison operators (<, >, ==): Overloading comparison operators help apply general searching, sorting, or strategic algorithms.

    - While playing games, to apply strategies, it is necessary to use general algorithms such as maximum (or minimum) valued coins, checking whether coins are in increasing or decreasing order, and so forth.

- Overload ostream (<<) operator: It is helpful to display coin objects like any other basic data type element.

    - For example, it is helpful to inspect coin object details.

Let's extend the gaming Coin class with operator overloading functions.

OVERLOAD OPERATORS FOR COIN CLASS OBJECTS

Define a new coin class in the `overloadcoin.cc` file.

1. Copy the following Coin class definition (Chapter 5's coin.h) into the `overloadcoin.cc` file.

    ```
    #include<iostream>
    using namespace std;
    class Coin
    {
        int state;
        int x,y,value;
        enum states {COLLECTED, AVAILABLE};
        public:
        Coin()
    ```

```
    {
        x = rand()%9+8;
        y = rand()%9+8;
        value = rand()%100;
        state = AVAILABLE;
    }
    int getX()
    {
        return x;
    }
    int getY()
    {
        return y;
    }
    int getValue()
    {
        return value;
    }
    void setValue(int ival)
    {
        value = ival;
    }
    int getState()
    {
        return state;
    }
    void setState(int istate)
    {
        state = istate;
    }
```

2. Define operator+ as a member function to overload + operator.

    a. Add two coin objects based on their internal data member value and return results as a new coin object.

    ```
    Coin operator+(Coin &c2)
    {
        Coin c3;
        c3.value = value + c2.value;
        return c3;
    }
    ```

3. Declare three friend operator functions for overloading >, <, == operators.

    ```
    friend bool operator>(Coin &c1, Coin &c2);
    friend bool operator<(Coin &c1, Coin &c2);
    friend bool operator==(Coin &c1, Coin &c2);
    ```

4. Declare another friend operator function for overloading ostream operator <<.

    ```
    friend ostream& operator<<(ostream &o, Coin &c);
    ```

    };

5. After defining the new Coin class, let's define a friend operator> function for comparing two Coin objects based on their data member value.

    ```
    bool operator>(Coin &c1, Coin &c2)
    {
        if(c1.getValue()>c2.getValue())
        {
            return true;
        }
    ```

CHAPTER 7 EASY-TO-USE SOFTWARE DEVELOPMENT USING OOP

```
        return false;
    }
```

6. Similarly, define a `friend operator` function for comparing two `Coin` objects based on their data member `value`.

```
    bool operator<(Coin &c1, Coin &c2)
    {
        if(c1.getValue()<c2.getValue())
        {
            return true;
        }
        return false;
    }
```

7. Similarly, define a `friend operator` function for comparing two `Coin` objects based on their data member `value`.

```
    bool operator==(Coin &c1, Coin &c2)
    {
        if(c1.getValue()==c2.getValue())
        {
            return true;
        }
        return false;
    }
```

8. Define `operator<<` function for displaying `Coin` objects based on their data member `value`.

```
    ostream& operator<<(ostream& o, Coin &c)
    {
        o<<c.getValue();
```

CHAPTER 7   EASY-TO-USE SOFTWARE DEVELOPMENT USING OOP

```
    return 0;
}
```

9. Test the code in main() as follows.

   a. Define three coin objects (c1, c2, and c3).

   b. Combine two objects, c1 and c2, into c3 using +.

   ```
   int main()
   {
       Coin c1;
       Coin c2;
       Coin c3;
       c3 = c1+c2;
   ```

   c. Print each coin object value ostream operator <<.

   ```
   cout<<"Coin1 value"<<c1<<"\n";
   cout<<"Coin2 value"<<c2<<"\n";
   cout<<"Coin3 value"<<c3<<"\n";
   ```

   d. Compare coin objects using <, > and == .

   ```
   if (c1>c2)
   {
       cout<<"Coin1 is high value"<<c1<<"\n";
   }
   if (c1<c3)
   {
       cout<<"Coin3 is high value"<<c3<<"\n";
   }
   if (c1==c2)
   {
   ```

CHAPTER 7 EASY-TO-USE SOFTWARE DEVELOPMENT USING OOP

```
            cout<<"Coin1 and Coin 2 are having same
            value"<<c1<<"\n";
        }
```

e. Create a magic coin from ten coin objects and print the magic coin value.

```
        Coin c[10];
        Coin magic;
        for (int i=0;i<10;i++)
        {
            magic = magic+c[i];
        }
        cout<<"Magic coin value"<<magic<<"\n";
    }
```

10. After saving all changes in overloadcoin.cc execute it and observe the results.

    a. Coin objects are added using + operator.

    b. Coin objects internal values are displayed using <<.

    c. Coin objects are compared using <, > , and ==.

    ```
    # g++ overloadcoin.cc -o overcoins
    # ./overcoins
    Coin1 value77
    Coin2 value35
    Coin3 value112
    Coin1 is high value77
    Coin3 is high value112
    Magic coin value483
    ```

Next, let's look at how to use operator overloading concepts for generic functions and data structures.

CHAPTER 7   EASY-TO-USE SOFTWARE DEVELOPMENT USING OOP

Generic Functions and Data Structures

In a function overloading example, you saw three maximum functions for three data types (int, float, and string). The logic of all three functions was the same, which means you did a lot of redundant work to solve these problems. Suppose you want to implement complex algorithms such as sorting, searching, and data structures to work on data type elements. Function overloading can lead to lots of redundant code. This section discusses C++ template concepts to write generic functions and data structures to work with data types without any redundant code.

Let's use a generic max function in C++ with the template syntax.

```
template<typename T>
T maxEle(T a, T b)
{
    if (a>b)
    return a;
    else
    return b;
}
```

It can be tested in main() as follows.

```
int max1 = maxEle(10,20);
float max2 = maxEle(10.5,45.56);
```

You should observe the following.

- Template data type T was passed as an argument to the maxEle function.

- In main(), actual data type elements were passed to test maxEle.

- Since only one template variable was used, it passed the same data type elements for both arguments.

CHAPTER 7 EASY-TO-USE SOFTWARE DEVELOPMENT USING OOP

To pass data type elements to each argument, you should define template function with multiple template variables as follows.

```
template<typename T1, typename T2, typename T3>
void sample ( T1 a, T2 b, T3 c)
{
}
```

You can test it with the variety of data types as follows.

```
sample(1,2,3);
sample(1,2.5,3.6);
sample(1.3,2.5,3.6);

template<typename T1, typename T2, typename T3>
void sample ( T1 a, T2 b, T3 c)
{
}
```

These examples should help you learn how to write generic functions to work over standard data types such as int, float, and char. Can you use these generic functions to work with class objects? Yes. However, you should use suitable operator functions in the respective class to work with generic functions or data structures.

For example, to use maxEle() over Coin class objects, you should overload necessary operators (>) used in maxEle() inside the Coin class as a member function or friend function.

```
Class Coin
{
    public:
    int v;
    bool operator>(Coin c2)
```

```
    {
        if (v>c2.v)
            return true;
        else
            return false;
    }
};
```

Next, let's practice a hands-on activity using generic functions over basic data types and the Coin class.

Practice with Generic Functions

Let's apply the following two generic algorithms as template functions.

- inIncreasingOrder(): This algorithm returns a given list of elements in ascending order or not.
  - It should work on all basic data type elements.
  - It should work on a list of coin elements.
- maxValue(): This algorithm should return a maximum element from a given list of elements.
  - It should work on all basic data type elements.
  - It should work on a list of coin elements.

Next, let's demonstrate these two generic algorithms as template functions.

CHAPTER 7   EASY-TO-USE SOFTWARE DEVELOPMENT USING OOP

GENERIC ALGORITHMS IMPLEMENTATION USING TEMPLATE FUNCTIONS

Let's implement the following template functions in genericfunc.cc file.

1. Include the following necessary header files for the tasks.

    a. Observe that you included coins.h file for testing generic functions with a list of coins.

    ```
    #include<iostream>
    #include<stdlib.h>
    #include"coins.h"
    using namespace std;
    ```

2. Implement inIncreasingOrder as template functions with two important arguments.

    a. Pointer to list of elements

    b. Size of list.

    c. It returns true when the input list of elements is in ascending order; otherwise, it returns false.

    ```
    template<typename T>
    bool inIncreasingOrder(T *c, int count)
    {
        bool order=true;
        for (int i=0;i<count-1;i++)
        {
            if (c[i]>c[i+1])
            {
                order = false;
                return order;
            }
    ```

```
    }
    return order;
}
```

3. Implement maxValue as template functions with two important arguments.

    a. Pointer to list of elements.
    b. Size of list.
    c. It returns the maximum value element from the input list of elements.

    ```
    template<typename T>
    T maxValue(T *c, int count)
    {
        T maxval = c[0];
        T max;
        for (int i=1; i<count; i++)
        {
            if (c[i]>maxval || c[i]==maxval)
            {
                maxval = c[i];
                max = c[i];
            }
        }
        return max;
    }
    ```

4. Test the generic functions in main() with the following list of elements.

    ```
    int main()
    {
    ```

CHAPTER 7   EASY-TO-USE SOFTWARE DEVELOPMENT USING OOP

a. List of integer elements

```
int v[10];
for (int i=0;i<10;i++)
{
  v[i] = i*20;
}
bool ret= inIncreasingOrder(v,10);
if (ret == true)
{
    cout<<"Values are in increasing order\n";
}
else
{
    cout<<"Values are not in increasing order\n";
}

int maxint = maxValue(v,10);
cout<<"Max int value  of array is "<<maxint<<
"\n";
```

b. List the float elements.

```
float fv[10];
for (int i=0;i<10;i++)
{
    fv[i] = i*10.5;
}
ret= inIncreasingOrder(fv,10);
if (ret == true)
{
    cout<<"Values are in increasing order\n";
}
```

```
    else
    {
        cout<<"Values are not in increasing order\n";
    }
```

c. List the Coin objects.

```
    float maxfloat = maxValue(fv,10);
    cout<<"Max float value of array is
    "<<maxfloat<<"\n";
    Coin c[10];
    bool res= inIncreasingOrder(c,10);
    if (res == true)
    {
        cout<<"Coins are in increasing order\n";
    }
    Coin max = maxValue(c,10);
    cout<<"Max valued coin is"<<max;
}
```

5. After saving all changes in genericfunc.cc execute it and observe the results.

   a. The generic functions can be used over all basic data types (int, float, etc.).

   b. The generic functions can be used over only class objects (included with suitable operator functions).

      i. It works only with Coin objects.

      ii. If you try with gun objects or bomb objects, these template functions return errors.

         ```
         # g++ genericfunc.cc -o genfunc
         # ./genfunc
         Values are in increasing order
         ```

```
Max int value  of array is 180
Values are in increasing order
Max float value  of array is 94.5
Coins are in increasing order
Max valued coin is 90
```

Next, let's look at a generic data structure.

Generic Data Structures

You should learn how to write generic classes to implement generic data structures.

First, let's look at a generic class in C++ using the `template` syntax.

```
template<typename T>
class DataStruct
{
    T container[10];
    public:
    void search(T e);
    T getEle();
    ..
};
```

It can be tested in `main()` as follows.

```
DataStruct<int> intd;
DataStruct<float> reald;
```

You should observe the following.

- Template data type T was passed as arguments to define the class.
- In main(), actual data types were passed to create DataStuct objects

Next, let's practice a hands-on activity with generic functions.

Practice Implementing a Generic Data Structure

The following generic data structure uses a template.

- Implement a generic data structure for creating the following dynamically sized data containers.
  - Basic data type elements (int, float, etc.) holding data containers.
  - Class objects holding data containers.
    - For example, create coins holding data containers.
- Every generic data structure should contain the following two data members:
  - Data elements holding container.
  - Size of the container.
- The following operations should be performed over the generic data structure holding data containers.
  - insert: A given data element should be inserted at the end of the given data container.
  - search: It should return true if a given element is present in the input data container; otherwise, it should return false.

CHAPTER 7   EASY-TO-USE SOFTWARE DEVELOPMENT USING OOP

- `print`: It prints all elements present in the data container.
- `getSize`: It should return the number of elements in the data container.

Next, let's walk through a generic data structure using a template.

GENERIC DATA STRUCTURE

Create a generic data structure and save it in the `gendatastruct.cc` file.

1. Include the following necessary header files for the tasks.

    a. The coins.h file for testing generic data structure with `Coin` objects.

    ```
    #include<iostream>
    #include<stdlib.h>
    #include"coins.h"
    using namespace std;
    template<typename T>
    ```

2. Define the `GenericDataStructure` with two important data elements: `storage` (Data elements holding container) and `size` (size of the storage).

    ```
    class GenericDataStructure
    {
        T *storage;
        int size;
        public:
    ```

a. Initialize GenericDataStructure objects storage default size using the following constructor.

   ```
   GenericDataStructure()
   {
       storage = (T *) malloc(1 * sizeof(T));
       size    = 1;
   }
   ```

b. Define the following destructor to clean up the memory space allotted for storage.

   ```
   ~GenericDataStructure()
   {
       storage = NULL;
       free(storage);
   }
   ```

c. Define the insert function to insert an element at the end of the storage.

   ```
   void insert(T e)
   {
       if (size == 1)
       {
           if (storage!=NULL)
           {
               storage[0] = e;
               size = size+1;
           }
       }
       else
       {
   ```

```
                storage = (T *) realloc(storage, (size+1) *
                sizeof(T));
                if (storage!=NULL)
                {
                    storage[size-1] = e;
                    size = size+1;
                }
            }
        }
```

d. Define the `search` function to check whether a given element is present in the `storage`.

```
bool search(T e)
{
    for (int i=0;i<size-1;i++)
    {
        if (storage[i] == e)
            return true;
    }
    return false;
}
```

e. Define the `print` function to display all elements present in the `storage`.

```
void print()
{
    for (int i=0;i<size-1;i++)
    {
        cout<<storage[i]<<"\n";
    }
}
```

f. Define the getSize function to return the number of elements present in the storage.

```
int getSize()
{
    return size-1;
}
};
```

3. You defined the generic data structure with necessary data members and member functions. Let's write its testing code in main().

4. Test the generic data structure using the following data type containers.

```
int main()
{
```

   a. Define integer holding data containers and test it.

```
GenericDataStructure<int> gd;
gd.insert(100);
gd.insert(10);
gd.insert(300);
gd.insert(40);
gd.insert(50);
gd.insert(60);
gd.insert(70);
gd.insert(400);
cout<<"Size of GD"<<gd.getSize()<<"\n";
gd.print();
```

b. Define Coin objects holding data containers and test them.

```
Coin c[10];
GenericDataStructure<Coin> gdc;
for (int i=0;i<10;i++)
{
    c[i].setValue(i);
    gdc.insert(c[i]);
}
gdc.print();
Coin sc;
sc.setValue(5);
if(gdc.search(sc) == true)
{
    cout<<"Coin found\n";
}

sc.setValue(6);
if(gdc.search(sc) == true)
{
    cout<<"Coin found\n";
}
}
```

5. Similarly, you can test other data type elements.

6. After saving all changes in gendatastruct.cc, execute it, and observe the results.

   a. The generic data structure can create containers for all basic data types (int, float, etc.).

   b. The generic data structure can be used over only class objects (included with suitable operator functions).

i. It works only with `Coin` objects.

ii. If you try with gun objects or bomb objects, these template functions return errors.

```
# g++ gendatastruct.cc -o gends
# ./gends
Size of GD8
100
10
..
0
1
..
9
Coin found
Coin found
```

Next, let's look at the Coin class to model opportunities in the gaming application.

Using Dynamic Polymorphism for Offering Common Interfaces

Usually, standard user-accessing interfaces must be offered to simplify accessing any software, and the number of interfaces should be minimal. From a C++ developer's perspective, defining standard user interfaces for accessing all similar objects, actions, tasks, functions, and operations is necessary. This section discusses the dynamic polymorphism concepts and how having standard user interfaces for a software application is helpful.

Unlike static polymorphism, dynamic polymorphism postone a function call linking with the correct function code during runtime. To apply dynamic polymorphism, developers must understand the following two concepts.

- Virtual functions
- Abstract classes

Let's start with virtual functions. For instance, to access a phone, you use standard user interfaces: call, answer, and message as standard user interfaces for accessing it. Similarly, to edit documents, you cut, copy, and paste as a standard user-accessing interface. To handle these situations in software development, virtual functions define standard user interfaces (one function prototype) for developing common actions, functions, tasks, and operations of related classes (base and derived classes) objects.

Using the virtual keyword before the member function prototype, you define virtual functions in a base class public section.

If you know the default implementation of objects in a software application, it is possible to define virtual member functions with the default code in base classes. Later, the virtual member functions are overridden in derived classes to create special behaviors.

In this case, users accessing standard interfaces should be defined with base class pointer arguments. Then, it is possible to invoke a specific object behavior by passing the object address to the base class pointer.

The Importance of Virtual Functions

Let's do the following activity to better understand the importance of virtual functions.

- Define a Phone class with a standard user interface function: `call()`.
- Define a Phonev2 class by inheriting the Phone class and redefine the `call()` with special behavior.

- Define a Phonev3 class by inheriting the Phone class and redefine the `call()` with special behavior.

- Create a standard user interface `call()` for accessing all phones. It should take a phone object as input and invoke the respective phone object call function.

FUNCTION OVERRIDING

Implement the function overriding activity code in the override.cc file.

1. Start by defining a Phone class with a sample `call` function.

   ```
   #include<iostream>
   using namespace std;
   class Phone
   {
       public:
       // virtual void call()
       void call()
       {
           cout<<"Normal calling..\n";
       }
   };
   ```

2. Define a new version phone class Phonev2 and override the sample `call` function to simulate the sample Phonev2 calling procedure.

   ```
   class Phonev2:public Phone
   {
       public:
       void call()
   ```

```
        {
            cout<<"Internet calling ..\n";
        }
    };
```

3. Define another version phone class, Phonev3, and override the sample call function to simulate a sample Phonev3 calling procedure.

```
    class Phonev3:public Phone
    {
        public:
        void call()
        {
            cout<<"Video callig ..\n";
        }
    };
```

4. Define a standard user interface for accessing any phone as follows.

   a. It takes an input argument: Phone objects pointing pointer.

   b. Inside the function body, invoke phone object-related code.

   ```
       void call(Phone *p)
       {
           p->call();
       }
   ```

5. Test the phone objects accessing using standard user interface call () in main().

   ```
   int main()
   {
   ```

CHAPTER 7　EASY-TO-USE SOFTWARE DEVELOPMENT USING OOP

a. Create an object for each phone class.

   Phone p1;
   Phonev2 p2;
   Phonev3 p3;

b. Invoke phone calling function from each phone object.

   p1.call();
   p2.call();
   p3.call();

c. Invoke phone calling function from a standard user interface.

   call(&p1);
   call(&p2);
   call(&p3);
   }

6. After saving all changes in override.cc, execute it and observe the results.

   a. Invoking phone calling functions from the specific object is working correctly.

   b. Invoking phone calling functions from the standard user interface leads to incorrect behavior.

      i. Only the Phone class call() is invoked.

         g++ override.cc -o phone
         ./phone
         Normal calling..
         Internet calling ..
         Video callig ..

Normal calling..
Normal calling..
Normal calling..

ii. How do you correct this behavior?

7. Let's make a Phone class `call()` a `virtual call()`. After saving all changes in `override.cc`, execute it, and observe the results.

    a. Invoking phone calling functions from the specific object is working correctly.

    b. Invoking phone calling functions from the standard user interface is working correctly.

    ```
    # g++ override.cc -o phone
    # ./phone
    Normal calling..
    Internet calling ..
    Video calling..
    Normal calling..
    Internet calling ..
    Video calling..
    ```

It means when a class member function is redefined in derived classes, it is necessary to make the base class member function as virtual function for developing polymorphism behavior. Defining a virtual function in a class means linking the correct code to the respective function call is postponed to runtime. Then, the respective function code is executed during runtime based on the object type. To minimize the number of interfaces of a software application and work correctly, you must use virtual functions in base classes.

Next, you learn how to handle when base classes do not provide default behavior for standard user-accessing interfaces.

The Importance of Pure Virtual Functions and Abstract Classes

When the base class does not offer any default behavior for standard user accessing interfaces, you define those standard user interfaces as pure virtual functions.

You declare one pure virtual function in a base class for each standard user accessing interface.

For example, to define standard user interfaces for Phone objects.

```
class Phone
{
    public:
    virtual void call() { print("calling");}
    virtual void answer()=0;
    virtual void message()=0;
}
```

The following are a few important details you must observe from the class.

- From the Phone class, in the public section, you can observe that a few function declarations are assigned with 0. These are nothing but pure virtual functions.

- Pure virtual functions must be declared in the public section and initialized with 0. Hence, it allows derived classes to implement pure virtual functions of the base class.

- Since the Phone class contains pure virtual functions, you cannot use it for creating objects.

CHAPTER 7 EASY-TO-USE SOFTWARE DEVELOPMENT USING OOP

- If a class contains a pure virtual function, you call it an abstract class. From abstract classes, you cannot create objects.

- Note: Besides virtual functions, it is possible to create pure virtual functions.

In derived classes, by extending from an abstract class, these virtual functions must be implemented to access these standards from derived class objects.

Next, to create standard user interfaces for phone objects, you can apply the following standard user interface functions with Base class pointer arguments as follows.

```
void call(Phone *p) ;
void answer(Phone *p);
void message(Phone *p);
```

Since base class (e.g., Phone) pointers were passed to each of these standard user interfaces, it is possible to pass any new derived class phone objects as arguments to invoke the special behavior (e.g., for Phonev2, Phonev3, .. PhonevN;).

To access new versions of phones, you need not change the user interfaces accessing code as follows.

You can use the following simple lines of code only.

The following allows access to Phonev2.

```
Phonev2 p1;
call(&p1);
answer(&p1);
message(&p1);
```

The following allows access to PhonevN.

```
PhonevN p2;
call(&p2);
answer(&p2);
message(&p2);
```

Next, let's do a hands-on activity for learning how to use dynamic polymorphism concepts.

Practice with Dynamic Polymorphism

Let's explore how to use dynamic polymorphism concepts to develop standard interfaces for a software application by implementing a variety of phone classes and providing standard user interfaces for simplifying any phone usage. Specifically, let's do the following activities.

- Define a Phone class with the following three standard accessing functions as pure virtual functions: call(), answer(), message().

- A Phonev2 class for simulating 2G phone functions

- A Phonev3 class for simulating 3G phone functions

- A Phonev4 class for simulating 4G phone functions

- Standard user interfaces for accessing any phone (2G/3G/4G)—specifically, standard interfaces for phone calls, answering, and messaging activities

Let's walk through these activities using abstract classes and pure virtual functions.

CHAPTER 7   EASY-TO-USE SOFTWARE DEVELOPMENT USING OOP

DYNAMIC POLYMORPHISM

Implement dynamic polymorphism activities in the dynpolymorph.cc file.

1. Start by defining the following abstract class for provisioning standard interfaces for various phones.

    a. Inside the Phone class, declare phone accessing functions as pure virtual functions.

    b. All pure virtual functions must be declared under the public section only.

    ```
    #include<iostream>
    using namespace std;
    class Phone
    {
        public:
        virtual void call()=0;
        virtual void answer()=0;
        virtual void message()=0;
    };
    ```

2. Define a Phonev2 by inheriting from the Phone abstract class.

    a. Implement sample 2G phone-specific functions.

    b. You must use all Phone accessing interfaces such as call(), answer(), and message().

    ```
    class Phonev2:public Phone
    {
        public:
        void call()
        {
    ```

```
            cout<<"2G calling ..\n";
        }
        void answer()
        {
            cout<<"2G call answering ..\n";
        }
        void message()
        {
            cout<<"Sending text message..\n";
        }
    };
```

3. Define a Phonev3 by inheriting from the Phone abstract class to create sample 3G phone-specific functions. All Phone accessing interfaces such as call(), answer(), and message() should be implemented.

```
    class Phonev3:public Phone
    {
        public:
        void call()
        {
            cout<<"3G callig ..\n";
        }
        void answer()
        {
            cout<<"3G call answering ..\n";
        }
        void message()
        {
            cout<<"Internet data messaging..\n";
        }
    };
```

CHAPTER 7   EASY-TO-USE SOFTWARE DEVELOPMENT USING OOP

4. Define a Phonev4 by inheriting from the Phone abstract class to create sample 4G phone-specific functions. All Phone accessing interfaces such as call(), answer(), and message() should be implemented.

```
class Phonev4:public Phone
{
    public:
    void call()
    {
        cout<<"4G callig ..\n";
    }
    void answer()
    {
        cout<<"4G call answering ..\n";
    }
    void message()
    {
        cout<<"Internet video messaging..\n";
    }
};
```

5. Apply the following standard user interfaces for accessing any type of phone.

```
void call(Phone *p)
{
    p->call();
}
void answer(Phone *p)
{
    p->answer();
}
```

```
void message(Phone *p)
{
    p->message();
}
```

6. Test different phones by accessing standard user interfaces from main().

    a. Create respective phone objects for 2G, 3G, and 4G phone simulating classes.

    b. Test each phone by accessing it using standard user interfaces: call(), answer(), and message().

    ```
    int main()
    {
        Phonev2 p2;
        Phonev3 p3;
        Phonev4 p4;
        call(&p2);
        call(&p3);
        call(&p4);
        answer(&p2);
        answer(&p3);
        answer(&p4);
        message(&p2);
        message(&p3);
        message(&p4);
    }
    ```

7. After saving all changes in dynpolymorph.cc, execute it, and observe the results.

    a. All phones are accessed using standard user interfaces.

    b. Calling a standard user interface with a specific phone object (e.g, 4g) invoked the right function (4g related functions).

    c. It is easier to access phones with standard user interfaces.

    ```
    # g++ dynpolymorph.cc - stdinterfaces
    # ./stdinterfaces
    2G calling ..
    3G callig ..
    4G callig ..
    2G call answering ..
    3G call answering ..
    4G call answering ..
    Sending text message..
    Internet data messaging..
    Internet video messaging..
    ```

Well done. From the results, you can observe that passing 2G phone object leads to 2G related functions are executed. Similarly, passing 3G or 4G objects lead to executing respective functions.

Summary

In this chapter, you practiced polymorphism approaches to develop easy-to-use software with standard interfaces. For example, you have explored when to use function overloading and template functions to save development time. You experimented with operator overloading and discovered its importance in creating generic functions and data structures. Finally, you practiced dynamic polymorphism constructs: virtual functions and abstract classes for implementing standard user interfaces to access software applications. You discovered polymorphism's importance in dealing with the complexity and ambiguity in designing software interfaces.

The next chapter focuses on design patterns to reuse common solutions for software development issues.

Practice: Hands-on Activities

1. Implement generic functions for the following.

    a. Sorting data elements

    b. Binary search algorithms

    c. Arranging a list of car objects in descending order based on their price

    d. Searching for a car based on registration number in a list of objects

2. Implement generic data structures for the following.

    a. A binary search tree to store data elements such as integers, strings, and car objects (based on registration numbers)

    b. A priority queue to store data elements such as integers, strings, and car objects (based on registration numbers)

    c. A stack to store data elements such as integers, strings, and car objects (based on registration numbers)

3. Handle the following tasks using dynamic polymorphism concepts.

    a. Implement an abstract class to declare standard interfaces for editing any document.

    b. Define a variety of document classes and create standard interfaces for edit operations.

4. Handle the following tasks using dynamic polymorphism concepts.

    a. Implement an abstract class to declare standard interfaces for accessing sensors.

    b. Define various sensor classes and create standard interfaces for accessing the sensor objects.

5. Handle the following tasks using dynamic polymorphism concepts.

    a. Implement an abstract class to declare standard interfaces for accessing guns in a gaming context.

    b. Define a variety of Gun classes and develop standard interfaces for accessing the gun objects.

CHAPTER 8

Design Patterns

You have learned important OOP concepts such as encapsulation, data hiding, inheritance, and polymorphism for handling software development challenges. This chapter introduces the design patterns and how they are useful to identify general solutions for common software development problems.

Usually, in software development, researchers observe repeated problems and common solutions to handle a group of problems. To save time in software development, repeatable solutions are formalized and grouped into design patterns. A design pattern is not a directly reusable algorithm or source code but a solution template to use in specific problem contexts. Developers can customize a design pattern solution template to handle specific problems.

Design patterns provide a variety of general software development solutions, such as handling complex systems design without violating OOP principles such as data hiding, reusing the code (inheritance), and polymorphism. Learning design patterns helps us solve tremendous time in handling ambiguities of software development and also helps us develop a reusable, extensible, and flexible software system. Design patterns are grouped into three major categories: creational patterns, structural patterns, and behavioral patterns. For instance, creational design patterns help handle challenges in classes and object creation; structural design patterns help handle challenges in implementing flexible and efficient software systems; and behavioral patterns help handle challenges in collaboration among software building blocks.

CHAPTER 8   DESIGN PATTERNS

Introduction to Design Patterns

Design patterns are template solutions for handling challenges in class creation, object creation, arranging classes into a hierarchy, combining subsystems to make larger systems, and providing clean solutions for complex object collaborations. Design pattern solutions use OOP concepts such as encapsulation, inheritance, object association, and composition. Design patterns are mainly classified into the following three categories.

- Creational design patterns
- Structural design patterns
- Behavioral design patterns

Creational Patterns

Creational patterns provide template solutions for classes and object creation mechanisms by ensuring the flexibility and reuse of existing classes.

This section discusses how to use inheritance, object composition, and aggregation to handle challenges in creating new classes or objects. Let's review the following creation patterns and their usage context.

- The **factory method**: It is defined in a base class to return the final product—creating objects. It is useful to hide the derived classes (final product) details.

- An **abstract factory**: It is defined in an abstract factory class to include multiple factory methods.

- **Builder**: It is defined in a builder class to handle complex objects construction process. Actual object-implementing class details are hidden in the builder class.

- **Prototype**: It is defined in a prototype class and includes an object's fields copying or cloning member function to create user-accessing objects.

- **Singleton**: It is defined in a singleton class to ensure that only one object is created from the singleton class. It is also possible to restrict that from a class number of objects to be created.

Structural Patterns

Structural patterns help developers to combine classes and compose objects flexibly and efficiently for developing large software systems.

Usually, structural pattern classes define references of other objects and common interfaces for accessing the necessary objects.

- **Adapter**: It is useful to create an adapter class and a compatible interface for collaborating incompatible objects.

- **Bridge**: It is useful to create abstract and implementation classes separately to enable parallel development activities. Instead of using inheritance, include necessary object references in abstract classes.

- **Composite**: It is useful to create a composite class to apply tree or hierarchical approaches to composing class objects and executing operations against the class objects.

- **Decorator**: It is useful to create a decorator class and includes references for class objects and standard interfaces to dynamically change the behavior of objects. Both the decorator class and its referring objects define the same accessing interface.

- **Facade**: It is useful to create a facade class to provide necessary simple interfaces to access a complex system containing multiple subsystems.

- **Flyweight**: It is useful to create a flyweight class to store the common state and unique state of objects separately to save them in random access memory (RAM).

- **Proxy**: It is useful to create a proxy class with real object references and defines the same accessing interface of the real object. Inside the proxy accessing interface, a request can be processed or saved for optimization before passing the request to the original real object.

Behavioral Patterns

Behavioral patterns help developers separate common algorithms from objects, simplify communication among different objects, and provide customized communication or collaboration. Let's discuss the following behavioral patterns and their usage.

- **Chain of responsibility**: It is useful to execute behaviors such as processing a user request through a series of class objects.

- **Command**: It is useful to model user requests as objects and manages the request objects for storing requests, delaying requests, redoing, and undoing requests.

- **Iterator**: It is useful to iterate through a list of complex objects to access.

- **Mediator**: It is useful to handle communication dependencies between multiple objects. Instead of directly communicating with objects, they communicate with a mediator object.

- **Memento**: It is useful to saves and restores an object's state without violating objects' data-hiding principles.

- **Observer**: It is useful to implement events handling **applications** using publish and subscribe methods. Provides interfaces for object subscription and publishing activities and maintains a list of subscribed objects.

- **State**: It is useful to model state machine behavior using related objects and their actions.

- **Strategy**: It is useful to implements algorithm as strategy objects. It is possible to involve strategies based on the usage context.

- **Template**: It is useful to define a system-wide algorithm as a template of steps in a class. Then, subclasses can use the necessary parts of the template algorithm to override or define specific behavior.

- **Visitor**: It is useful to define additional behaviors in specific classes of the inheritance hierarchy.

Next, let's practice a few design patterns.

Learning Creational Design Patterns

In the process of developing software from subsystems and their classes, it is necessary to create objects from various classes to perform various tasks in the software. However, it is not easy to create objects in the presence of many classes with dependencies due to the following challenges.

- Object creation involves a lot of its internal data configurations and initializations.

- Necessary to hide classes' private data members and member functions to ensure data-hiding features.

- Need to implement a variety of objects from the same procedure.
- Copying objects should be simplified without depending on source objects.
- Reduce the build time of objects and reuse the existing objects.
- Strict enforcement on the number of objects to be created.

This section explains how creational design patterns help create suitable objects from classes by following OOP principles and flexibly reusing them. Let's quickly check the types of creational design patterns and their uses.

- **Factory method**: The **factory method** is useful to create final product-related objects and return them. The factory method is declared in abstract classes, and implementation is done in end-product classes. It eliminates the need to reveal the specific derived class (product) details.
    - It is useful to hide details of actual derived classes and their dependent classes for creating end-product objects.
    - It helps in easily reusing the existing objects.
- **Abstract factory** contains multiple factory methods to hide multiple classes and their dependent class details.
    - It is a general solution for hiding multiple end-user objects accessing class details.
    - Abstract factory classes are also helpful in returning objects for end-product creation.

- The **Builder pattern** hides the complex end product object creation process. The complex object construction process from multiple dependent objects is separated into a builder class.

    - It is useful to separate the internal objects of the end product object from the construction process. Hence, extending or changing the end product object creation process is easier.

    - It is helpful in easily constructing special products from multiple objects.

    - It is useful to hide the complex object construction process.

- The **prototype pattern** helps implement objects copying code to construct prototypes without depending on the source classes.

    - It is helpful in easily applying proof of concept models by customizing the object's initialization and copying code.

    - It is useful to eliminate unnecessary subclasses that only differ in the configuration of constructors.

- The **singleton pattern** is useful to enforce rules on the number of objects to be created per class. The singleton pattern procedure enforces rules on the number of objects created from a singleton class.

    - Restricting your application to run with only one shared object from a specific class is helpful.

    - It is also helpful to restrict a specific number of class objects available during an application execution.

CHAPTER 8   DESIGN PATTERNS

You know solutions for handling object creation challenges in software development from the list of creational design patterns and quick discussion. Practicing all these patterns is beyond the scope of this book.

Next, let's start with exploring how to use the factory method creational design using C++.

The Factory Method

Let's look at a use case that features drone products based on end-user requirements. In this context, consider the following rules to design drone classes.

- All manufacturers must define standard interfaces (userControl()) for providing drone objects access to users.

- All varieties of drone objects should have common interfaces to interact with and control the drone objects. However, the drone object and its accessing interfaces should be hidden from the end user.

- All users of drones should access final drone product objects from standard interfaces (userContol()) only.

To realize the requirement to offer access to drone objects, hiding the actual drone object classes from the end user is necessary. Besides, developers should offer drone sellers a variety of drone objects by implementing the drone seller-recommended standard accessing interfaces using factory methods.

Let's walk through a hands-on activity using the factory method pattern.

CHAPTER 8   DESIGN PATTERNS

FACTORY METHOD

This hands-on activity uses code snippets in the factory.cc file.

1. To model a variety of drones, define the following abstract classes.

   a. Define an abstract class called Drone to declare all common controls for all varieties of drone objects.

   b. Define sample control operations related to drones by declaring pure virtual functions. We included only one control, it is possible to include multiple control functions. These are implemented by drone objects creating classes.

   ```
   #include<iostream>
   using namespace std;
   class Drone
   {
           public:
           virtual ~Drone() {}
           virtual void Control() const = 0;
   };
   ```

2. Define an example actual drone objects creating class as following.

   a. Define a base class called MonitoringDrone to create an example of monitoring drone objects by inheriting the Drone abstract class.

   b. Define the control function by using sample code.

   ```
   class MonitoringDrone : public Drone
   {
           public:
           void Control() const override
   ```

CHAPTER 8   DESIGN PATTERNS

```
        {
                cout<<"Drone1 control\n";
        }
};
```

3. To enforce the use case rule, such as not allowing end users to access drone objects directly and allowing only through drone seller-recommended interfaces, define the following abstract class called DroneSeller.

   a. Declare a virtual function called DroneFactory to create drone objects. The factory method allows manufacturers to create specific drone objects and return them to callers. It defines actual user accessing controls (userControl). Based on requirements, we can include multiple user controls here.

   b. Define drone sellers to provide user-accessing interfaces.

   ```
   class DroneSeller
   {
           public:
           virtual ~DroneSeller(){};
           virtual Drone* DroneFactory() const = 0;

           void userControl() const
           {
                   Drone* drone = this->DroneFactory();
                   drone->Control();
                   delete drone;
           }
   };
   ```

CHAPTER 8 DESIGN PATTERNS

4. Define the following concrete class called ManufacturerA to apply DroneFactory to return custom drone objects from manufacturers.

   a. Define DroneFactory to create an example monitoring drone object and return it. It is the factory method to return monitoring drone objects to sellers.

   ```
   class ManufacturerA : public DroneSeller
   {
           public:
           Drone* DroneFactory() const override
           {
                   return new MonitoringDrone();
           }
   };
   ```

5. Let's access end products called monitoring drones from end-user code.

   a. Declare a DroneSeller pointer to get monitoring drone objects from ManufacturerA.

   b. Access monitoring drone objects from the end user code.

   c. Test these tasks in main().

   ```
   void ClientCode(const DroneSeller& udrone)
   {
       cout << "Client:";
       udrone.userControl();
   }
   int main()
   {
      std::cout << "Drone: Launched with the Manufacturer\n";
   ```

```
            DroneSeller* udrone = new ManufacturerA;
            ClientCode(*udrone);
            std::cout << std::endl;

            delete udrone;
            return 0;
        }
```

6. Let's execute `factory.cc` and observe the following.

    a. A drone from ManufacturerA is created.

    b. The user got the drone object and accessed it from a standard interface called `userControl`.

    ```
    # g++ factory.cc -o factory
    # ./factory
    Drone: Launched with the Manufacturer
    Client:Drone1 control
    ```

Well done. You have used factory methods to return sample drone objects and accessed them using standard interfaces. Readers can do the following practice tasks.

Practice Tasks

Next, do the following tasks by extending the use case to practice the factory method and understand its importance.

- Introduce another variant of drone objects and including multiple controls from another manufacturer (Manufacturer B).

- Think of creating multiple drone objects and returning them from the factory method.

- You can observe that new requirements can be easily applied in new variant drone classes and manufacturer classes.

- Drone sellers can easily return a user-requested drone object from the factory returned drone objects by different manufacturers.

- Moreover, end user code need not be changed to access and control a new drone product.

Next, let's practice another important creational design pattern called the singleton pattern.

The Singleton Pattern

Let's consider creating an application where you want to have only a single database object to execute the application task. All other objects must share only the single database object. The following are the requirements for the use case.

- The application should have only a single database object.

- The application is not allowed to create multiple database objects.

- There is a provision in the database object creation class to return the necessary number of objects.

To implement the proposed application, use the singleton pattern that lets the application have only one instance database object and provides global access to the unique single database object.

The following hands-on activity uses the singleton pattern approach.

CHAPTER 8   DESIGN PATTERNS

SINGLETON

Let's use code snippets in the `singleton.cc` file.

1. Start by defining a singleton pattern class. Define a `DataBase` class as follows.

   a. Define a private static database object pointer to hold a dynamically created database object address.

   b. Define a private field called record to insert into a sample database object.

   ```
   #include<iostream>
   #include<thread>
   using namespace std;
   class DataBase
   {
        private:
        static DataBase* dbo;
        string record;
   ```

   c. Define a **private constructor** to initialize database record value to avoid multiple database object creation in nonmember functions of the DataBase class. For example, the application is not allowed to create objects.

   ```
   DataBase(const std::string value)
   {
        record = value;
   }
   ```

424

d. **Disable default and copy constructors** using the following lines of the code. It also useful to avoid creating multiple database objects inside the class member functions.

```
public:
DataBase(DataBase &other) = delete;
void operator=(const DataBase &) = delete;
```

e. Define the following member functions to access database record values.

```
std::string getRecord()
{
        return record;
}
void setRecord(string val)
{
        record = val;
}
```

f. Declare a unique member function: **static member function** to return the **globally sharable single database object**.

```
        static DataBase *GetInstance(std::string
        value);
};
```

2. Define and initialize static data member dbo.

   `DataBase* DataBase::dbo= nullptr;`

3. Implement the **static member function** to create **a single database object** and set a user passed record.

   a. You can observe that for the first time calling this static function only a new database object is created.

CHAPTER 8   DESIGN PATTERNS

    b. Further calls to this static function return only the existing database object address to the callers.

    c. You can restrict the number of database objects created in this static member function. For instance, you can create a N number of database objects and return to applications.

    d. Except for this member function, no other member function or external member function is allowed to create database objects.

```
DataBase *DataBase::GetInstance(std::string value)
{
    if(dbo==nullptr)
    {
        dbo = new DataBase(value);
    }
    dbo->setRecord(value);
    return dbo;
}
```

4. Let's test your code in main as follows.

    a. Call the static member function GetInstance to get a single database object and set a sample record. Collect the database object pointer in db1.

    b. Call GetInstance again to insert another sample record in it. Collect the database object pointer in db2.

    c. Print the database record using getRecord from db1 and db2.

```
int main()
{
    DataBase* db1 = DataBase::GetInstance
    ("Record1");
    DataBase* db2 = DataBase::GetInstance
    ("Record2");
```

```
cout<<db1->getRecord()<<"\n";
cout<<db2->getRecord();
return 0;
}
```

5. Let's execute `single.cc` and observe the following.

    a. Observe the attempt to create two database instances.

    b. But, due to the singleton pattern there is only one database instance.

    c. Hence, accessing the database anytime is printing the latest record details only.

    ```
    # g++ single.cc -o single
    # ./single
    Record2
    Record2
    ```

Next, let's continue practicing.

Practice Tasks

Next, do the following tasks by extending the use case to practice the singleton pattern and understand its importance.

1. Change your `Database` class to create only a fixed number of database objects.

2. Access the fixed number of objects from the client code to test them.

3. Check that your application is allowed to use more than the fixed number of objects available in your application.

Next, let's learn another category of design patterns called structural design patterns.

CHAPTER 8   DESIGN PATTERNS

Structural Design Patterns

Creating larger software systems involves inheriting multiple classes, aggregating, and composing a variety of objects. During this process, developers may end up with lots of redundant code, introducing multiple interfaces for interactions with the system, leading to inconsistent codes and increasing the memory size of objects. Structural design patterns offer important reusable solutions for handling the following challenges.

- Making use of existing classes and interfaces by handling the incompatibility issues.

- Developing larger systems form subsystems and offer their services access using only standard interfaces.

- Divide the complex or monolithic systems into subsystems.

- Supporting layers approach for implementing complex systems such as operating systems and protocol stacks.

- Introducing and integrating necessary services to existing systems without changing the subsystems and their classes.

- Reducing the object runtime memory size.

This section explores how structural design patterns are helpful to combine subsystems, non-subsystem classes and objects into complex software systems. The structural design patterns approaches make the complex systems design and code flexible to make any extensions or enhancements by minimizing the redundant code, reusing the common access interfaces, and allowing the system to be easily integrated with incompatible systems or non-subsystem services.

Let's quickly review the types of structural design patterns and their uses.

- **Adapter**: This pattern is helpful to integrate services available outside the main system and access incompatible objects' services through the system's common interfaces. As part of using the adapter pattern, create an adapter class to do the following.
    - Use the adapter pattern to access a system or an existing class service in case of incompatible interfaces.
    - It is especially useful to access a common service of a non-subsystem or an existing class across the many classes of the main system.
    - If you cannot include the common service in any of the superclasses of the main system, adapter classes are necessary.
- **Facade**: This design pattern offers simplified interfaces to use a set of subsystems together and eliminates the need of complex interfaces. It also helps you to design a complex system by combining multiple subsystems in terms of layers. Usually, you define facade pattern classes with multiple subsystem objects and integrate them logically to realize the complex services.
    - Use the facade pattern to design protocol stacks with simplified standard interfaces for accessing underlying subsystems or layers services.

- Use the facade pattern to simplify the design of complex monolithic systems.
- Use the facade pattern to reuse the smaller subsystems and build a larger system.

- **Decorator**: This design pattern helps you to add new functionalities to existing class objects, including the object's reference and their accessing standard interfaces inside a decorator class. Then, you can use the reference of objects in the decorator class to add new functionalities for the objects at runtime.
  - Use the decorator pattern to define runtime functionalities to existing objects.
  - Use the decorator pattern to dynamically add multiple behaviors to an object.
  - The decorator pattern is typically used when it is not possible to use inheritance for extending object functionalities.

- **Composite**: This design pattern helps you to compose multiple objects in a hierarchical manner (tree-like structure) and execute their member functions as per the parent and child relationship defined in the composite class. Usually, to use a composite pattern, you define a composite class, and inside the class objects are linked in a tree structure manner to execute their behaviors.
  - Use the composite pattern for a parent-child approach to recursively connect multiple objects.

- Use the composite pattern when you need to get a result from multiple objects formed as a tree to process the input in a hierarchical manner and return results.

- Use the composite pattern to recursively connect objects and execute system behaviors.

- **Bridge**: This design pattern helps you to organize several system classes into separate inheritance hierarchies. Classes are organized into hierarchies, which allows developers to work in parallel on their respective class hierarchies. You can use necessary object aggregation in class hierarchies to perform coordination tasks between objects.

  - Use the bridge pattern to divide an application into multiple class hierarchies.

  - Use the bridge pattern when there is a need for parallel development of class hierarchies.

  - Use the bridge pattern to dynamically change objects at runtime.

- **Proxy**: This design pattern helps you to hide an original application object and expose an alternate object (proxy) for the original object. To use this, you define a proxy class, and inside the class an original object is created for handing over user requests through the proxy object. Moreover, users interact with the original application server and proxy server using the same service interface.

- Use the proxy pattern to implement new services before handing over the user requests to the original application.

- For instance, you can use the proxy pattern to cache user requests, responses to the requests, locally executing the remote service, etc.

- You can also use the proxy objects to control the application object lifecycle, such as automatically cleaning up the unused server objects in the system.

- **Flyweight**: This design pattern helps you to run more system objects in the limited available main memory (RAM) To execute this pattern, let's separate the common data members of objects' states into a separate shared object, and the shared object is referenced during execution time by all objects of the system.

  - Use the flyweight pattern to optimally utilize the available limited RAM.

As part of learning structural design patterns, let's use the facade pattern to build complex systems from the smaller subsystems.

The Facade Pattern

The facade pattern helps you to flexibly develop a larger system with simplified interfaces from existing subsystems. Let's discuss using the facade pattern to implement a protocol stack (larger system) from existing layers (subsystems).

CHAPTER 8   DESIGN PATTERNS

- Every layer (subsystem) can be accessed independently with its own interfaces. For example, the networking layer (layer 3) should provide interfaces related to network packet transmission and reception. Similarly, **every layer** should provide their unique **interfaces** for transmitting and receiving respective layer packets.

- Every layer can be accessed individually through its interfaces.

- Our sample network protocol stack should provide simplified interfaces for end users for **sending** (send()) and **receiving** (recv()) packets through all layers of the protocol stack based on protocol rules. That means the end user of the protocol stack (larger system) should be aware of only using **send()** and **recv()** interfaces.

- Our protocol should be easily extended with the necessary layers. These changes should be hidden from end users.

THE FACADE PATTERN

Let's implement the hands-on activity using code snippets in the facade.cc file.

1. Define subsystem-related classes for creating layers objects.

    a. Define a sample Layer1 class to handle bits sending and receiving tasks.

    b. Define sample functions to handle layer1 transmission and reception tasks.

433

CHAPTER 8   DESIGN PATTERNS

   c. Define simplified codes in Layer1Send and Layer1Recv functions for handling transmission and reception of frames, respectively.

```cpp
#include<iostream>
using namespace std;
class Layer1
{
    public:
    std::string Layer1Send() const
    {
        return "Layer1: Encode and Send\n";
    }
    std::string Layer1Recv() const
    {
        return "Layer1: Decode and Recv!\n";
    }
};
```

2. Define a sample Layer2 class to handle frames sending and receiving tasks.

   a. Define sample functions to handle layer2 frames addressing, checking related transmission and reception tasks.

   b. Define simplified codes in Layer2Send and Layer2Recv functions for handling transmission and reception of frames, respectively.

```cpp
class Layer2
{
    public:
    std::string Layer2Send() const
    {
        return "Layer2: Frame with Host Address and Send!\n";
```

```
            }
            std::string Layer2Recv() const
            {
                    return "Layer2: Check address and recv
                    frame!\n";
            }
    };
```

3. Define a sample Layer3 class to handle network packets sending and receiving tasks.

   a. Define sample functions to handle layer 3 network addressing, checking, routing-related transmission, and reception tasks.

   b. Define simplified codes in Layer3Send and Layer3Recv functions for handling transmission and reception of network packets, respectively.

```
    class Layer3
    {
            public:
            std::string Layer3Send() const
            {
                    return "Layer3: Create a Packet with
                    Network Address and Route it!\n";
            }
            std::string Layer3Recv() const
            {
                    return "Layer3: Check Soure network
                    address and recv the packet!\n";
            }
    };
```

CHAPTER 8   DESIGN PATTERNS

4. Define a sample protocol stack class to handle transmission and reception of end-user data through underlying layers. It is the facade class.

   a. Define **a sample protocol stack** with pointers to **underlying layers (subsystem) objects**.

   ```
   class ProtocolStack
   {
           protected:
           Layer1 *layer1;
           Layer2 *layer2;
           Layer3 *layer3;
   ```

   b. Define a sample protocol stack constructor to initialize pointers with layers (subsystem) objects.

   ```
   public:
   ProtocolStack(Layer1 *l1,Layer2 *l2,
   Layer3 *l3)
   {
           layer1 = l1;
           layer2 = l2;
           layer3 = l3;
   }
   ```

   c. Define a **simplified interface** called Send for sending users data through underlying protocol stack layers. End users need to know only the Send interface for accessing the protocol stack (facade).

   ```
   std::string Send()
   {
           std::string packet = "Packet send flow:\n";
           packet += layer3->Layer3Send();
           packet += layer2->Layer2Send();
   ```

CHAPTER 8   DESIGN PATTERNS

```cpp
        packet += layer1->Layer1Send();
        return packet;
    }
```

d. Define a **simplified interface** called Recv for receiving user data through underlying protocol stack layers. End users need to know only the Recv interface for accessing the protocol stack (facade).

```cpp
        std::string Recv()
        {
            std::string packet = "Packet recv flow:\n";
            packet += layer1->Layer1Recv();
            packet += layer2->Layer2Recv();
            packet += layer3->Layer3Recv();
            return packet;
        }
};
```

5. Test your simplified protocol stack from end users accessing code as follows.

   a. Define client code function for sending and receiving user data using protocol stack pointer

   ```cpp
   void ClientCode(ProtocolStack *facade)
   {
       std::cout << facade->Send();
       std::cout << facade->Recv();
   }
   ```

CHAPTER 8 DESIGN PATTERNS

b. Define the main code as follows to construct a sample protocol stack from underlying protocol layers. Then, pass the protocol stack pointer to the client code executing function.

```
int main()
{
        Layer1 *layer1 = new Layer1;
        Layer2 *layer2 = new Layer2;
        Layer3 *layer3 = new Layer3;
        ProtocolStack *facade = new
        ProtocolStack(layer1,
        layer2,layer3);
        ClientCode(facade);

        delete facade;

        return 0;
}
```

6. Let's execute facade.cc and observe the following.

   a. A sample protocol stack with three layers is created.

   b. A protocol stack is accessed using simple interfaces send and recv only.

   ```
   # g++ facade.cc -o facade
   # ./facade
   Packet send flow:
   Layer3: Create a Packet with a Network Address and
   Route it!
   Layer2: Frame with Host Address and Send!
   Layer1: Encode and Send
   Packet recv flow:
   ```

CHAPTER 8 DESIGN PATTERNS

```
Layer1: Decode and Recv!
Layer2: Check address and recv frame!
Layer3: Check Soure network address and recv
the packet!
```

By following the facade pattern, you developed a protocol stack using layers and accessed it using simple and standard interfaces. Next, let's continue practicing.

Practice Tasks

Next, do the following tasks by extending the use case to practice the facade pattern and understand its importance.

1. Introduce new layers, such as layer 4 for handling sample transport layer tasks and layer 5 for handling application layer tasks.

2. Integrate new layers with your protocol stack. Test your new protocol task.

3. Observe that your changes are limited to only the protocol stack class. In main(), you can still interact with all layers using standard Send and Recv interfaces.

Next, let's learn another interesting structural pattern to extend a system with a subsystem to offer new features without altering the existing system accessing interfaces.

CHAPTER 8   DESIGN PATTERNS

The Proxy Server Pattern

The proxy server pattern helps you to extend a large system without changing the existing system accessing interfaces. Let's explore using the proxy server pattern to extend an existing application server with new features. As part of this activity, let's consider the following rules.

- An existing application server must be accessible with its original interfaces (e.g, Request()).

- Extend the application server with new features, such as caching user requests.

- The new features must be available through only the new subsystem called the proxy server.

- Even after extending the application server with new features, the server must be accessible with only the application server's original interfaces (e.g., Request().

- The original and extended application servers must be accessible to end users using the same interface (e.g., Request()).

PROXY SERVER

The hands-on activity code snippets are executed in the `proxy.cc` file.

1. Define an abstract class called `Server` to define application servers accessing interfaces.

    a. For example, declare a pure virtual function called `Request` as a server accessing interface.

    ```
    #include <iostream>
    #include <string>
    using namespace std;
    ```

CHAPTER 8   DESIGN PATTERNS

```
class Server
{
    public:
    virtual void Request(string request)
    const = 0;
};
```

2. Define your sample application server as follows.

   a. Define a class called `ApplicationServer` by implementing abstract class `Server` interfaces.

   b. Define user request data as a private member.

   c. Define a public function to access user-requested data.

   ```
   class ApplicationServer : public Server
   {
       string request;
       public:
       void Request(string input) const override
       {
           std::cout << "Application server
           Handling request.\n";
       }
       string getInput()
       {
           return request;
       }
   };
   ```

CHAPTER 8 DESIGN PATTERNS

3. Define **the proxy server** pattern to provide special features before accessing the application server.

   a. Define a class called Proxy to create the application server accessing function called Request().

   ```
   class Proxy : public Server
   {
   ```

   b. Implement a **special feature sample function** called cacheRequest to cache user-requested data.

   ```
   private:
   ApplicationServer *as;
   bool cacheRequest(ApplicationServer *as) const
   {
           std::cout << "Proxy: caches requesting details"<<as->getInput()<<"\n";
           return true;
   }
   ```

   c. Define a proxy constructor to create a local application server object. Here, you can control the lifecycle of the local application server object.

   ```
   public:
   Proxy(ApplicationServer *as) : as(new ApplicationServer(*as))
   {

   }
   ```

   d. Implement your virtual function Request to **offer caching service** before sending the user request to the **actual application server**.

```
        void Request(string request) const override
        {
                cacheRequest(as);
                as->Request(request);
        }
```

e. Define destructor to delete dynamically created local application server objects automatically.

```
        ~Proxy()
        {
                delete as;
        }
};
```

4. Define client code to test accessing the application server.

```
void ClientCode(const Server &ser,string input)
{
        ser.Request(input);
}
```

5. Define the `main()` code to test accessing the application server from the end user.

   a. Create an application server object.

   b. Access the application server directly and test results.

   c. Access the application server through the proxy server and test results.

```
int main()
{
        std::cout << "Client: Executing the client
        code with a real subject:\n";
        ApplicationServer *ras = new ApplicationServer;
```

```
            string inp;
            ClientCode(*ras,inp);
            std::cout << "\n";
            std::cout << "Client: Executing the same
            client code with a proxy:\n";
            Proxy *proxy = new Proxy(ras);
            ClientCode(*proxy,inp);

            delete ras;
            delete proxy;
            return 0;
        }
```

6. Let's execute `proxy.cc` and observe the following.

    a. The application server is accessible using a standard interface (ser.Request()) only.

    b. When the application server is accessed without a proxy object, user-requested data is not cached.

    c. When the application server is accessed with the proxy object, caching user-requested data is done.

    ```
    # g++ proxy.cc -o proxy
    #./proxy
    Client: Executing the client code with a real
    subject:
    Application server Handling request.

    Client: Executing the same client code with a proxy:
    Proxy: caches requesting details
    Application server Handling request.
    ```

You used the proxy pattern to extend existing application server functionalities. Next, practice the following tasks.

Practice Tasks

Next, do the following tasks by extending the use case to practice a proxy pattern and understand its importance.

1. Introduce additional tasks such as authentication check, and caching responses too.

2. Test original application server access through the updated proxy server object.

3. Observe that your changes are limited to only the proxy class. The user code and actual application server classes need not be changed.

Next, let's discuss behavioral design patterns to handle challenges in large system object communication and carefully separate the system algorithms into specific classes to dynamically reuse them.

Behavioral Design Patterns

One of the complex tasks in constructing larger software systems is providing communication and collaborating with subsystem (classes) objects. It is helpful to quickly develop and deliver evolving requirements of the system. This section studies interesting behavioral design patterns to learn how to deal with complexities in designing object communication and collaboration activities. Understanding behavioral design patterns is helpful in carefully separating and assigning systems behaviors and objects responsibilities.

Behavioral design patterns offer important reusable solutions for handling the following challenges.

- Providing flexible ways to pass messages between objects.

- Dynamically creating service chains by linking objects.

- Dynamically deciding services to be executed based on objects.
- Providing a clean hierarchy among objects to exchange messages.
- Dynamically handling the objects' runtime-generated events.
- Defining generic system-wide algorithms and procedures.

Let's start with behavioral design pattern roles that address the complexity of subsystems, objects, services (algorithms), and communication in larger systems.

- **Chain of responsibility**: The pattern allows multiple objects to handle the request without linking the multiple classes together. This pattern helps you to easily create runtime service chains among multiple objects. Let's define a chain of responsibility pattern using a class to link the next server object.
    - Use this pattern to create service chains among a variety of objects.
    - Use this pattern to enable multiple service chains to handle user requests.
    - Use this pattern to eliminate the need to couple multiple server objects together.
    - Use this pattern to make users unaware that multiple servers are handling their requests.

- **Command**: This design pattern helps you to convert high-level commands into commands handling objects. Establish one-way connections between commands sending and receiving objects to apply a command pattern.

    - Use the command pattern to divide complex command execution responsibility among specific objects.

    - Use the command pattern to log command history, queue command execution, and enable the undo and redo commands.

- **Mediator**: This pattern helps you to avoid mutual and multiple dependencies among subclasses of a system. It is useful to provide clean communication among objects. It is implemented through a single object called a *mediator* object to provide multiple objects for intercommunication.

    - Use the mediator pattern to avoid changes in multiple class hierarchies.

    - Use the mediator pattern when you want to reuse components of another system.

    - Use the mediator pattern to offer a flexible and clean way of communicating with objects.

- **Observer**: This pattern is useful to execute event-based applications, particularly publish and subscription approaches.

    - Use the observer pattern to develop an event-based application that creates new events and handles events dynamically.

- Use the observer pattern to introduce new events, prioritize events, and schedule events of an application in a flexible manner.

- Consider using the observer pattern to apply smart application requirements.

- **Template method**: This pattern helps you to define a common algorithm for the entire system in superclasses and lets subclasses extend specific algorithm steps. You implement the template pattern by inheritance and polymorphism principles.

    - Use this pattern to avoid a lot of redundant code among subclasses.

    - Use this pattern to easily introduce new objects with specialized behavior without changing the logical order of the system's common algorithm steps.

- **Strategy**: This pattern helps you pack system algorithms into specific objects and allow subsystems or classes to link them during runtime based on various contexts. You apply algorithms in specific classes and define a context of objects to link with specific algorithms using the generic algorithm object holding pointers.

    - Use the strategy pattern to eliminate redundant code of algorithms among multiple classes. It helps provide consistent algorithm availability for all system objects.

CHAPTER 8 DESIGN PATTERNS

- Use the strategy pattern based on specific context to dynamically decide the algorithm to be linked with an object.

- Use the strategy pattern to eliminate many if-else or switch case code to execute specific algorithms.

- **State**: This pattern is useful to apply the finite state machines concept. Finite state machines are helpful in modeling behaviors of protocols, smart devices, automated machines, and so forth. You can implement state machine transition behavior by linking different objects in the system, passing messages between objects, and changing the system's behavior.

    - Use the state pattern to implement systems designed based on finite state machines.

    - State pattern helps you to reduce the redundant code among objects by carefully moving related code into specific objects. Transitions can execute specific object behavior through object pointers.

    - Use the state pattern to easily remove clumsy code, which invokes various objects and multiple if-else condition checks.

- **Iterator**: This design pattern is useful to traverse data elements of any complex data structure, such as trees, lists, and graphs, without exposing their underlying structure.

    - Use the iterator pattern to simplify data element accessing of complex data structures for users.

    - Use the iterator pattern to eliminate redundant data elements and traversal codes.

CHAPTER 8   DESIGN PATTERNS

- Use the iterator pattern to introduce new complex data structures.

- **Memento**: This design pattern is useful to you save and restore an object's state (including private data members). It is useful to execute undo and redo operations related to the object.

  - Use the memento pattern when there is a need to save snapshots of object states for applying history, redo, and undo commands to the objects.

  - Use the memento pattern to access and copy object states from external functions without violating the object's data-hiding principles.

- **Visitor**: This pattern helps you to include additional behavior in class hierarchies in a flexible manner.

  - Use the visitor pattern to apply additional behaviors in specific classes of inheritance hierarchy.

  - Use the visitor pattern to separate the additional tasks of the application.

Let's practice using behavioral design patterns to handle challenges in objects, message exchange, and common algorithms by eliminating redundant code.

The Chain of Responsibility Pattern

The chain of responsibility pattern is useful to implement dynamic service chains for handling user requests. The service chain defines a list of server objects in a specific order to handle user requests. Mainly, the chain of responsibility eliminates the need for users to directly couple server objects in the service chain. Let's discover how to use the chain of responsibility in the following tasks.

- There are multiple servers, such as authentication, compression, and caching, to implement different service chains.

- Server objects should not be directly coupled to allow the creation of service chains in a flexible manner.

    1. End users should define required service chains dynamically. For example, users can define service chains using multiple servers' processing orders, such as **authentication ➤ cache**, **compression ➤ cache**, **authentication ➤ compress ➤ cache,** and so on.

    2. As per the service chain order, user requests must be processed through all the servers in the service chain.

    3. Moreover, users should submit the input request to the system using a single common interface (e.g., ProcessRequest()).

CHAPTER 8   DESIGN PATTERNS

CHAIN OF RESPONSIBILITY

Let's use the hands-on activity code snippets in the `chainofservers.cc` file.

1. Define **server common interfaces** in an abstract class called `RequestHandler` to allow specific servers to implement the interface in their concrete classes. This is the crucial class for applying a chain of responsibility pattern.

    a. Declare a virtual function called `ProcessRequest` to allow concrete server classes to execute it.

    b. Define another important virtual function called `SetNextServer` to dynamically allow a server object to set its next processing server object address.

    ```
    #include<iostream>
    #include<vector>
    using namespace std;
    class RequestHandler
    {
        public:
        virtual RequestHandler *SetNextServer
        (RequestHandler *handler) = 0;
        virtual void ProcessRequest(string
        request) = 0;
    };
    ```

2. Defien a class called **RequestHandlerImpl** by inheriting from `RequestHandler` to do the following. This **class is useful to realize chain of responsibility pattern** tasks.

    a. Declare a `RequestHandler *nextServer` to hold the next server objects to process user requests in a service chain.

CHAPTER 8   DESIGN PATTERNS

```
class RequestHandlerImpl: public RequestHandler
{
    private:
    RequestHandler *nextServer;

    public:
    RequestHandlerImpl() : nextServer(nullptr)
    {
    }
```

b. Define SetNextServer to allow servers to set their next servers.

```
    RequestHandler *SetNextServer(RequestHandler *handler)
    {
        nextServer = handler;
        return handler;
    }
```

c. Implement ProcessRequest to pass user requests to the target server for processing through the service chain.

```
    void ProcessRequest(string request)
    {
        if (nextServer)
        {
            nextServer->ProcessRequest(request);
        }
    }
};
```

CHAPTER 8   DESIGN PATTERNS

3. Define server object classes.

   a. For example, define AuthRequestHandler class by inheriting from RequestHandlerImpl to implement authentication server processing tasks. Here, sample authentication server tasks were defined.

   b. At the end of the server processing tasks, pass user requests to a possible target server object of the service chain using RequestHandlerImpl::ProcessRequest.

   ```
   class AuthRequestHandler: public RequestHandlerImpl
   {
           public:
           void ProcessRequest(string request)
           {
                   cout<<"Authentication check..!\n";
                   RequestHandlerImpl::ProcessRequest
                   (request);
           }
   };
   ```

4. You can similarly define another server by creating a class called CompressRequestHandler by inheriting from RequestHandlerImpl.

   a. Implement ProcessRequest to define compression server tasks.

   b. At the end of the server processing tasks, pass user requests to a possible target server object of the service chain using RequestHandlerImpl::ProcessRequest.

   ```
   class CompressRequestHandler : public
   RequestHandlerImpl
   {
   ```

CHAPTER 8 DESIGN PATTERNS

```
    public:
    void ProcessRequest(string request)
    {
        cout<<"Data Compressed..!\n";
        RequestHandlerImpl::ProcessRequest
        (request);
    }
};
```

5. You can define another server class called CacheRequestHandler by inheriting from RequestHandlerImpl.

   a. Implement ProcessRequest to define cacher server handling tasks.

   b. At the end of the server processing tasks, pass user requests to a possible target server object of the service chain using RequestHandlerImpl::ProcessRequest.

```
class CacheRequestHandler : public RequestHandlerImpl
{
    public:
    void ProcessRequest(string request)
    {
        cout<<"Request Cached..!\n";
        RequestHandlerImpl::ProcessRequest
        (request);
    }
};
```

CHAPTER 8   DESIGN PATTERNS

6. Define client testing code to test service chain execution.

    ```
    void ClientCode(RequestHandler &handler)
    {
        string input = "data";
        handler.ProcessRequest(input);
    }
    ```

7. Define your main() code to define dynamic service chains using server objects.

    a. Define all your server objects and hold their pointers in respective server class pointers.

    b. Define a sample service chain using SetNextServer().

    c. Test the service chain by calling client code with inputs of one of the server objects.

    ```
    int main()
    {
        AuthRequestHandler *auth = new AuthRequestHandler;
        CompressRequestHandler *compress = new CompressRequestHandler;
        CacheRequestHandler *cache = new CacheRequestHandler;
        auth->SetNextServer(compress)->SetNextServer(cache);

        ClientCode(*auth);
        ClientCode(*compress);
        ClientCode(*cache);

        delete auth;
        delete compress;
    ```

CHAPTER 8　DESIGN PATTERNS

```
        delete cache;

        return 0;
    }
```

8. Let's test chainofresp.cc and observe the following.

    a. A sample service chain with three server objects is created.

    b. User requests are processed through the three server objects based on the service chain order.

    c. You can set new service chain orders and test them to observe more results.

    ```
    # g++ chainofresp.cc -o cor
    # ./cor
    Authentication check..!
    Data Compressed..!
    Request Cached..!
    Data Compressed..!
    Request Cached..!
    Request Cached..!
    ```

The chain of responsibility pattern created a service chain using three different server objects. Next, let's practice the following tasks.

Practice Tasks

Next, do the following tasks by extending the use case to practice the chain of responsibility pattern and understand its importance.

1. Introduce a new server, such as encryption.

2. Create new service chains by including your new server.

3. You can easily flexibly create new service chains without affecting existing class code.

4. Client requests can be processed through new service chains without changing the service chain accessing the interface.

Next, let's learn another important behavioral pattern called the template method to define system-level common algorithms and be able to change specific steps of the algorithm in subclasses as per requirements.

The Template Method

Template method pattern is useful to develop system-level common algorithms. It eliminates redundant code in general algorithm steps among system subclasses. Moreover, this specific pattern allows various objects to have a consistent algorithm executing steps and their own steps for introducing specialized behavior. Let's look at how to use the template method pattern to apply general algorithm steps for game characters' behaviors in a gaming world. Consider the following rules to execute the general algorithms for gaming characters in this task.

- Players and enemies must be implemented as separate classes in the gaming application.

- Assume players and enemies have similar plans of action to play the game. For example, players' or enemies' common plan of action steps to **observe** the gaming world, **explore paths**, and then **react to weapons, opponents, wealth,** and **secrets**.

- Players and enemies have the **same observation** and **exploration paths** and plan of action steps.

CHAPTER 8   DESIGN PATTERNS

- However, Players and enemies have **unique procedures** to implement steps such as **reacting with weapons**, **opponents**, **wealth** and **secrets**.

- Eliminate redundant code of plan of action algorithm steps and allow gaming characters to behave their own way.

THE TEMPLATE METHOD

Let's use the hands-on activity code snippets in the templatemethod.cc file.

1. Define the **general gaming character plan of action steps** in the following class.

   a. Define an abstract class called GameCharacter to create algorithm steps in a logical order inside PlanOfAction(). It is the template method. The steps in the method are overridden by player and enemy gaming characters.

   ```
   #include<iostream>
   using namespace std;
   class GameCharacter
   {
         public:
         void PlanOfAction()
         {
               Observes();
               ExplorePaths();
               ReactToOpponents();
               ReacToWeapons();
   ```

459

```
            ReacToWealth();
            ReacToSecrets();
    }
```

b. Implement **common steps** in the **plan of action algorithm**, such as **observing, exploring paths**, and actions against opponents. It reduces redundant code in player and enemy classes.

```
protected:
void Observes()
{
    std::cout << "Observing gaming evniornment\n";
}
void ExplorePaths()
{
    std::cout << "Exploring paths to move
    forward\n";
}
void ReactToOpponents()
{
    std::cout << "Attacking..\n";
}
```

c. **Declare the following virtual functions** to allow concrete classes, such as **players and enemies**. For example, define virtual functions such as **reacting to weapons, wealth, and secrets**.

```
        virtual void ReacToWeapons() = 0;
        virtual void ReacToWealth()  = 0;
        virtual void ReacToSecrets() {}
};
```

CHAPTER 8   DESIGN PATTERNS

2. Define a class called Player to implement player characters' plan of action algorithm-specific steps. It is inherited from the GameCharacter abstract class.

    a. ReacToWeapons defines a player's specific behavior in the PlanOfAction algorithm.

    b. ReacToWealth defines a player's specific behavior in the PlanOfAction algorithm.

    c. ReacToSecrets defines a player's specific behavior in the PlanOfAction algorithm.

```cpp
class Player : public GameCharacter
{
    protected:
    void ReacToWeapons()
    {
        std::cout << "Check opponents and run towards the weapons\n";
    }
    void ReacToWealth()
    {
        std::cout << "Check any danger events and run towards the wealth\n";
    }
    void ReacToSecrets()
    {
        std::cout << "Carefully explore paths and get the secret\n";
    }
};
```

CHAPTER 8   DESIGN PATTERNS

3. Define another class called Enemy to implement enemy characters' plan of action algorithm-specific steps. It is inherited from the GameCharacter abstract class.

   a. ReacToWeapons defines the enemies' specific behaviors in the PlanOfAction algorithm.

   b. ReacToWealth defines the enemies' specific behaviors in the PlanOfAction algorithm.

   c. ReacToSecrets defines the enemies' specific behaviors in the PlanOfAction algorithm.

   ```
   class Enemy : public GameCharacter
   {
           protected:
           void ReacToWeapons()
           {
                   std::cout << "Immediately jump and run towards the weapons\n";
           }
           void ReacToWealth()
           {
                   std::cout << "By attacking players and try to grab the wealth\n";
           }
   };
   ```

4. Define the following simple client code to execute the player or enemy's plan of execution.

   ```
   void ClientCode(GameCharacter *gc)
   {
           gc->PlanOfAction();
   }
   ```

CHAPTER 8   DESIGN PATTERNS

5. Define the `main()` testing code to execute the player's and enemies' game plan of action.

    a. Define a player object and pass it to the client code to execute the player's game plan of action.

    b. Define an enemy object and pass it to the client code to execute the enemy's game plan of action.

    ```
    int main()
    {
            std::cout << "Player actions:\n";
            Player *p1 = new Player;
            ClientCode(p1);
            std::cout << "\n";
            std::cout << "Enemy actions:\n";
            Enemy *e1 = new Enemy;
            ClientCode(e1);
            delete p1;
            delete e1;
            return 0;
    }
    ```

6. Let's execute template.cc and observe the following.

    a. Observe that player and enemy objects are created to test their sample plan of action.

    b. Observe that the player object's plan of action is distinct from the enemy object's plan of action.

    ```
    # g++ template.cc -o template
    # ./template
    Player actions:
    Observing gaming environment
    Exploring paths to move forward
    ```

463

CHAPTER 8　DESIGN PATTERNS

```
Attacking..
Check opponents and run toward the weapons
Check any danger events and run toward the wealth
Carefully explore paths and get the secret

Enemy actions:
Observing gaming environment
Exploring paths to move forward
Attacking..
Immediately jump and run toward the weapons
By attacking players and try to grab the wealth
```

The template method was used to define sample game players and enemies' common plan of action as a game algorithm. Next, let's continue to do tasks.

Practice Tasks

Next, do the following tasks by extending the use case to practice the template method pattern and understand its importance.

1. Introduce new steps in the common algorithm of the system superclass and you can observe that new algorithm behavior is available in subclasses.

2. Change new steps in subclasses as per your choice.

3. Observe that your code does not lead to redundancy in the common algorithm logical steps and is consistent across all subclasses.

4. You may also attempt to create new game characters and reuse the common algorithm defined in the superclass.

Summary

In this chapter, you learned the importance of design patterns—specifically, when and how to use them to address software development issues. Although you have not explored every design pattern, you have experimented with creational, structural, and behavioral patterns in important use cases. The hands-on activities taught you the importance of design patterns in solving software development issues without violating OOP principles.

The next chapter discusses event-driven programming for developing smart applications and simulators.

CHAPTER 9

Event-Driven Programming

In past chapters, you have learned OOP principles and approaches to easily handle ambiguities and issues with reusable, extendible, and easily usable software. On the other hand, to deploy software applications over the Internet, you use client-server or distributed applications architecture. These software applications' major challenges are handling service failures, changing existing services, introducing new services, and replicating existing services to handle scalability issues. However, software must be flexible for any enhancements and extensions to handle these challenges. Moreover, novel software such as IoT, smart applications, gaming software, and distributed applications must be designed and developed to meet scalability, reliability, and flexibility expectations.

To handle these challenges, it is necessary to deploy software from decoupled software components to offer scalable, reliable, and easily manageable services. Hence, failure of a component does not affect other components and enables flexibility in handling requests.

To support the decoupled software components colloboration, event-driven programming approaches use events as primary ways for communication and carrying out the software activities and transactions. Specifically, event-driven programming involves suitable events management and handling, and asynchronous methods for messages exchange. In event-driven programming, to carry out software

CHAPTER 9   EVENT-DRIVEN PROGRAMMING

application transactions, interactions among software components are modeled as publishing events, subscribing to events, and handling suitable events. For example, placing or canceling an order can be modeled as events in an online novel shopping application. Hence, the shopping application events can be handled flexibly to implement new services such as fast delivery, dynamic pricing, and allowing customers to change their address. This chapter explores event-driven programming approaches based on loosely coupled and decoupled components.

The chapter covers the following.

- The importance of event-driven programming
- Event-driven programming structure
- A quick practice of event-driven programming
- Design a simulator

The Importance of Event-Driven Programming

Over the Internet, client and server architecture are used for deploying most of the software applications. Usually, client-server software applications were developed to process user requests and synchronously send responses. Mainly, these applications are facing issues in case of delayed responses, server failures, missing request messages, error handling, and updating services. To handle these issues, software architecture must be flexible to introduce any changes.

Distributed application architectures have evolved to offer highly scalable, reliable, and easily updatable software services. To support distributed application architecture, software components must be decoupled, components should be assigned with a single responsibility

CHAPTER 9 EVENT-DRIVEN PROGRAMMING

only, and easier to collaborate with other components. In recent software development evolutions, distributed applications have been designed based on microservices architecture. Unlike monolithic application architecture (client and server), in microservice architecture, software interactions are seen as exchanging messages between producers and consumers. Complex software applications are carefully decomposed into multiple services to implement microservice application architecture to easily collaborate and carry out application tasks. As a producer, a software component usually generates events with necessary data for other components. On the other hand, consumer software components consume data and respond to events.

Event-driven programming approaches play a key role in supporting distributed applications and deploying microservice applications. Basically, event-driven programming addresses the software services' reliability, scalability, and update issues. To handle these challenges, event-driven programming supports decoupled software components communication and collaboration by offering publish and subscribe, and asynchronous methods of messages exchange.

In summary, event-driven programming focuses on modeling suitable event services, subscribing to the events, publishing events, managing events using suitable message queues, and handling the scheduling and executions of events.

Key Concepts

Event-driven programming's primary goal is to provide flexibility in connecting decoupled software components (services or microservices) to carry out software tasks and support scalable, reliable, and easily updatable services. Hence, it should enable a flexible deployment environment for distributed applications such as IoT, novel smart applications, gaming applications, and Internet applications.

CHAPTER 9   EVENT-DRIVEN PROGRAMMING

To work with event programming, you must understand its key concepts.

- Producers and consumers
- Events
- Events management
- Asynchronous messaging

Producers and Consumers

To enable the decoupling of services and offering collaboration among services, developers can view complex application services as producer and consumer services. An application performing an action means one of its services (producer) produces data or events for another service to complete the action. Here, you can observe producers publishing events and data.

On the other hand, consumer services check for notifications to events with suitable data to carry out the application actions. It means consumer services either subscribe to get notifications or do polling activity to retrieve events and inspect data for proceeding with an application action. A service can perform both producer and consumer roles in software tasks. Hence, in event-driven programming you usually see complex applications services as producers/consumers. As part of handling producer and consumer activities, you need to understand the events and data exchanged between producer and consumer services.

Events

Events are key to initiating actions from a software application and carrying out tasks. Let's discuss a few important details of events.

Usually, an application state changes, actions, transactions, and operations are modeled as events. Events can be represented as important messages with necessary fields to perform actions of a software application. An event carries important details such as source and destination identifiers, type of event, priority, data, lifetime, and actions. Based on application tasks, events can be modeled by carefully choosing necessary fields. In event-driven programming, producers generate events, and consumers consume events for the software's actions. For example, you can find the following events: clicking any GUI components, a customer sending a request to perform a transaction, and receiving inputs from various actors and components in a software application.

Events can be classified into the following categories based on their characteristics.

- **Prioritized events**: Based on the priority of events, scheduling, and execution policies are defined.

- **Persistent or nonpersistent**: Persistent events are stored permanently. Nonpersistent events are destroyed once they are processed.

- **Unicast, multicast, or broadcast messages**: Unicast events are delivered to a single destination. Multicast events are delivered to a group of destinations. Broadcast events are delivered to all.

- **Repeatable and nonrepeatable**: Repeatable events can be handled multiple times and nonrepeatable events are handled only once.

From the event characteristics, you observe that events must be managed and handled using suitable data structures.

Events Management

In event-driven programming, queues are set up to store and manage events. Event queues are the major resources accessed by producers, consumers, and event handlers. Usually, all producer-generated events need to be stored in a suitable queue for further processing and consumers should subscribe for the interested events. Hence, consumers can inspect and pull the events from the event queues without waiting, or event handlers can notify the event's subscribers (consumers). Event handlers set up event queues and apply scheduling policies to execute events, handle failures of events, and replay events.

Standard message brokers have evolved to offer reliable, scalable, and fault-tolerant event management. For instance, to deploy novel distributed applications, IoT and smart applications, developers are using **RabbitMQ** and **Apache ActiveMQ**. On the other hand, developers are using Apache Kafka to store persistent events. It helps log all event handling, failure of event handling, and replaying events.

Asynchronous Methods for Message Exchange

To enable the decoupling of services and flexible ways for message exchange, it is necessary to avoid blocking of services in sending and receiving messages. Moreover, a decoupled service to send a request need not assume whether destination services are running. It means a decoupled service should be able to send requests to another service independent of the destination service running status (active, blocked, or stopped).

In event-driven programming to enable asynchronous methods of message exchange, publish and subscribe policies are implemented. A decoupled service can publish its events independent of the receiver state. Producer services can send events to event queues and leave the rest to the application behavior for handling events. It avoids unnecessary blocking of producer services.

Similarly, consumers (another decoupled service) can subscribe with an application for only interested events. Later, consumer services can be notified about events from the event handlers. On the other hand,

CHAPTER 9   EVENT-DRIVEN PROGRAMMING

consumer services can poll event queues and inspect events for receiving and handling them independently. It means consumer services need not wait to receive events or responses from other services.

In summary, publish and subscribe policies enable producer and consumer services to exchange messages flexibly using event queues and offer nonblocking approaches to exchange messages. Moreover, having suitable event queues allows storing events permanently, and handling the events at decoupled services convenience for reliable event processing.

Advantages and Use Cases

Before practicing event-driven programming, let's discuss its advantages.

- It enables easier to change, update, and introduce new services in software applications.

- It is easier to scale necessary services of software applications.

- In case of failure of a service do not affect the entire application. Event-driven programming enables flexible event delivery options: delayed execution, retries and replays of events.

- Event-driven programming offers asynchronous ways to message between producers and consumers. Hence, it avoids unnecessary blocking of services on waiting responses and sending messages.

- It is possible to analyze events and introduce new services quickly.

- It is possible to use events to update the service state and handle any critical updates quickly.

- Event-driven programming offers software flexibility in terms of changes to decoupled services.
- Enables and supports novel distributed applications.
- Enables novel application architectures such as microservices.

In summary, event-driven programming supports the following important use cases.

- Distributed applications deployment
- Microservices based applications
- Serverless applications deployment
- Novel cloud services, such as Function as a Service
- Novel smart and IoT applications
- Future generation core networks (5G and 6G service-based architecture)
- Real-time data analytics services

This section explained the importance of event-driven programming and its concepts. Next, let's discuss event-driven programming structures.

Structure

This section teaches the basic programming constructs to implement event-based applications. You learn how to connect the event programming constructs to develop event-based applications such as gaming applications, real-world smart applications, and simulators. In general, event-based programming includes the following programming constructs.

CHAPTER 9   EVENT-DRIVEN PROGRAMMING

- **Events**: An event is a basic programming construct of event-based programming. Usually, an event is associated with a unique identifier (id) and code to be executed as a response to handling the event. Events can be viewed as special messages to communicate between software components (objects). In OOP, events are implemented with the help of classes.
    - For instance, an IoT sensor generates a warning event for a smart application then the smart application handles the warning event by executing the corresponding event code.
    - In gaming applications, characters generate events, and the application reacts to the events by executing the necessary action code.
    - In network simulators, network equipment generates events such as packet generation and packet drop, the network simulator executes the event corresponding code.
- **Event handlers**: To manage and handle events, event handlers are implemented as classes. The primary task of event handlers is to manage events received from the objects (producers) and store them in suitable event queues for consumers. In general, event handlers are for subscribing to and handling events. To handle a variety of events, use the following types of queues in event handler classes.
    - General queues are for handling the events according to a first come/first serve policy.

- Priority queues are used for handling the events based on the event's priority.
- Based on application requirements, event handlers may use multiple types of queues.

- **Events scheduling policies**: Another primary task of event handlers is to schedule events and execute them with destination objects.
  - It involves accessing events from queues based on queue principles and executing them with specific objects (consumers).
  - It is possible to implement custom events scheduling policies to meet application requirements.
  - Event handlers schedule events from all available event queues and execute with specific objects (consumers).

Let's learn basic approaches to using events and event handlers in C++.

Using C++ for Events and Event Handlers

This section examines two important event programming constructs.

- Events classes in C++
- Events management and handling classes in C++

EVENTS AND MANAGEMENT CLASSES

For example, you can use the following code snippets in the events.h file to model application events.

1. Define **an event class** with the following basic data members and member functions **to model application events.**

    a. Define event id for uniquely identifying events of the application.

    b. Define the event id accessing functions.

    c. Declare a **virtual function** to **handle a variety of events** and corresponding code at runtime based on object type.

    ```
    #include<iostream> #include<queue>
    #include<vector>
    #include<experimental/random>
    using namespace std;
    class Event
    {
          unsigned int eventid;
          public:
          Event (unsigned int id)
          {
                eventid = id;
          }
          unsigned int getEventId()
          {
                return eventid;
          }
          virtual void handleEvent () = 0;
    };
    ```

CHAPTER 9   EVENT-DRIVEN PROGRAMMING

2. Define an example of an **event management and handling class** as follows.

   a. Declare an **event identifier** data member.

   b. Declare suitable **event queues** for managing events, such as normal or priority queues.

   c. Declare a suitable number of event queues.

   ```
   class EventHandler
   {
       protected:

       unsigned int eid;
       std::priority_queue<Event*,
       std::vector<Event *, std::allocator<Event*> >,
       eventComparator> equeue1;
       std::priority_queue<Event*,
       std::vector<Event *, std::allocator<Event*> >,
                   eventComparator> equeue2;
   ```

3. Execute the event handler constructor to initialize necessary data members.

   ```
   public:
       EventHandler ()
       {
           eid = 0;
       }
   ```

4. The following example event subscription functions can be executed to handle the subscription of events from publishers.

   a. To store or insert events into the event queue.

   b. Based on event id, allow or disallow event subscriptions.

CHAPTER 9   EVENT-DRIVEN PROGRAMMING

c. Event handlers can select the specific event queues based on event ids to store events.

```
void subscribeEvent (Event* newEvent)
{
        if (newEvent->getEventId()>=0)
        {
                cout<<"Event inserted\n";
                cout<<"event id "<<newEvent->
                getEventId()<<"\n";
                equeue1.push(newEvent);
        }
}
```

5. Define example event schedulings and execution policies as follows.

   a. For example, design a simple policy that executes events from the equeue1 and then executes events from the equeue2.

   b. After handling events, delete the corresponding events from the queue.

```
void executeEventOnTarget()
{
        while (! equeue1.empty ())
        {
                Event * nextEvent =
                equeue1.top ();
                equeue1.pop ();
                eid = nextEvent->getEventId();
                nextEvent->handleEvent ();
                delete nextEvent;
        }
```

CHAPTER 9   EVENT-DRIVEN PROGRAMMING

```
                  while (! equeue2.empty ())
                  {
                          Event * nextEvent =
                          equeue2.top ();
                          equeue2.pop ();
                          eid = nextEvent->getEventId();
                          nextEvent->handleEvent ();
                          delete nextEvent;
                  }
          }
    };
```

Well done. You have learned the basic programming constructs events and event handlers for event-based applications.

Next, let's discuss application events and subscribe from the interested classes using event handlers.

Implementing Application Events and Subscribing to Classes

Let's discuss how to execute application events using an event class.

SAMPLE APPLICATION EVENTS IMPLEMENTATION

Use the following code snippets in the `customevents.h` file.

1. Include events modeling class from `events.h` to implement the following **application events**.

2. Define an **application event class**, such as **sampleEvent1**, by **inheriting** from the **Event** class as follows.

CHAPTER 9   EVENT-DRIVEN PROGRAMMING

a. In your application event constructor (sampleEvent1()), initialize all necessary data members of sampleEvent1 and Event.

b. **Implement an event-handling virtual function** with necessary actions to handle the application-specific events.

```
#include"events.h"
using namespace std;
class sampleEvent1 : public Event
{
      public:
      sampleEvent1 (unsigned int eid):Event(eid)
      {
      }
      void handleEvent()
      {
            cout<<"Sample event 1 handling\n";
      }
};
```

3. Similarly, define **another application event** class, such as sampleEvent2 by inheriting from the Event class as follows.

   a. Initialize all necessary data members in sampleEvent2().

   b. Implement an event-handling virtual function with necessary actions to handle the application events in sampleEvent2.

```
class sampleEvent2 : public Event
{
      public:
      sampleEvent2 (unsigned int eid):Event(eid)
      {
      }
```

481

CHAPTER 9 EVENT-DRIVEN PROGRAMMING

```
            void handleEvent()
            {
                    cout<<"Sample event 2 handling\n";
            }
    };
```

Next, let's learn how to subscribe and handle application events.

APPLICATION EVENTS SUBSCRIPTION HANDLING CLASS

Use the following code snippets in the `subscribers.h` file.

1. Define **sample IoT application events** handling class by inheriting from the `EventHandler` class as follows.

    a. Define your application events handling class with all necessary data members and member functions.

    b. Define a default constructor to initialize necessary data members.

    c. Define a parameter constructor to handle the subscription for application events.

```
    class IoTSensors: public EventHandler
    {
            EventHandler ih;
            public:
                    IoTSensors()
                    {
                    }
                    IoTSensors(EventHandler &eh)
                    {
```

```
                    eh.subscribeEvent (new
                    sampleEvent1 (2));
                    eh.subscribeEvent (new
                    sampleEvent2 (10));
                    eh.subscribeEvent (new
                    sampleEvent1 (3));
                    eh.subscribeEvent (new
                    sampleEvent2 (20));
            }
    };
```

2. Do the following to test your event handling code.

    a. Include `subscribers.h` for accessing subscriber classes.

    b. Define the `EventHandle` object to pass it to the custom class and initiate events scheduling and execution.

    c. Define necessary objects of your application classes: as defined in subscriptions for events in constructors, event subscriptions are done as soon as objects get created.

This section walked you through important programming constructs such as `Events` and `EventHandlers`.

Next, let's practice event-driven programming through simple activities.

Quick Practice

This section features a quick exercise for developing and testing a simple event driver program using event-driven programming constructs.

CHAPTER 9 EVENT-DRIVEN PROGRAMMING

As part of this activity, you do the following tasks.

1. Define events, creating a class with necessary data members and virtual functions.

2. Define events handling class with a priority queue to schedule events based on the event's id order (in ascending order).

3. Define application events by inheriting from the Event class.

4. Test your sample code by subscribing to sample events of the applications in the main() code. It helps in understanding how two decpoupled applications events are handled to carry out specific tasks.

Let's start with a sample application events class and the events handling classes.

SAMPLE APPLICATION EVENTS HANDLING CODE

Use the following code snippets in the events2.h file.

1. Define an application-specific event class with the following basic data members and member functions.

    a. Define event id for uniquely identifying events of the application.

    b. Define event id accessing functions.

    c. Declare a virtual function to handle application events at runtime based on object type.

    ```
    #include<iostream>
    #include<queue>
    #include<vector>
    ```

```
#include <experimental/random>
using namespace std;
class Event
{
        unsigned int eventid;
        public:
        Event (unsigned int id)
        {
                eventid = id;
        }
        unsigned int getEventId()
        {
                return eventid;
        }
        virtual void handleEvent () = 0;
};
```

2. Define an example event handling class as follows.

   a. Declare an event identifier data member.

   b. Declare a priority queue for handling events based on the event's id order. The lowest id event should be executed first from the event queue.

   ```
   struct eventComparator
   {
           bool operator() (Event * left, Event * right)
           {
                   return left->getEventId() > right->getEventId();
           }
   };
   ```

CHAPTER 9   EVENT-DRIVEN PROGRAMMING

```
class EventHandler
{
    protected:
    unsigned int eid;
    std::priority_queue<Event*,
    std::vector<Event *, std::allocator<Event*> >,
    eventComparator> equeue;
```

3. Using the event handler constructor initialized necessary data members as follows.

```
public:
    EventHandler ()
    {
        eid = 0;
    }
```

4. To handle the subscription of events from producers of software components, implement the following function.

   a. Insert events into the priority queues.

   b. Do not process the events with id >100.

```
void subscribeEvent (Event* newEvent)
{
    if (newEvent->getEventId()<= 100)
    {
        cout<<"Event inserted\n";
        cout<<"event id "<<newEvent->
        getEventId()<<"\n";
        equeue.push(newEvent);
    }
}
```

5. Define sample events scheduling and execution function as follows.

```
void executeEventOnTarget()
{
    while (! equeue.empty ())
    {
        Event * nextEvent = equeue.top ();
        equeue.pop ();
        eid = nextEvent->getEventId();
        nextEvent->handleEvent ();
        delete nextEvent;
    }
}
};
```

This activity used the base `Event` and `EventHandler` classes for application-specific events. Next, let's use these classes to handle events.

Next, let's look at two sample application events to test a simple event-handling program.

CUSTOM EVENTS SUBSCRIPTION AND TESTING

Use the following code snippets in the `eventstest.cc` file.

1. Include your `events2.h` class to execute application-specific events.

2. Define your custom event class, such as `sampleEvent1` by inheriting from the `Event` class as follows.

    a. Initialize all necessary data members of `sampleEvent1`.

CHAPTER 9   EVENT-DRIVEN PROGRAMMING

  b. Apply the event handling virtual function with the necessary actions to handle the application events.

```
#include"events2.h"
using namespace std;
class sampleEvent1 : public Event
{
    public:
    sampleEvent1 (unsigned int eid):Event(eid)
    {
    }
    void handleEvent()
    {
        cout<<"Sample event 1 handling\n";
    }
};
```

3. Define another sample event class, such as sampleEvent2 by inheriting from the Event class as follows.

  a. Initialize all necessary data members of sampleEvent2.

  b. Implement the event handling virtual function with necessary actions to handle the event.

```
class sampleEvent2 : public Event
{
    public:
    sampleEvent2 (unsigned int eid):Event(eid)
    {
    }
    void handleEvent()
    {
        cout<<"Sample event 2 handling\n";
    }
};
```

CHAPTER 9   EVENT-DRIVEN PROGRAMMING

4. To test your event-based application, do the following in main().

   a. Define an EventHandler object to subscribe for custom events.

   b. Subscribe for ten sample events of each custom event using the loop.

      i. Create sample application events objects by passing event ids (e.g., sampleEvent1 id =2, sampleEvent2 id = 4).

      ii. Pass the sample application events objects in the member function: subscribeEvent of EventHandler object eh.

   c. Schedule the execution of events using the event handler object and its member function. executeEventOnTarget().

   ```
   using namespace std;
   int main ()
   {
           EventHandler eh;
           for (int i=0;i<10;i++)
           {
                   cout << "Generating events " << i << '\n';
                   eh.subscribeEvent (new sampleEvent1 (2));
                   eh.subscribeEvent (new sampleEvent2 (4));
           }
           eh.executeEventOnTarget();
           return 0;
   }
   ```

   d. Let's test the sample events-based applications and observe the results.

   ```
   # g++ eventstest.cc -o eventstest
   # ./eventstest
   Generating events 0
   Event inserted
   ```

```
event id 2
Event inserted
event id 4
Generating events 1
Event inserted
event id 2
Event inserted
event id 4
..
Generating events 9
Event inserted
event id 2
Event inserted
event id 4
Sample event 1 handling
Sample event 1 handling
..
Sample event 2 handling
Sample event 2 handling
```

From the results, you can observe that two decoupled applications events are handled according to their event id order in executing main tasks. Here sample events with id 2 are executed first, then id 4 events are executed. You should test it by changing event ids of the applications to observe event order execution. Specifically, test results when applications events with id >100 are subscribed to the event handler.

Next, let's design a simple simulator using the event-based programming constructs.

CHAPTER 9   EVENT-DRIVEN PROGRAMMING

Hands-on Activity: Design a Simulator

In this hands-on activity, you learn how to implement a simple simulator using event-driven programing constructs for simulating the behavior of a smart application comprising two decoupled services from IoT sensors and smart vehicles. Simplified services of IoT sensors and smart vehicles are defined to simulate our sample smart application. The smart application uses simplified **IoTSensorsHandler** and **SmartVehiclesHandler** classes **to realize the smart application behavior.**

Let's do the following tasks to simulate smart application behaviors.

1. The proposed simple smart application includes IoTSensorsHandler objects and SmartVehiclesHandler objects.

2. Define an **IoTSensorsHandler** class with sample functionalities and it is useful for subscribing to **warning** and **emergency** events.

   a. Create **two custom smart application events** called **warning** (event id = 4) and **emergency (event id =2).**

   b. **E**mergency events must be handled before **warning events** during the smart application execution. Hence, events must be inserted in a priority queue.

   c. Define the IoTSensorsHandler class with a **sample function** to **react to smart vehicle events.**

3. Define a **SmartVehiclesHandler** class with sample functionalities and it is useful for subscribing to **data** and **aggregate** events.

   a. Define two custom events called data (event id = 5) and aggregate (event id = 6).

   b. Data events must be handled before aggregate events during the smart application execution. Hence, these events also must be inserted in a priority queue.

CHAPTER 9 EVENT-DRIVEN PROGRAMMING

4. SmartVehiclesHandler objects are associated with specific IoTSensorsHandler objects. After receiving data events, a SmartVehiclesHandler generates additional events to IoTSensorsHandler objects.

5. During **smart application execution**, **events** are generated for IoTSensorsHandler and SmartVehiclesHandler objects. Based on the priority of event ids, the events should be handled.

6. Simulate all the events of the proposed smart application and test it.

7. Further develop the proposed sample smart application by implementing the following.

    - A IoTSensorsHandler class **to subscribe** and handle **warning** and **emergency** events

    - A SmartVehiclesHandler class **to subscribe** and handle **data** and **aggregate** events

8. Test the smart application events simulation by creating sample IoTSensorsHandler and SmartVehiclesHandler objects.

IoTSensorsHandler Events

This section examines the following three concepts through related activities.

- Uses the events.h class to create smart application events such as "emergency" and "warning".

- Generates the smart application events as warningEvent and emergencyEvent classes.

- Implements IoTSensorsHandler for subscriptions and handling the warning and emergency events.

CHAPTER 9 EVENT-DRIVEN PROGRAMMING

Let's go over inheriting an event class for a smart application warning and emergency events.

IOT SENSORS CUSTOM EVENTS

Let's use the following code snippets in `subscribers1.h` file.

1. Define a `warningEvent` class to implement warning events.

   a. Define `warningEvent` class by inheriting the `Event` class.

   b. Define constructors of the `warningEvent` class to initialize the event id (e.g, warning event Id = 4) and any important data members.

   c. Implement sample warning event handling code to be executed on receiving warning events.

   d. Inside, the warning event handling code checks the event id and executes the code.

```cpp
#include"events.h"
using namespace std;
class warningEvent : public Event
{
    public:
    warningEvent (unsigned int eid):Event(eid)
    {
    }
    void handleEvent()
    {
        if (getEventId() == 4)
        {
            cout<<"Handle IoT sensor  warning "<<getEventId()<<"\n";
        }
```

CHAPTER 9 EVENT-DRIVEN PROGRAMMING

```
                else
                {
                        cout<<"Handle warning \n";
                }
        }
};
```

2. Define an emergencyEvent class to implement emergency events.

   a. Define the emergencyEvent class by inheriting the Event class.

   b. Define constructors of the emergencyEvent class to initialize the event id (e.g, emergency event Id = 2) and any important data members.

   c. Implement sample emergency event handling code to be executed on receiving emergency events.

   d. Inside, the emergency event handling code checks the event id and executes the code.

```
class emergencyEvent : public Event
{
        public:
        emergencyEvent (unsigned int eid):Event(eid)
        {
        }
        void handleEvent()
        {
                if (getEventId() == 2)
                {
                        cout<<"Handle IoT sensor emergency "<<getEventId()<<"\n";
                }
```

```
                else
                {
                    cout<<"Handle emergency \n";
                }
            }
        };
```

3. Implement the `IoTSensorsHandler` event handling code as follows.

    a. Define the `IoTSensorsHandler` class by inheriting the `EventHandler` class.

    b. Define the default `IoTSensorsHandler` constructor to initialize its data members.

    c. Define another `IoTSensorsHandler` constructor with `EventHandler` class object for subscribing to warning and emergency events. Assign emergency events with high priority compared to warning events.

    ```
    class IoTSensorsHandler: public EventHandler
    {
            EventHandler ih;
            public:
                    IoTSensorsHandler()
                    {
                    }
                    IoTSensorsHandler(EventHandler &eh)
                    {
                            eh.subscribeEvent (new
                            emergencyEvent (2));
                            eh.subscribeEvent (new
                            emergencyEvent (2));
    ```

CHAPTER 9 EVENT-DRIVEN PROGRAMMING

```
                    eh.subscribeEvent (new
                    emergencyEvent (2));
                    eh.subscribeEvent (new
                    emergencyEvent (2));
                    eh.subscribeEvent (new
                    warningEvent (4));
                    eh.subscribeEvent (new
                    warningEvent (4));
                    eh.subscribeEvent (new
                    warningEvent (4));
                    eh.subscribeEvent (new
                    warningEvent (4));
            }
```

4. Define another important member function in the IoTSensorsHandler class to react to smart vehicle data events.

    a. On receiving a data event from a SmartVehiclesHandler object, the IoTSensorsHandler object handles it as an emergency event.

    ```
                void actOnEvent()
                {
                        cout<<"React to smart vehicle event\n";
                        ih.subscribeEvent (new
                        emergencyEvent (2));
                        ih.executeEventOnTarget();
                }
        };
    ```

Next, let's define another two smart application events to be handled by SmartVehiclesHandler objects.

CHAPTER 9 EVENT-DRIVEN PROGRAMMING

SmartVehiclesHandler Custom Events

This section examines the following three concepts.

- Using the events.h class to create new smart application events such as data and aggregate to be handled by SmartVehiclesHandler

- Implementing the new smart application events as dataEvent and aggregateEvent classes

- Implementing SmartVehiclesHandler for subscriptions and handling the warning and emergency events

Let's start with custom events classes inheriting the event class.

SMART VEHICLE CUSTOM EVENTS

Use the following code snippets in the subscribers2.h file.

1. Define a dataEvent class to execute smart application data events.

   a. Define the dataEvent class by inheriting the Event class.

   b. Define constructors of the dataEvent class to initialize the event id (e.g, data event Id = 5) and any important data members.

   c. Implement sample data event handling code to be executed on receiving data events.

   d. Inside, data event handling code inside the handleEvent to check the event id and execute the code using a specific IoTSensorsHandler object.

      i. IoTSensorsHandler object handles it as an emergency event.

497

CHAPTER 9 EVENT-DRIVEN PROGRAMMING

```
using namespace std;
class dataEvent : public Event
{
    IoTSensorsHandler s1;
    public:
    dataEvent (IoTSensorsHandler &s,unsigned int
    eid):Event(eid)
    {
        s1 = s;
    }
    void handleEvent()
    {
        if (getEventId() == 5)
        {
            cout<<"Handle Vehicle critical
            sensor data "<<getEventId()<<"\n";
            s1.actOnEvent();
        }
        else
        {
            cout<<"Handle Vehicle normal
            data \n";
        }
    }
};
```

2. Define an `aggregateEvent` class to implement data aggregation events.

   a. Define the `aggregateEvent` class by inheriting the `Event` class.

   b. Define constructors of the `aggregateEvent` class to initialize the event id (e.g, aggregate event Id = 6) and any important data members.

CHAPTER 9 EVENT-DRIVEN PROGRAMMING

c. Implement sample aggregate event handling code inside the handleEvent to be executed on receiving aggregate events.

```
class aggregateEvent : public Event
{
      public:
      aggregateEvent (unsigned int eid):Event(eid)
      {
      }
      void handleEvent()
      {
            if (getEventId() == 6)
            {
                  cout<<"Handle Vehicle sensors data
                  aggregating "<<getEventId()<<"\n";
            }
            else
            {
                  cout<<"Handle Vehicle data
                  checking \n";
            }
      }
};
```

3. Implement a SmartVehiclesHandler event handling code as follows.

   a. Define the SmartVehiclesHandler class by inheriting the EventHandler class.

   b. Define the default SmartVehiclesHandler constructor to initialize the SmartVehiclesHandler class data members, if any.

499

CHAPTER 9   EVENT-DRIVEN PROGRAMMING

c. Define another `SmartVehiclesHandler` constructor with an `EventHandler` class object for subscribing to data (id = 5) and aggregating (id = 6) events. Assign data events with high priority compared to aggregate events.

d. As defined in subscribing to events code in the constructor, hence all `SmartVehiclesHandler` objects subscribed to data and aggregate events.

```
class SmartVehiclesHandler: public EventHandler
{
      public:
      SmartVehicle(EventHandler &eh)
      {
            IoTSensorsHandler sensor1;
            IoTSensorsHandler sensor2;
            eh.subscribeEvent (new dataEvent
            (sensor1,5));
            eh.subscribeEvent (new dataEvent
            (sensor2,5));
            eh.subscribeEvent (new
            aggregateEvent (6));
            eh.subscribeEvent (new
            aggregateEvent (200));
/
      }
};
```

Well done. You have implemented `IoTSensorsHandler`, `SmartVehiclesHandler`, and smart application events.

Next, let's simulate the sample smart application and test it.

CHAPTER 9　EVENT-DRIVEN PROGRAMMING

SmartApplication Simulation

This section goes through the following activities.

- Using `subscribers1.h` and `subscribers2.h` to subscribe events with `IoTSensorsHandler` and `SmartVehiclesHandler` objects.

- Defining a sample number of `IoTSensorsHandler` and `SmartVehiclesHandler` objects to simulate sample application warning, emergency, data, and aggregate events.

- Defining an `EventHandle` object for scheduling and executing `IoTSensorsHandler` and `SmartVehiclesHandler` objects generating events.

Let's start with `main()`.

> **SMART APPLICATION SIMULATION**

Use the following code snippets in the smartapptest.cc file.

1. Do the following tasks in `main()`.

    a. Define an `EventHandling` object for executing the `IoTSensorsHandler` and `SmartVehiclesHandler` handling events.

    b. Define a suitable number of `IoTSensorsHandler` objects by assigning the event handling object.

      i. As defined in the event subscription in the constructor code, sample warning and emergency events are subscribed with `IoTSensorsHandler` objects.

c. Define a suitable number of SmartVehiclesHandler objects by assigning the event handling object.

   i. As defined in the event subscription in the constructor code, sample data, and aggregate events are subscribed with SmartVehiclesHandler objects.

d. Schedule execution of all IoTSensorsHandler and SmartVehiclesHandler handling events using executeEventOnTarget.

```
#include"subscribers.h"
#include"subscribers2.h"
using namespace std;
int main ()
{
        EventHandler eh;
        IoTSensorsHandler i1(eh);
        SmartVehiclesHandler sv(eh);
        eh.executeEventOnTarget();
        return 0;
}
```

2. Test your code using the following commands and observe the results.

```
# g++ smartapptest.cc -o smartapp
# ./smartapp
Event inserted
event id 2
Event inserted
event id 2
..
event id 4
Event inserted
```

```
event id 4
Event inserted
..
event id 5
Event inserted
..
Event inserted
event id 200
Handle IoT sensor emergency 2
Handle IoT sensor emergency 2
..
Handle IoT sensor  warning 4
Handle IoT sensor  warning 4
```
Handle Vehicle critical sensor data 5
Reacto to smart vehicle event
```
Event inserted
event id 2
```
Handle IoT sensor emergency 2
Handle Vehicle critical sensor data 5
Reacto to smart vehicle event
Event inserted
event id 2
Handle IoT sensor emergency 2
```
Handle Vehicle sensors data aggregating 6
Handle Vehicle data checking
```

The results show emergency events are handled first, and then warning events are handled. Moreover, smart vehicle data events are raising emergency events, which are handled by `IoTSensorsHandler` objects immediately. These results are shown by highlighting respective messages.

CHAPTER 9   EVENT-DRIVEN PROGRAMMING

Summary

This chapter explained the importance of event-driven programming for handling challenges in novel applications and application architectures such as microservices. You have learned important programming constructs for event-driven applications. Specifically, you practiced event-driven programming for implementing sample smart application simulators. In summary, you learned about event-driven programming activities in publish-subscribe software development, asynchronous ways to collaborate with objects, and designing novel games and smart applications.

The next chapter explores using Python and Solidity to implement OOP concepts.

Practice: Hands-on Activities

1. List the events generated in the following applications.

    a. Smart energy management

    b. Smart home

    c. Smart environment monitoring

2. Describe various approaches to handle the following smart application-generated sample events.

    a. Smart energy management application

    b. Smart home application

    c. Smart environment monitoring application

CHAPTER 9 EVENT-DRIVEN PROGRAMMING

3. List possible publishers and subscribers in the following applications.

   a. Weather forecast application

   b. Any social network

   c. Any online shopping application

4. Simulate the following simple smart home application.

   a. Your smart home application needs to handle the following events.

      i. When a visitor comes, a surveillance camera should raise an event.

      ii. Generate warning events in case any house-hold device is running for a longer time.

      iii. Generate emergency events in case of gas leakage, unexpected fire detection, and water leakage.

   b. Simulate the necessary number of events and event handler classes to implement a smart home application.

   c. Test your smart home application by generating sample events.

CHAPTER 10

A Brief Introduction to OOP in Python and Solidity

In previous chapters, you practiced OOP by doing hands-on activities related to software application development. Mainly, you have practiced OOP concepts through C++ language. Moreover, having a good understanding of OOP principles and knowledge, you can easily learn any OOP language. This chapter introduces two important OOP languages: Python and Solidity. Specifically, you quickly learn Python and Solidity basic programming constructs related to OOP and practice them through various hands-on activities. Learning Python enables you to work in important computer science fields such as data science, machine learning (ML), and artificial intelligence (AI). On the other hand, learning Solidity helps you explore popular decentralized applications such as blockchain.

Discussing Python and Solidity in depth is beyond the scope of this book. However, this chapter exposes you to the growing interest in technology.

This chapter covers the following topics.

- Introduction to other important OOP languages
- Learning Python basic programming constructs for OOP

- Quickly practicing Python way of OOP
- Learning Solidity basic programming constructs for OOP
- Quickly practicing Solidity way of OOP

Other Important OOP Languages

There are many popular OOP languages. OOP principles are primary concepts for developing software applications in many programming languages such as C++, C#, Java, Python, Visual Basic .NET, JavaScript, PHP, Ruby, Emerald, and Solidity.

Python is known for its popularity in many domains, such as web applications, data science applications, AI and ML applications, and network applications. Hence, it helps you easily practice OOP concepts in Python and strengthen your programming skills to advance your career in advanced computer science fields. Moreover, Python is simple to learn.

Solidity is a primary language for developing complex distributed applications such as blockchain. Solidity programming constructs are discussed to explain how fundamental OOP concepts are helpful to learning any new OOP language. Moreover, Solidity programming syntax is similar to C++. Hence, it helps you easily learn Solidity programming.

The Importance of Python Programming

Python is one of the most popular high-level programming languages. Basically, it is a scripting language. Hence, to run Python programs, you need a Python interpreter. Python programs are executed in terms of line by line. It was invented by Guido van Rossum in 1991. Python supports multiple programming approaches such as procedural, imperative,

CHAPTER 10   A BRIEF INTRODUCTION TO OOP IN PYTHON AND SOLIDITY

dynamically typed, and object-oriented. Hence, writing Python scripts is simple and easier to understand. Let's check Python language's few important features.

- It is platform-independent. Python programs can be deployed over Windows or Linux operating systems using Python interpreters.

- It is dynamically typed. There is no need to declare data types of variables. During runtime, the actual data type of variables is decided.

- Python supports OOP features such as classes, data encapsulation, hiding, inheritance, and polymorphism.

- Moreover, Pythons supports a rich set of built-in data types and libraries for simplifying the programming related to advanced computer science fields such as ML, AI, data science, and networking.

- Python programming syntax is highly simplified and easier to use.

Python language simplified the development activities of the following applications.

- Useful for developing web applications, scientific applications, and a variety of software applications.

- Python has a rich set of libraries for developing data science and analytical applications.

- Python offers AI, ML, and data analysis tools.

- Python supports many libraries for designing networking and security applications and tools.

CHAPTER 10   A BRIEF INTRODUCTION TO OOP IN PYTHON AND SOLIDITY

The Importance of Solidity Programming

Blockchain technology and its applications have recently been primary security solutions for many domains. Blockchain technology applies a secured distributed ledger over peer-to-peer network nodes to carry out and store transactions using cryptographic hashing algorithms. Blockchain technology plays a key role in securing a wide range of applications such as finance, healthcare, government services, IoT, and many others. Ethereum is one of the popular decentralized blockchain platforms that offers deployment of blockchain application transactions as smart contracts. For example, you can implement the following transactions as smart contracts: buying or selling products on the Internet, exchanging digital currency between online accounts, managing digital records, and so forth.

Developers can understand a smart contract as a combination of application state variables and programming logic to store, access, or update state variables. C++ programmers can view smart contracts as the implementation of classes. Gavin Wood, the co-founder of Ethereum, invented the Solidity programming language to create smart contracts. The smart contracts are deployed and tested using an Ethereum Virtual Machine (EVM). To learn the development of blockchain applications Solidity programming is highly helpful. This chapter covers the basics of Solidity for creating smart contracts and testing them using the online browser Remix.

You should learn Solidity for the following reasons.

- Solidity's syntax is similar to C++ and JavaScript. Hence, it is easier to explore and learn Solidity.

- Solidity is based on OOP principles. It supports data encapsulation, data hiding, inheritance, and polymorphism.

CHAPTER 10   A BRIEF INTRODUCTION TO OOP IN PYTHON AND SOLIDITY

- Solidity supports reentrancy checks, a safe math library, a crypto library, and access control in robust smart contracts.

- Solidity smart contracts can easily deployed and tested using online tools such as Remix browser.

In summary, smart contracts are similar to C++ classes. Hence, a smart contract can be reused, extended, and collaborated with other contracts.

The next section starts by exploring Python methods in OOP.

Python Basic Programming Constructs for OOP

This section briefly discusses Python programming syntax in OOP constructs and principles. You learn the following.

- Basic Python programming constructs, such as variables, conditional statements, loops, and functions

- Python OOP constructs, such as classes, objects, constructors, and destructors

- Ways to implement inheritance and polymorphism concepts in Python

Let's start with learning basic Python programming constructs.

Python Basic Programming Constructs

Let's start with learning Python programming constructs such as variables, conditional statements, loops, and functions.

CHAPTER 10   A BRIEF INTRODUCTION TO OOP IN PYTHON AND SOLIDITY

QUICK REVIEW ON PYTHON BASIC PROGRAMMING CONSTRUCTS

- Python 3.8.10 is the version used in this book.

- Python variable declarations, input, and output statements do not end with any terminators.

- Python is a dynamically typed language. Hence, you need not declare data types of variables before using them, and actual data types of Python variables are determined during runtime (execution).

```
iv = 10
fv = 10.5
sv = "abc"
lv = [10,20,30]
```

For example, the `iv` data type is an integer, the `fv` data type is a float, the `sv` data type is a string, and the `lv` data type is a list.

1. The `input()` function is used in Python for taking inputs into variables. It converts user inputs into a string and returns the string. Hence, you must convert the string into a suitable data type for performing arithmetic operations using `eval()`.

2. To print values of variables, use the `print()` function.

```
iv = input("Enter integer")
iv = eval(iv)+12
print("Value:",iv)
fv = input("Enter float number")
fv = eval(fv)+12
print(fv)
```

3. To write conditional statements, use if else blocks as follows.

   a. **if** or **else** statements must **end** with a colon.

b. Observe that under the if or else statements, you should write all relevant **lines of code in a block** with the **same indentation** (for example, a tab space).

```
if iv>20:
    print("iv is greater than 20")
else:
    if iv>10:
        print("iv is greater than 10 but less than 20")
    else:
        print("iv is lesser than 10")
        print("iv is lesser than 10..")
```

4. To write loop statements, use for statements as follows.

   a. In the following loop statements, **for, in**, and **range** are keywords.

   b. **for** statements must **end** with a colon.

   c. Use range to define loop starting value, end value, and step value.

   d. Write all for loop relevant **lines of code in a block** with the **same indentation** as follows.

   ```
   for i in range(0,5,1):
       print(i)
       print(i+1)
   ```

   e. If you use a range without a starting value, end value, and step value, then the default start value =0 and end value =n-1.

   ```
   for i in range(5):
       print(i)
       print(i+1)
   ```

f. If you want to iterate through a list of elements (lv), use the following syntax.

    ```
    for e in lv:
        print(e*e)
    ```

g. Similarly, Python supports while loops also.

5. Use the **def** keyword to define a Python **function**, and its signature must **end** with a colon.

    a. It is possible to assign default values to function arguments.

    b. It is possible to return multiple variables from a Python function.

    c. For example, define the following maxfun with indentation rules as follows.

    ```
    def maxfun(a,b):
        if a>b:
            return a
        else:
            return b
    ```

    d. To call the function, use the following lines.

        i. As maxfun returns a value, collect results into a suitable python variable.

        ```
        c=maxfun(20,40)
        print(c)
        ```

Python is a highly popular scripting language and it offers many library functions.

Next, let's discuss important Python programming constructs for OOP.

CHAPTER 10   A BRIEF INTRODUCTION TO OOP IN PYTHON AND SOLIDITY

Python OOP Constructs

Let's start by learning Python programming constructs to define classes, data members, member functions, and objects.

PYTHON OOP CONSTRUCTS

---

1. To define a **class** in Python, use the `class` keyword followed by the class name, and it ends with a colon.

    a. Inside the class, it is necessary to declare **data members** and **initialize them** with suitable values.

    b. Define suitable **data members accessing functions.** Every member function is defined with a special argument (`self`). It is similar to `this` pointer in C++. You should define member functions inside of the class only.

    c. To access data members of objects, use `self` arguments inside the member functions as shown in the following.

    ```
    class Class_Name:
        field1 = None
        field2 = None
        ..
        def setField1(self,f1):
            self.field1 = f1
        def getField1(self):
            return self.field1
        def setField2(self,f2):
            self.field2 = f2
        def getField2(self):
            return self.field2
    ```

515

2. To create an **object** from the class, use the following syntax. You should observe object creation involves calling a constructor of the class.

   ```
   obj1 = Class_Name()
   ```

3. To access an object data member, do the following.

   a. Through the class member functions.

   ```
   obj1.setField1(10)
   iv = obj1.getField1()
   ```

   b. Directly accessing the data members using the object.

   ```
   obj1.field1 = 10
   iv = obj1.field1
   ```

4. If you are accessing data members directly with the object, what about the data-hiding feature of OOP?

5. Python does **not offer access specifiers** such as private, public, and protected. By default, all data members are public. However, for hiding data members' access to external functions, Python supports hiding data members using special variable names as follows.

   a. Each **data member is declared** with a variable name prefixed with a **double underscore** (__). These special variables (data members) work as private data members.

   b. You can even define member functions as private ones using the (__) prefix with function names.

   c. By default, Python class **data members (without __ prefix)** and **member functions (without __ prefix)** are **publicly accessible.**

```
class Class_Name:
    __field1 = None
    __field2 = None
    ..
    def setField1(self,f1):
        self.__field1 = f1
    def getField1(self):
        return self.__field1
```

6. Accessing private data members of a class is possible only through public member functions as follows.

```
obj1 = Class_Name()
obj1.setField1(10)
iv = obj1.getField1()

obj2 = Class_Name()
obj2.setField2(10)
iv = obj2.getField2()
```

Next, let's discuss Python programming constructs for constructors and destructors.

PYTHON PROGRAMMING CONSTRUCTS FOR CONSTRUCTORS AND DESTRUCTORS

1. Unlike C++ constructors, in Python, constructors are defined with a special name **__init__(self)** to initialize data members and execute start-up activities on object creation.

2. To define the default constructor for a class, use the following syntax.

```
class Class_Name:
    def __init__(self):
```

```
            field1 = None
            field2 = None
            print("Initialized with none")
```

3. A default constructor is invoked when an object is created for the class as follows.

   ```
   obj = Class_Name()
   ```

4. To define the default parameterized constructor for a class, use the following syntax.

   ```
   class Class_Name:
       def __init__(self, f1, f2):
           field1 = f1
           field2 = f2
           print("Initialized with custom values")
   ```

5. A parameterized constructor is invoked when an object is created for the class as follows.

   ```
   obj = Class_Name(1,2)
   ```

6. Note: **Python does not support multiple constructors in a class**. Moreover, constructors cannot be overloaded.

7. However, to define a destructor for a class, Python uses a special **__del__(self)** function as follows.

   a. A destructor is invoked automatically when an object is destroyed.

   b. Only one destructor is allowed in a Python class.

   ```
   class Class_Name:
       def __del__(self):
           print("Destructor..")
   ```

Next, let's discuss ways to apply inheritance concepts in Python.

CHAPTER 10   A BRIEF INTRODUCTION TO OOP IN PYTHON AND SOLIDITY

Python OOP Constructs for Inheritance

Let's start with learning Python programming constructs for applying inheritance concepts: base classes, derived classes, and inheritance approaches.

PYTHON PROGRAMMING CONSTRUCTS FOR INHERITANCE

1. Define a sample base class as follows.

   ```
   class Base_Class:
       def __init__(self):
           self.field1 = None

       def setField1(self,f1):
           ..sample code
       def getField1(self):
           ..sample code
   ```

2. To define a new class from an existing base class, you should define a sample-derived class as follows.

   a. Observe the syntax for inheritance in class Derived_Class(**Base_Class**).

   ```
   class Derived_Class(Base_Class):
       def __init__(self):
           self.field2 = None
       def setField2(self,f1):
           ..sample code
       def getField2(self):
           ..sample code
   ```

3. Similar to C++ classes, Python-derived class objects can access and reuse the base class code as follows.

```
obj = Derived_Class()
obj.setField1(10)  #base class code
obj.getField1()    #base class code
obj.setField2(10)
obj.getField2()
```

Next, let's check whether Python supports inheritance approaches.

PYTHON SUPPORTING INHERITANCE APPROACHES

1. Python supports **multilevel inheritance** approaches as follows: Base_Class -> Derived_Class1 -> Derived_Class2

   ```
   class Base_Class:
       def __init__(self):
           self.field1 = None

   class Derived_Class1(Base_Class):
       def __init__(self):
           self.field2 = None
   class Derived_Class2(Derived_Class1):
       def __init__(self):
           self.field3 = None
   ```

2. Python supports **hierarchical inheritance** approaches as follows: Derived_Class1 <- Base_Class -> Derived_Class2

   ```
   class Derived_Class1(Base_Class):
       def __init__(self):
           self.field2 = None
   ```

CHAPTER 10   A BRIEF INTRODUCTION TO OOP IN PYTHON AND SOLIDITY

```
class Derived_Class2(Base_Class):
    def __init__(self):
        self.field3 = None
```

3. Python supports **multiple** and **hybrid inheritance approaches** as follows.

```
class Derived_Class1(Base_Class):
    def __init__(self):
        self.field2 = None

class Derived_Class2(Base_Class):
    def __init__(self):
        self.field3 = None
class Child_Class3(Derived_Class1,Derived_Class2):
    def __init__(self):
        self.field4 = None
```

Observe two combinations of inheritance approaches: Child_Class3 is inherited from two derived classes (known as *multiple inheritance*), and derived classes are inherited from a base class (known as *hierarchical inheritance*).

Next, let's discuss important Python programming constructs for polymorphism concepts.

Python OOP Constructs for Polymorphism

Python does not support function overloading in classes but supports the following polymorphism methods.

- Operator overloading
- Function overriding
- Abstract classes and abstract methods

CHAPTER 10   A BRIEF INTRODUCTION TO OOP IN PYTHON AND SOLIDITY

PYTHON POLYMORPHISM (OPERATOR OVERLOADING)

Python does not support function overloading concepts, but it supports operator overloading.

1. Python supports overloading all arithmetic, assignment operators, and comparison operators.

2. For example, to overload arithmetic operators such as +, -, *, /, you need to overload the following **built-in functions** in a class.

    a. __add__(self, other)

    b. __sub__(self, other)

    c. __mul__(self, other)

    d. __truediv__(self, other)

    Here, observe that all these functions are taking two arguments: self refers to the Left Hand Side (LHS) operand of the operator, and other refers to the operator's Right Hand Side (RHS) operand.

3. To overload unary operators (e.g., +, -, ~), you must overload the following **built-in functions** in a class.

    a. __neg__(self)

    b. __pos__(self)

    c. __invert__(self)

4. To overload comparison operators (>, <, ==, etc.), you need to overload the following **built-in functions** in a class.

    a. __lt__(self, other)

    b. __gt__(self, other)

    c. __eq__(self, other)

5. For example, to overload < operator to compare two player objects' scores, you need to overload a suitable built-in function in the Player class as follows.

```
class Player:
    def __init__(self,pscore):
        self.score=pscore
    def __lt__(self,other):
        if self.score < other.score:
            return self
        else:
            return other
```

Next, let's learn how to override member functions in derived classes for polymorphism concepts in Python.

MEMBER FUNCTION OVERRIDING IN PYTHON

1. Let's define a fun() function in a BaseClass as follows.

    ```
    class BaseClass:
        def fun(self):
            print("..")
    ```

2. To override the fun() function in a DerivedClass, you can define it as follows.

    a. Observe that DerivedClass is inherited from the BaseClass.

    b. Redefine func() in DerivedClass to override the BaseClass definition.

    ```
    class DerivedClass(BaseClass):
        def fun(self):
            print("..")
            print("..")
    ```

3. Involve the correct member functions from respective class objects as follows.

   ```
   ob1 = BaseClass()
   ob1.fun() # it invokes base class fun()
   ob2 = DerivedClass()
   ob2.fun() # it invokes derived class fun()
   ```

4. Suppose you want to call the `BaseClass` version of the overridden function (`fun()`), then you can invoke it using the Python built-in super class object: `super()`.

   ```
   class DerivedClass(BaseClass):
       def fun(self):
           super().fun() #invokes the BaseClass fun()
           print("..")
           print("..")
   ```

Next, let's discuss abstract classes and pure virtual functions (abstract methods) in Python that support declaring standard interfaces.

PYTHON WAY FOR ABSTRACT CLASSES AND METHODS

1. In Python, you should import a module called abc to implement abstract classes and abstract methods. The **ABC** module is an **Abstract Base Classes (ABC)** module.

2. For example, to define an abstract class called `Interfaces` with suitable standard interfaces declaration for application controls access, you should define `Interfaces` as follows.

   a. Observe that the abc module was imported.

   b. Declare each of the interfaces by prefixing with @abstractmethod.

CHAPTER 10   A BRIEF INTRODUCTION TO OOP IN PYTHON AND SOLIDITY

c. No interface code is defined (e.g., `pass` is no action).

```
from abc import ABC, abstractmethod
class Interfaces:
    @abstractmethod
    def control1(self):
        pass
    @abstractmethod
    def control2(self):
        pass
    @abstractmethod
    def control3(self):
        pass
```

3. You should do the following to define Application1 with standard interface definitions for all controls.

```
class Application1(Interfaces):
    def control1(self):
        print("..")
    def control2(self):
        print("..")
    def control3(self):
        print("..")
```

4. Define another Application2 with only a few standard interface definitions as follows.

```
class Application2(Interfaces):
    def control1(self):
        print("..")
    def control3(self):
        print("..")
```

5. By creating objects for Application1 and Application2, you can access and test their respective application interfaces.

Let's practice how to use abstract classes in the next section.

CHAPTER 10   A BRIEF INTRODUCTION TO OOP IN PYTHON AND SOLIDITY

Practicing OOP in Python

This section practices OOP concepts using Python scripts. Python is used to implement the following.

- classes and objects
- data encapsulation and data hiding principles
- inheritance approaches
- polymorphism concepts

Let's start by discussing classes.

Using Python for Encapsulation and Data-Hiding Features

This section describes how to define Python classes by following data encapsulation and data-hiding principles.

> **DATA ENCAPSULATION**
>
> 1. Use the Python 3.8.10 version for testing all activities in this book. Use the following command; it displays a Python prompt and then you can execute all Python commands.
>
>    ```
>    # python3
>    >>>
>    ```
>
> 2. To write a Python script, you can use any text editor and save the file name with the .py extension (sample.py). Use the following command to run the script.
>
>    ```
>    #python3 sample.py
>    ```

CHAPTER 10   A BRIEF INTRODUCTION TO OOP IN PYTHON AND SOLIDITY

3. Note: Follow the indentation rules while executing all the Python scripts.

4. To show how to execute Python classes by combining related data members and member functions, do the following simple activity in the player.py file.

   a. Define a Python class called Player with sample data member's jersey number and name.

   b. Define suitable member functions for accessing Player class data members.

   c. For example, to access each data member, execute suitable set and get member functions as follows.

```
class Player:
        jno = None
        name = None
        def setJno(self,pjno):
                if pjno>=0 and pjno<=100:
                        self.jno = pjno
        def getJno(self):
                return self.jno
        def setName(self,pname):
                self.name = pname
        def getName(self):
                return self.name
```

5. After defining the Player class, test it by creating two objects.

   a. For each object, assign values to data members (jersey number and name) and print them using member functions of the Player class.

   ```
   p1 = Player()
   p1.setJno(10)
   ```

```
p1.setName("Sachin")
print("Player Jersey Number:",p1.getJno())
print("Player Name:",p1.getName(),p1.name)

p2 =  Player()
p2.setJno(7)
p2.setName("Dhoni")
print("Player Jersey Number:",p2.getJno())
print("Player Name:",p2.getName())
```

b. Observe that you can access object data members' values directly as follows.

```
p1.jno=101
p1.name="Sachin T"
print("Player Jersey Number:",p1.getJno())
print("Player Name:",p1.getName(),p1.name)
```

6. Save player.py and execute it using the following command.

   a. Observe that each player object has its own data, and the data is accessible through member functions

   #python3 player.py
   Player Jersey Number: 10
   Player Name: Sachin Sachin
   Player Jersey Number: 7
   Player Name: Dhoni

   b. Observe that by default, all data members and member functions are public. Hence, it is possible to access p1 object details directly (without member functions).

   Player Jersey Number: 101
   Player Name: Sachin T Sachin T

Next, let's discuss data-hiding principles in Python classes.

CHAPTER 10 A BRIEF INTRODUCTION TO OOP IN PYTHON AND SOLIDITY

DATA HIDING

1. To show how to implement data-hiding principles, do the following simple activity in the dh_player.py file.

    a. Define a Python class called `Player` with sample private data member's jersey number and name using __ variable names such as __jno and __name.

    b. Define suitable public member functions for accessing `Player` class private data members. Do not include __ in front of member function names such as `setJno`, `getJno`, and so on.

    ```
    class Player:
        __jno = None
        __name = None
        def setJno(self,pjno):
            if pjno>=0 and pjno<=100:
                self.__jno = pjno
        def getJno(self):
            return self.__jno
        def setName(self,pname):
            self.__name = pname
        def getName(self):
            return self.__name
    ```

2. After defining the `Player` class, test it by creating Player objects `p1` and `p1`.

    a. Access values of `Player` object's data members using set and get member functions as follows.

    ```
    p1 = Player()
    p1.setJno(10)
    p1.setName("Sachin")
    ```

529

```
print("Player Jersey Number:",p1.getJno())
print("Player Name:",p1.getName())

p2 = Player()
p2.setJno(7)
p2.setName("Dhoni")
print("Player Jersey Number:",p2.getJno())
print("Player Name:",p2.getName())
```

b. Access values of p1 object's data members directly as follows.

```
p1.__jno=101
p1.__name="Sachin T"
print(p1.__jno)
print(p1.__name)
```

c. Access values of p1 object's using member functions and test its values.

```
print("Player Jersey Number:",p1.getJno())
print("Player Name:",p1.getName())
```

3. Save dh_player.py and execute it using the following command.

   a. Observe that player objects' private data members are accessed using public member functions successfully.

   #python3 dh_player.py
   Player Jersey Number: 10
   Player Name: Sachin
   Player Jersey Number: 7
   Player Name: Dhoni

   b. Observe that player objects p1 private data members are not updated when the external function accesses its data members directly.

   101
   Sachin T

CHAPTER 10   A BRIEF INTRODUCTION TO OOP IN PYTHON AND SOLIDITY

c. p1 object holds its old details only.

Player Jersey Number: 10
Player Name: Sachin

Next, let's practice using Python constructors and destructors.

QUICK EXPERIMENT ON PYTHON CONSTRUCTORS AND DESTRUCTORS

1. Let's look at whether Python allows multiple constructors. Use the following sample code in `constdest.py`.

   ```
   class Player:
       def __init__(self):
           jno = None
           name = None
           print("Initialized with none")
       def __init__(self,pno,pname):
           self.jno = pno
           self.name = pname
           print("Initialized with custom values")
   ```

2. Create suitable objects to invoke constructors as follows.

   ```
   p1 = Player(1,"sachin")
   p2 = Player() #throws error
   ```

3. Run the code and observe the following. If a parameter constructor is defined in a Python class, you cannot invoke the default constructor.

   ```
   #python3 constdest.py
   ..
   TypeError: __init__() missing 2 required positional arguments: 'pno' and 'pname'
   ```

CHAPTER 10   A BRIEF INTRODUCTION TO OOP IN PYTHON AND SOLIDITY

4. Let's remove the parameter constructor, check the following code, and observe the following.

   a. On object creation, the constructor code gets executed automatically.

   b. On object deletion, the destructor code gets executed automatically.

```
class Player:
    def __init__(self):
        jno = None
        name = None
        print("Initialized with none")
    def __del__(self):
        print("Object destroyed")
p2 = Player()
#python3 constdest.py
Initialized with none
Object destroyed
```

Next, let's practice inheritance concepts in Python.

Using Python to Implement Inheritance

Let's do the following activity that combines various inheritance approaches in Python.

1. Implement cricket player maintenance classes.

2. Define classes to maintain batsman, bowler, and all-rounder player details.

3. To avoid duplicate code and reuse the existing code, use inheritance approaches.

- For example, all players have common details such as jersey number and name. These details are maintained in the player class.
- The Batsman class inherits from the player class to maintain batsman-specific details.
- The Bowler class inherits from the player class to maintain batsman-specific details.
- The Allrounder class inherits from batsman and bowler classes to maintain the all-rounder player details.

INHERITANCE APPROACHES IN PYTHON

1. Let's go through implementing inheritance approaches. Do the following simple activity in the inheritance_player.py file.

    a. Define a Python class called Player with sample private data member's jersey number and name using __ variable names such as __jno and __name.

    b. Initialize Player class data members using a constructor.

    c. Define suitable public member functions for accessing Player class private data members.

    ```
    class Player:
        def __init__(self):
            self.__jno = 0
            self.name = ""
    ```

CHAPTER 10 A BRIEF INTRODUCTION TO OOP IN PYTHON AND SOLIDITY

```
            def setJno(self,pjno):
                if pjno>=0 and pjno<=100:
                    self.__jno = pjno
            def getJno(self):
                return self.__jno
            def setName(self,pname):
                self.name = pname
            def getName(self):
                return self.name
```

2. Inherit a Batsman class from the Player class.

    a. Declare and initialize Batsman class data members (runs and centuries) using a constructor.

    b. Define suitable public member functions for accessing Batsman class data members (runs and centuries).

```
        class Batsman(Player):
            def __init__(self):
                self.runs = 0
                self.centuries = 0

            def setRuns(self,ptotal):
                if ptotal>=0:
                    self.runs = ptotal
            def getRuns(self):
                return self.runs
            def setCenturies(self,pcent):
                if pcent>=0:
                    self.centuries = pcent
            def getCenturies(self):
                return self.centuries
```

3. Inherit a Bowler class from the Player class.

    a. Declare and initialize Bowler class data members (wkts)

using a constructor.

b. Define suitable public member functions for accessing Bowler class data members (wkts).

```
class Bowler(Player):
    def __init__(self):
        self.wkts = 0
    def setWkts(self,ptotal):
        if ptotal>=0:
            self.wkts = ptotal
    def getWkts(self):
        return self.wkts
```

4. Implement an AllRounder class by inheriting from the BatsMan and Bowlers classes.

   a. Define a default constructor to initialize AllRounder class inherited fields.

   b. Do not implement any more member functions. Test how the AllRounder class objects reuse existing codes of Player, Batsman, and Bowler classes.

   ```
   class AllRounder(Batsman,Bowler):
       def __init__(self):
           pass
   ```

5. After defining all classes, create objects for each class and test them.

   a. Create a Batsman object (b1) and check how it is reusing Player class code.

   b. Invoke Player and Batsman member functions using the object b1 for accessing its data members (jno, name, runs, and centuries).

   ```
   b1 = Batsman()
   ```

```
b1.setJno(10)
b1.setName("Sachin")
b1.setRuns(20000)
b1.setCenturies(200)
print("Player Jersey Number:",b1.getJno())
print("Player Name:",b1.getName())
print("Player Total runs:",b1.getRuns())
print("Player Centuries:",b1.getCenturies())
```

c. Create a Bowler object (b2) and check how it is reusing the Player class code.

d. Invoke Player and Bowler member functions using the object b2 for accessing its data members (jno, name, and wkts).

```
b2 = Bowler()
b2.setJno(6)
b2.setName("Srinath")
b2.setWkts(500)
print("Player Jersey Number:",b2.getJno())
print("Player Name:",b2.getName())
print("Player Total wickets:",b2.getWkts())
```

e. Create an AllRounder object (a) and check how it reuses the Player class code.

f. Invoke Player, Batsman, and Bowler member functions using the object a for accessing its data members (jno, name, runs, centuries, and wkts).

```
a = AllRounder()
a.setJno(7)
a.setName("Dhone")
a.setRuns(18000)
a.setCenturies(150)
a.setWkts(50)
```

```
print("Player Jersey Number:",a.getJno())
print("Player Name:",a.getName())
print("Player Total runs:",a.getRuns())
print("Player Centuries:",a.getCenturies())
print("Player Total wickets:",a.getWkts())
```

6. Save inheritance_player.py and execute it using the following command.

   a. The Batsman object reuses the Player code to access the jersey number and name.

   ```
   #python3 inheritance_player.py
   Player Jersey Number: 10
   Player Name: Sachin
   Player Total runs: 20000
   Player Centuries: 200
   ```

   b. The Bowler object reuses the Player code to access the jersey number and name.

   ```
   Player Jersey Number: 6
   Player Name: Srinath
   Player Total wickets: 500
   ```

   c. The AllRounder object reuses the Player, Batsman, and Bowler classes code to access jersey numbers, names, runs, centuries, and wickets.

   ```
   Player Jersey Number: 7
   Player Name: Dhone
   Player Total runs: 18000
   Player Centuries: 150
   Player Total wickets: 50
   ```

Next, let's look at polymorphism concepts in Python.

CHAPTER 10   A BRIEF INTRODUCTION TO OOP IN PYTHON AND SOLIDITY

Using Python for Polymorphism

This section explains how to create abstract classes and methods for standard user interfaces for Python application access.

As part of this activity, implement the following.

1. A simple player class as an abstract class with three abstract methods for declaring sample standard accessing interfaces such as play, stop, and stats.

2. A Batsman class with suitable code for abstract methods (play, stop, and stats)

3. A Bowler class with suitable code for abstract methods (play, stop, and stats)

4. Test accessing these standard interfaces by all Player objects from a sample user-defined function called play().

> **POLYMORPHISM IMPLEMENTATION**
>
> 1. Define a `Player` abstract class with the following abstract methods in the poly_player.py file.
>
>   a. Play plays player (Batsman or Bowler) specific actions.
>
>   b. Stop stops player (Batsman or Bowler) specific actions.
>
>   c. Stat displays player (Batsman or Bowler) specific details.
>
>    ```
>    from abc import ABC, abstractmethod
>    class Player:
>        @abstractmethod
>        def play(self):
>            pass
>        @abstractmethod
>    ```

```python
    def stats(self):
        pass
    @abstractmethod
    def stop(self):
        pass
```

2. Define a Batsman class and implement batsman-specific sample codes for play, stats, and stop as follows.

```python
class Batsman(Player):
    def play(self):
        print("Batting")
    def stats(self):
        print("Total runs scored")
    def stop(self):
        print("Player out")
```

3. Define a Bowler class and execute batsman-specific sample code for play, stats, and stop as follows.

```python
class Bowler(Player):
    def play(self):
        print("Bowling")
    def stats(self):
        print("Total wickets taken")
    def stop(self):
        print("Overs over!")
```

4. Define a user-defined function for testing a variety of player object controls.

```python
def Play(p):
    p.play()
    p.stats()
    p.stop()
```

5. Create a batsman object (b1) and pass it to user user-defined Play function for testing the batsman object actions.

   ```
   b1=Batsman()
   Play(b1)
   ```

6. Create a bowler object (b2) and pass it to user user-defined Play function for testing the bowler object actions.

   ```
   b2=Bowler()
   Play(b2)
   ```

7. Save poly_player.py and execute it using the following command.

   a. Observe that the Batsman actions are invoked based on the object type.

   ```
   #python3 poly_player.py
   Batting
   Total runs scored
   Player out
   ```

   b. Observe that the Bowler actions are invoked based on the object type.

   ```
   Bowling
   Total wickets taken
   Overs over!
   ```

This activity implemented the base `Event` and `EventHandler` classes for application-specific events. Soon, you'll use these classes to handle application sample events.

The next section explores Solidity and OOP.

Solidity Basic Programming Constructs for OOP

Solidity has a rich set of programming constructs for writing smart contracts. Covering all the topics is beyond the scope of the book. This section examines the following Solidity programming constructs for writing basic smart contracts and the role of OOP principles.

- Solidity basic programming constructs
- Solidity smart contracts
- Solidity programming constructs for inheritance and polymorphism

Let's start with learning Solidity basics.

Solidity Basics

Let's start with learning the basic programming constructs of Solidity, including the following basic syntax.

- Solidity data types and variables
- Solidity commenting styles
- Solidity conditional statements and loop statements
- Ways to define functions in Solidity
- Ways to define smart contracts (similar to C++ classes) in Solidity

CHAPTER 10   A BRIEF INTRODUCTION TO OOP IN PYTHON AND SOLIDITY

SOLIDITY BASIC PROGRAMMING CONSTRUCTS

1. In Solidity, all programming statements must end with ;.

2. Solidity most of the programming constructs syntax is similar to C++ programming constructs.

3. Solidity supports single-line comments as well as multiline comments.

    a. `// a = b+c;`

    b. `/* a =1; a=b+c; */`

4. Like popular languages such as C and C++, Solidity programming also supports basic and complex data types—such as `int, unit, bool, enum, struct, string`, and `mapping`—to handle a variety of data elements. For example, you can define data type variables as follows.

    a. `int a=-10; unit b =200; string name = "abc";`

    b. To declare structures: `struct student = { int a; bool choice; string name;};`

    c. To declare arrays: `int [5]list;`

    d. To declare dictionaries: `mapping (unit=>string) names;`

    e. Supports special data types.

        i. To manage contracts address: `address owner;`

        ii. To declare dynamic data types: `var i=3; var s="abc";`

5. Solidity programming conditional and loop syntax is similar to C and C++.

    a. if (a>b) { max =a;} else {max=b;}

    b. for (i =0; i<10; i++) { a=a+i;}

6. Solidity programming supports defining functions inside contracts.

    a. Define a function with suitable visibility modes (public, private, internal, and external):

    function funName(int a) **public returns (uint)**
    {
            return data1;
    }

    b. From this sample function definition, you should know the following details.

        i. Any function definition starts with a keyword: function

        ii. Functions take arguments after the function name inside ( )

        iii. Function visibility modes (e.g., public, private, internal, external) should be defined after arguments.

        iv. The type (view, pure, constant) of function can be defined.

        v. Finally, the function return type should be defined using the returns keyword.

Next, let's learn how to write smart contracts in Solidity.

CHAPTER 10 A BRIEF INTRODUCTION TO OOP IN PYTHON AND SOLIDITY

Smart contracts are very similar to C++ classes and objects. The upcoming activity discusses defining smart contracts (classes) and creating instances (objects) to interact with smart contracts.

SOLIDITY SMART CONTRACT DEFINITION

1. In Solidity programming, smart contracts can be defined similarly to C++ classes.

2. Usually, a smart contract contains state variables (data members) and functions to access state variables and carry out transactions (member functions).

3. Hence, to define a smart contract the following syntax is useful.

   a. The Pragma line indicates Solidity compiler versions.

   b. contract is the keyword used to define smart contracts in Solidity.

   ```
   pragma solidity >=0.8.2 <0.9.0;
   contract ContractName
   {
        //sample state variables (data members)
        uint public data1;
        uint private data1;
        //Sample state accessing functions (member functions)
        function setData1(uint d) public
        {
             data1 = d;
        }
   }
   ```

CHAPTER 10   A BRIEF INTRODUCTION TO OOP IN PYTHON AND SOLIDITY

```
function getData1() public view returns (uint)
{
    return data1;
}
}
```

c. In Solidity, smart contracts are implemented based on data encapsulation and data hiding principles of OOP.

d. From this sample contract definition, you must know the following details.

  i. Smart contract state variables and accessing functions can be defined together under the contract name.

  ii. To access the contract, you can create an instance as follows.

  ```
  ContractName sample = ContractName();
  sample.setData1(10);
  uint a = sample.getData1();
  ```

  iii. You can observe that creating an instance of a smart contract and accessing it is the same as C++ object creation and accessing processes.

e. Smart contract definition includes OOP data hiding principles using visibility modes (similar to C++ visibility modes).

  i. If you include `public` visibility with state variables or member functions in a contract, then using the contract instance, other contracts can access the contract's `public` data members or member functions. It is similar to C++ public visibility only.

CHAPTER 10   A BRIEF INTRODUCTION TO OOP IN PYTHON AND SOLIDITY

ii. If you include `private` visibility data members (member function) in a contract then other contracts can access these private data members (member functions) using `public` member functions of the contract only. It is similar to C++ private visibility only.

iii. If you include `internal` visibility data members in a contract, only inherited contacts from the contract can access these internal data members. `Internal` visibility is similar to protected visibility in C++.

Next, let's learn Solidity programming constructs for inheritance concepts.

Solidity Inheritance Programming

This section explores the syntax of Solidity programming for using inheritance approaches. It discusses the importance of OOP inheritance in reusing the existing contract and how to define a base contract and derived contracts.

REUSE SMART CONTRACT USING SOLIDITY INHERITANCE SYNTAX

1. Solidity programming supports the following OOP inheritance approaches for reusing existing smart contracts and defining new smart contracts.

2. **Single-level inheritance** approach.

    contract BaseContract
    {
    　　//sample state variables (data members)
    　　uint public data1;

    　　//Sample state accessing functions (member functions)

```solidity
        function setData1(uint d) public
        {
            data1 = d;
        }
        function getData1() public view returns (uint)
        {
            return data1;
        }
}
contract DerivedContract is BaseContract
{
        //sample state variables (data members)
        uint public data2;

        //Sample state accessing functions (member
        functions)
        function setData2(uint d) public
        {
            data2 = d;
        }
        function getData2() public view returns (uint)
        {
            return data2;
        }
}
```

a. Observe that a new contract (derived contract) is created from the base contract using **is** keyword.

b. You can create instances (objects) of derived contracts and access them as follows.

```solidity
DerivedContract dc = DerivedContract();
dc.setData1(10);
dc.setData2(20);
uint a = dc.getData1(); //reuse
uint b = dc.getData2();
```

CHAPTER 10   A BRIEF INTRODUCTION TO OOP IN PYTHON AND SOLIDITY

- c. You can observe that accessing derived contracts is the same as using derived classes in C++.
- d. The derived contract instance can reuse the code of the base contract.

3. Similarly, in Solidity programming **multilevel inheritance** approach can be implemented as follows.

```
contract BaseContract
{
}
contract DerivedContract1 is BaseContract
{
}
contract DerivedContract2 is DerivedContract1
{
}
```

4. Similarly, in Solidity programming **multiple inheritance** approach can be implemented as follows.

```
contract DerivedContract1
{
}
contract DerivedContract2
{
}
contract DerivedContract3 is DerivedContract1, DerivedContract2
{
}
```

5. Solidity programming allows a combination of multiple and multilevel inheritance approaches.

Next, let's learn Solidity programming constructs for applying polymorphism concepts.

Solidity Polymorphism Programming

Solidity supports function overloading and function overriding concepts similar to C++. This section explains the syntax of Solidity programming for applying polymorphism concepts. It covers the following.

- **Abstract classes and pure virtual functions**: These constructs help define common interfaces for accessing contracts. Later, derived contracts can apply those interfaces in their own way.

- **Interfaces**: Solidity supports defining standard accessing interfaces for contracts. Later, new contracts can implement the interfaces.

SOLIDITY AND POLYMORPHISM

1. Solidity supports abstract classes and virtual functions similar to C++ with few syntax differences.

2. For example, the following syntax is used to define an abstract class with virtual functions in solidity.

   ```
   abstract contract SampleContract
   {
           function sampleVirtualFun(uint n1) public virtual
           returns (uint);
   }
   ```

   You should use the `abstract` keyword to declare an abstract contract and define at least one virtual function using the `virtual` keyword.

Similar to C++, it is not possible to create instances from abstract contracts. You should implement the abstract class virtual functions in a derived contract as follows. The virtual function must be in the derived contract using the **override** keyword.

```
contract SampleContract is SampleImpl
{
    function sampleVirtualFun(uint n1) override public
    returns (uint)
    {
        ..
    }
}
```

3. Solidity also supports interfaces for defining standard interfaces for accessing contracts as follows.

```
interface MyInterfaces
{
    function myaccessFun1(uint) external  returns (uint);
    function myaccessFun2(uint) external  returns (uint);
}
```

You should use the `interface` keyword to define an interface contract and declare the necessary number of access functions using the `external` keyword. Similar to C++, it is not possible to create instances from interface contracts. Hence, you should use the interface access functions in a derived contract as follows.

```
contract MyInterImple is MyInterfaces
{
    function myaccessFun1(uint n1) public view
    returns (uint)
    {
```

```
    }
    function myaccessFun1(uint n1) public view
    returns (uint)
    {
    }
}
```

Next, let's discuss a few important unique Solidity programming constructs.

SOLIDITY OTHER IMPORTANT PROGRAMMING CONSTRUCTS

1. Solidity also supports constructors to initialize state variables of contract. However, solidity constructors are usually used for initializing activities only.

    a. Only one constructor is allowed per contract.

    b. In an inheritance context, contract constructors work similarly to C++ only.

    ```
    constructor() public
    {
        //initialize state variables
    }
    ```

2. Solidity supports a unique way of extending function capabilities using modifier functions. Basically, modifier functions allow you to restrict function executions based on checking important constraints.

    ```
    uint256 internal number;

    modifier isAdmin
    {
        require(admin == msg.sender);
        _;
    }
    ```

3. Solidity supports defining events as follows.

    a. You defined a sample event called `highPrice`.

    b. Inside the `priceCheck` function, it raises a `highPrice` event based on `currentPrice` input.

    ```
    contract itemPricing
    {
        uint8 price;
        event highPrice(bool returnValue);
        function priceCheck(uint8 currentPrice) public
        returns (bool)
        {
            if (currentPrice>=price)
            {
                highPrice(true);
                return true;
            }
        }
    }
    ```

Well done. You have learned basic Solidity programming constructs for writing smart contracts.

The next section practices writing smart contracts, deploying, and testing using the Remix browser.

Practicing OOP in Solidity

To practice Solidity programming, let's use an online Remix editor. You can access it through any Internet browser using the following link: https://remix.ethereum.org/. The following topics are discussed in this section.

CHAPTER 10   A BRIEF INTRODUCTION TO OOP IN PYTHON AND SOLIDITY

- Remix editor options for executing and deploying solidity contracts
- Implement smart contracts by following OOP principles using Solidity
- Extend smart contracts using inheritance
- Practice solidity polymorphism ways

Using the Remix Editor for Practicing Solidity

Remix offers an elegant browser with simple user interfaces. Remix allows writing, saving, and compiling the solidity files to correct syntax errors. It also allows you to deploy and test the successfully compiled contracts over online Ethereum runtime environments using a variety of EVMs. Let's check important options of the Remix browser for implementing and testing sample smart contracts using solidity programming.

REMIX BROWSER OPTIONS

1. To access an online Remix browser, a good Internet connection is mandatory. Open the following URL in your Internet browser.

   https://remix.ethereum.org/

2. It opens a Remix browser in various panels (see Figure 10-1).

    a. To implement smart contracts, observe the **FILE EXPLORER** panel on the LHS of the Remix browser. Under FILE EXPLORER, click on the **contracts** folder icon. It shows existing sample solidity files for reference. Observe these options in the LHS panel of Figure 10-1.

CHAPTER 10   A BRIEF INTRODUCTION TO OOP IN PYTHON AND SOLIDITY

   b. To create a new Solidity file, select the **contracts** folder, and it shows options for creating a new Solidity file (**Create new file**), renaming, and deleting existing files. (Observe these options in the RHS panel of Figure 10-1.) Click the **Create new file** icon to open a new solidity file.

   c. Save your new Solidity file (for example, you created **mycontr.sol** file under the **contracts** folder). Observe it in the bottom pane of Figure 10-1.

Figure 10-1. Remix Browser and important panels to interact with it

   d. Write your smart contract code in mycontr.sol. It is saved automatically.

   e. To compile your solidity file, just click on the green-colored play button icon shown in the bottom panel of Figure 10-1.

CHAPTER 10   A BRIEF INTRODUCTION TO OOP IN PYTHON AND SOLIDITY

f. If there are no compilation errors, you can deploy the smart contract by clicking on the **deploy and run** option (the fifth icon from the top) shown in the LHS panel in Figure 10-2.

g. On successfully deploying your smart contract, the Remix browser opens the **DEPLOY & RUN TRANSACTIONS** panel (see RHS panel in Figure 10-2).

h. Under the DEPLOY & RUN TRANSACTIONS panel, click on the **CONTRACT** drop-down box to select your smart contract (mycontr.sol) and click the **Deploy** button. Under **CONTRACT**, all smart contracts are defined in the Solidity file).

i. It displays all publicly accessible functions of your smart contract to interact with them (see Figure 10-2).

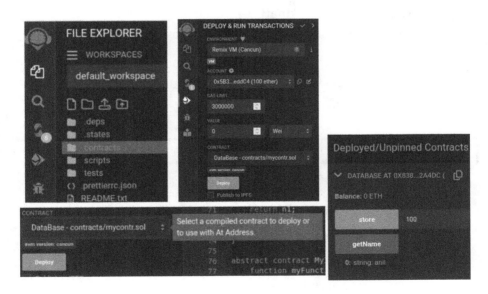

Figure 10-2. Remix browser smart contract deployment options

CHAPTER 10   A BRIEF INTRODUCTION TO OOP IN PYTHON AND SOLIDITY

3. Using the Remix browser for writing, compiling, deploying, and testing smart contracts is simple.

4. Practice writing sample smart contracts using Remix.

Let's practice by writing a smart contract using Solidity and testing OOP principles.

Practicing with Smart Contracts

Let's do the following activities to learn how to execute smart contracts by following OOP principles.

1. Implement a smart contract called `MySecretData` to store and access sample secret data.

2. Access the existing smart contract (`MySecretData`) from a new smart contract called `MyProfile`.

3. Update `MySecretData` with `private`, `public` and `internal` state variables for understanding Solidity visibility modes.

IMPLEMENT SMART CONTRACTS BY FOLLOWING OOP PRINCIPLES

1. Do the following activities using Remix in a solidity file (mycontract.sol).

2. Define `MySecretData` with a sample secret field (`data1:state variable`) and implement publicly accessing functions for storing and retrieving the secret field (`data1`).

```
pragma solidity >=0.8.2 <0.9.0;
contract MySecretData
{
```

CHAPTER 10 A BRIEF INTRODUCTION TO OOP IN PYTHON AND SOLIDITY

```
    uint data1;
    function setData1(uint d) public
    {
        data1 = d;
    }
    function getData1() public view returns (uint)
    {
        return data1;
    }
}
```

3. Compile and deploy it using the Remix browser.

   a. To deploy and test it, select your smart contract (MySecretData) under the CONTRACT drop-down box and deploy it, as shown in Figure 10-3.

Figure 10-3. Deploying MySecretData smart contract

   b. Test your contract (see Figure 10-4) by setting and accessing sample secret values using public access functions (setData1 and getData1).

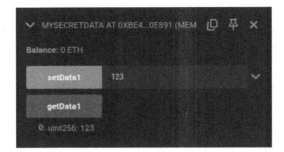

Figure 10-4. *MySecretData smart contract test results*

    4. In the same Solidity file, define another smart contract called `MyProfile` to access the `MySecretData` instance.

        a. Create an object of `MySecretData` and access it in member functions (`setProfile` and `getProfileData`) of `MyProfile`.

        b. Define a sample state variable (`profile`) specific to `MyProfile`.

```
contract MyProfile
{
    string profile;
    MySecretData ms = new MySecretData();
    function setProfile(string memory i) public
    {
        ms.setData1(200);
        profile = i;
    }
    function getProfile() public view returns
    (string memory)
    {
        return profile;
    }
}
```

CHAPTER 10 A BRIEF INTRODUCTION TO OOP IN PYTHON AND SOLIDITY

```
        function getProfileData() public view
        returns (uint)
        {
            return ms.getData1();
        }
}
```

5. Compile and deploy it using the Remix browser.

   a. To deploy and test it, select the smart contract (`MyProfile`) under the CONTRACT drop-down box and deploy it as follows.

   b. Test your contract (see Figure 10-5) by setting and accessing sample secret and profile values using public access functions (`setProfile`, `getProfile`, and `getProfileData`).

Figure 10-5. *MyProfile smart contract test results*

6. Modify `MySecretData` to learn Solidity visibility modes (`public, private, and internal`).

   a. Define a state variable with each visibility mode.

CHAPTER 10   A BRIEF INTRODUCTION TO OOP IN PYTHON AND SOLIDITY

    b. Define publicly accessible functions for accessing all state variables.

    c. For public state variables (data2), there is no need for publicly accessible functions. But, for private (data1) and internal state variables (data3) you should define publicly accessible functions.

```solidity
pragma solidity >=0.8.2 <0.9.0;
contract MySecretData
{
      uint internal data1;
      uint public data2;
      uint private data3;
      function setData1(uint d) public
      {
            data1 = d;
      }
      function getData1() public view returns (uint)
      {
            return data1;
      }
      function setData2(uint d) public
      {
            data2 = d;
      }
      function getData2() public view returns (uint)
      {
            return data2;
      }
      function setData3(uint d) public
      {
            data3 = d;
      }
```

CHAPTER 10   A BRIEF INTRODUCTION TO OOP IN PYTHON AND SOLIDITY

```
        function getData3() public view returns (uint)
        {
            return data1;
        }
    }
```

7. Compile and deploy it using the Remix browser.

   a. To deploy and test it, select your smart contract (MySecretData) under the CONTRACT drop-down box and deploy it as follows.

   b. Test your contract (see Figure 10-6) by setting and accessing sample secret values using public access functions (setData1, setData2, setData3, getData1, getData2, and getData3).

   c. Observe that data2 (public state variable) can be accessible without publicly accessible functions, too.

Figure 10-6. *MySecretData smart contract test results*

This hands-on activity shows that a Solidity contract works similarly to a C++ class. Using contract definition with visibility modes (public, private, and internal), Solidiy offers data encapsulation and data hiding features of OOP.

Let's practice using inheritance principles to extend smart contracts in Solidity.

Extending Smart Contracts Using Inheritance

Let's do the following activities to learn to use smart contracts by following OOP principles.

1. Implement a smart contract called MySecretProfile from MySecretData using an inheritance approach.

    a. Do not execute any code in MySecretProfile.

    b. Test reusing the codes of MySecretData from the MySecretProfile contract instance (object).

2. Change MySecretProfile to include public, private, and internal state variables and understand how visibility mode works in the inheritance context.

3. Include a public constructor in the derived contract (MySecretProfile) to initialize the state variables of the base contract.

4. Practice function overloading and multiple inheritance approaches by defining multiple contracts.

CHAPTER 10   A BRIEF INTRODUCTION TO OOP IN PYTHON AND SOLIDITY

SOLIDITY BASICS

1. Implement the following contracts in a Solidity file (mycontract.sol).

2. Create a contract called MySecretProfile from an existing contract, MySecretData, using an inheritance approach as follows.

    a. Observe that inheriting a contract from an existing contract is done by using is keyword as follows.

    b. No code is used in the new contract (MySecretProfile). But it inherits existing contract (MySecretData) code into it. Hence, creating an instance of MySecretProfile allows you to access all publicly accessible functions of the MySecretData contract.

    ```
    contract MySecretProfile is MySecretData
    {

    }
    ```

3. Compile and deploy it using the Remix browser.

    a. To deploy and test it, select your smart contract (MySecretProfile) under the CONTRACT drop-down box and deploy it as follows.

    b. Observe that from the MySecretProfile instance (see Figure 10-7), it is possible to access all MySecretData public accessible state variables and functions (data2, setData1, setData2, setData3, getData1, getData2, and getData3).

CHAPTER 10   A BRIEF INTRODUCTION TO OOP IN PYTHON AND SOLIDITY

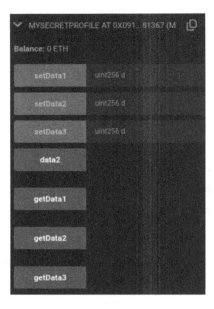

Figure 10-7. MySecretProfile smart contract test results

4. Modify `MySecretProfile` with a new publicly accessible function `setSecretData`.

   a. Inside `setSecretData`, access `public` and `internal` variables of `MySecretData` from the `MySecretProfile`. However, `private` state variables cannot be accessed.

   b. It means internal visibility allows inheriting variables into derived contracts only. You can relate Solidity's `internal` visibility mode with C++ `protected` visibility mode.

   c. Define a `public constructor` to initialize `public` and `internal` variables of `MySecretData`. Unlike C++ constructors, Solidity constructors are defined using the `constructor()` function. Moreover, you cannot overload constructors in Solidity.

```
contract MySecretProfile is MySecretData
{
    function setSecretData(uint d) public
    {
        data1 = d;
        data2 = d;
        //data3 = d;
        uint d1 = getData1()+getData2()+getData3();
    }
    constructor() public
    {
        data1 = 300;
        data2 = 200;
    }
}
```

5. Practice function overloading and multiple inheritance approaches.

   a. Define two sample secret contracts (Secrets and Secrets2).

   b. In the Secrets contract, overload the mySecret function for generating a variety of secrets.

   c. In the Secrets2 contract, overload the mySecret2 function for generating a variety of secrets.

   d. Define another contract, Secrets3, from Secrets and Secrets2 using multiple inheritance approaches.

   ```
   contract Secrets
   {
       function mySecret() public view returns
       (string memory)
       {
           return "abcdef";
       }
   ```

```solidity
        function mySecret(uint i) public view
        returns (uint)
        {
                return 100+20;
        }
        function mySecret(int i) public view
        returns (int)
        {
                return -100+i;
        }
}
contract Secrets2
{
        function mySecret2() public view returns
        (string memory)
        {
                return "abcdefghi";
        }
        function mySecret2(uint i) public view
        returns (uint)
        {
                return 100+200;
        }
        function mySecret2(int i) public view
        returns (int)
        {
                return -300+i;
        }
}
```

CHAPTER 10 A BRIEF INTRODUCTION TO OOP IN PYTHON AND SOLIDITY

6. After defining Secrets and Secrets2 contracts, define a Secrets3 contract using the multiple inheritance approach as follows.

   ```
   contract secrets3 is Secrets, Secrets2
   {
   }
   ```

7. Compile and deploy (secrets3) using the Remix browser (see Figure 10-8).

Figure 10-8. *Secret3 smart contract test results*

a. To deploy and test it, select your smart contract (Secrets3) under the CONTRACT drop-down box and deploy it as follows.

b. Observe that from the Secrets3 instance (see Figure 10-8), it is possible to access all public accessible state variables and functions of Secrets and Secrets2 are accessible (mySecret and mySecret2).

c. Observe that mySecret and mySecret2 are displayed three times each due to function overloading. You can test them using sample data.

Next, let's practice polymorphism concepts in Solidity.

Using Solidity for Polymorphism

Let's discuss polymorphism in Solidity using abstract classes, virtual functions, and interfaces.

1. As you learned from C++ abstract classes, defining base classes with virtual functions is possible. Then, it is possible to create virtual functions in derived classes. It helps in defining common interfaces for application access. Solidity also supports abstract contracts and virtual functions.

   a. Learn how to execute sample abstract contracts and virtual functions in Solidity.

   b. Define virtual functions in a derived contract.

2. Solidity also supports pure virtual functions to declare standard interfaces of future contracts. It is possible to implement pure virtual functions in derived contracts.

a. Learn the Solidity method of defining interfaces with pure virtual functions.

b. Design interfaces using derived contracts.

SOLIDITY ABSTRACT CONTRACT AND INTERFACES

1. Implement the following contracts in a Solidity file (mycontract.sol).

2. Define a sample abstract contract (MySecrets) with a virtual function and sample function as follows.

```
abstract contract MySecrets
{
        function mySecretFunctions(uint n1) public virtual
        returns (uint);
        function mySecret() public view returns
        (string memory)
        {
                return "abc";
        }
}
```

3. Define a sample derived contract (MySecretImple) from MySecrets and execute a virtual function as follows.

```
contract MySecretImpl is MySecrets {
        function mySecretFunctions(uint n1) override public
        view returns (uint)
        {
                uint n;
                n = n1*200;
                return n;
        }
}
```

4. Compile and deploy (`MySecretImpl`) using the Remix browser.

   a. You cannot deploy abstract classes: `MySecrets`.

   b. To deploy and test `MySecretImpl`, select your smart contract (`MySecretImpl`) under the CONTRACT drop-down box and deploy it as follows.

   c. Observe that from the `MySecretImpl` instance (see Figure 10-9), it is possible to access all public accessible functions (`MySecret()`) of `MySecrets`.

   d. Observe that `mySecretFunctions` is accessible from `MySecretImpl`.

   e. You can test `mySecretFunctions()` and `mySecret()` with sample inputs as follows.

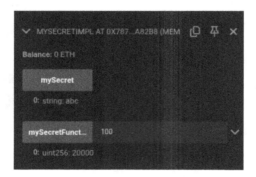

Figure 10-9. MySecretImpl smart contract test results

CHAPTER 10   A BRIEF INTRODUCTION TO OOP IN PYTHON AND SOLIDITY

5. let's define a sample `interface` (`MySecretInterfaces`) in the same solidity file as follows.

   a. Define two sample pure virtual functions in the `interface`.

   ```
   interface MySecretInterfaces
   {
           function mySecFunction1(uint)
           external   returns (uint);
           function mySecFunction2(uint)
           external   returns (uint);
   }
   ```

   b. Implement the sample interface's pure virtual functions by defining a contract from the interfaces as follows.

   ```
   contract MySecretInterImpl is MySecretInterfaces
   {
           function mySecFunction1(uint n1) public view
           returns (uint)
           {
               n1 = n1*100;
               return n1;
           }
           function mySecFunction2(uint n1) public view
           returns (uint)
           {
               n1 = n1*200;
               return n1;
           }
   }
   ```

571

CHAPTER 10   A BRIEF INTRODUCTION TO OOP IN PYTHON AND SOLIDITY

    c. Define another sample contract for sample interfaces as follows.

```
contract MySecretInterImpl2 is MySecretInterfaces
{
    function mySecFunction1(uint n1) public view
    returns (uint)
    {
        n1 = n1*300;
        return n1;
    }
    function mySecFunction2(uint n1) public view
    returns (uint)
    {
        n1 = n1*400;
        return n1;
    }
}
```

6. Compile and deploy (MySecretInterImpl1) using the Remix browser.

    a. You cannot deploy interfaces: MySecretInterfaces

    b. To deploy and test MySecretInterImpl1, select your smart contract (MySecretInterImpl1) under the CONTRACT drop-down box and deploy it as follows.

    c. Observe that from the MySecretInterImpl1 instance (see Figure 10-10), it is possible to access mySecFunction1 and mySecFunction2.

    d. Test these functions using sample values.

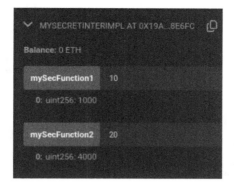

Figure 10-10. *MySecretInterImpl smart contract test results*

    e. Similarly, you can deploy `MySecretInterImpl1` and test it.

Well done. You have practiced working with important OOP concepts in Solidity.

Summary

This chapter explored the role of OOP principles in Python and Solidity programming. Learning Python helps you experiment with trending computer science technologies such as AI/ML, data science, and Solidity, which helps you explore the development of blockchain applications. Although all features of Python and Solidity were not covered, the basics and OOP features in this book help you start exploring these languages.

    The book covered the primary concepts of OOP for developing software systems. Unlike other books, it mainly focused on learning OOP concepts by solving suitable real-world hands-on activities.

    Thanks a lot for choosing this book to learn OOP concepts. The concepts covered should help you learn and excel in OOP languages.

Index

A

Abstract data types (ADT), 52, 64
Access specifiers, 50
ADT, *see* Abstract data types (ADT)

B

Behavioral design patterns
    chain of responsibility
        pattern, 446
        CacheRequestHandler, 455
        chainofresp.cc, 457
        chainofservers.cc file, 452
        client testing code, 456
        CompressRequest
          Handler, 454
        dynamic service chains, 456
        RequestHandlerImpl, 452
        server object classes, 454
        service chains, 451
        tasks, 450, 457
    commands handling
        objects, 447
    iterator pattern, 449
    mediator object, 447
    memento pattern, 450
    observer pattern, 447
    reusable solutions, 445
    state pattern, 449
    strategy pattern, 448
    subsystems/objects/services/
        communication, 446
    template method
        GameCharacter abstract
          class, 461, 462
        general algorithm steps, 458
        main() testing code, 463
        player/enemy gaming
          characters, 459, 460
        tasks, 464
        template.cc, 463
        templatemethod.cc file, 459
        virtual functions, 460
    template pattern, 448
    visitor pattern, 450
Blockchain technology, 508, 510, 573

C

C++ programming
    access control modes
        C objects, 90–92
        C++ objects, 93–99

INDEX

C++ programming (*cont.*)
    external functions, 87, 95
    internal data members, 87–90
  constructors/destructors, 113–167
  object interactions
    activities, 77
    animal objects, 82–84
    customer objects, 77–79
    gun objects, 84–86
    item objects, 80–82
  OOP programming constructs
    access specifier, 50
    class declaration, 50–54
    data encapsulation, 50
    features, 44
    input/output statements, 48, 49
    keywords, 45
    member functions, 52
    operators, 46
    program structure, 62–64
    sensor objects, 55–57
    string class, 57–60
    vector class, 60–62
  polymorphism (*see* Polymorphism)
  real-world entities
    customer class/transactions, 66–68
    gaming applications, 65
    item objects, 69–71
    animal objects, 71–74
    principles, 64
    gun class, 74–77
  smart applications
    activities, 100
    findNearestSensorTo() function, 104, 105
    getHighTempSensors() function, 103
    getLowBatterySensors() function, 103
    getLowBatterySensors() function, 103
    IoTSensor class, 100–109
    set/get member functions, 101, 102 (*see also* Friend member functions/friend classes)
Constructors/destructors
  C++ programming
    Bomb() function, 121
    compiler, 128–130
    copy constructors, 124, 125
    details, 122
    main() code, 122
    parameterized constructors, 126
    rules, 120
    supports, 123–128
  definition, 113
  handling startup sequence
    activities, 130
    existing bombs, 137–139
    gaming bombs, 130–132
    secret file, 134–136

INDEX

hands-on activity, 150, 151
IoT sensors, 151–162
Sensor.txt files, 161
startup sequence, 120
Creational design patterns
abstract factory, 416
builder class, 417
classes/objects, 412, 413
creation patterns, 412
dependencies, 415
factory method, 416
    abstract class, 420
    design drone classes., 418
    end-user code, 421
    features, 418
    hands-on activity, 419–423
    requirement, 418
    rules, 418
    tasks process, 422
prototypes, 417
singleton class, 417
singleton pattern approach, 423–427

D

Design patterns
behavioral patterns, 414, 445–464
categories, 412
creational patterns (*see* Creational design patterns)
learning design patterns, 411
software development solutions, 411
structural design patterns, 428–445
structural patterns, 413, 414
Destructors
activities, 143
Bomb class, 140, 142
definition, 113
deleting dynamical objects, 148–150
details, 142
hands-on activity, 143–148, 162, 163
IoTSensor class, 163–166
member functions, 140
shutdown activities, 139
smart application, 162 (*see also* Constructors/destructors)

E

Ethereum Virtual Machine (EVM), 510
Event-driven programming
advantages, 473, 474
application events class/events handling classes, 484–487
application events implementation, 480–482
asynchronous methods, 472, 473
characteristics, 471

INDEX

Event-driven programming (*cont.*)
  components, 467
  design/simulator
    emergency events, 494
    IoTSensorsHandler
      events, 492–496
    smart application, 491
    warning events, 493
  distributed application
    architectures, 468, 469
  events, 470, 471
  features, 483
  key concepts, 470
  management events, 472
  message exchange, 472
  producer/consumer
    services, 470
  scheduling and execution
    function, 487
  SmartApplication
    simulation, 501–503
  SmartVehiclesHandler
    events, 497–500
  software applications, 467
  structure
    application events, 480–483
    event handlers, 475
    management/handling
      classes, 476–480
    model application
      events, 477
    programming
      constructs, 474
    schedule events, 476
  subscription handling class,
    482, 483
  testing code, 487–490
EVM, *see* Ethereum Virtual
  Machine (EVM)

F

Friend member functions/
  friend classes
  access secret locations, 178–181
  Authenticated objects, 174
  class concept, 174–177
  concepts, 177
  constant
    external/object
      functions, 208
    pointers, 169, 212–224
    variables/objects, 208–212
  external functions/classes, 170
  features, 170
  friend classes, 182–187
  game implementation, 177
  main() function, 172
  pass arguments
    activities, 190
    arrays, 189, 193–197
    destination function,
      188, 189
    memory blocks, 197–199
    objects to functions, 190–192
    reference variables, 189
  pointers
    activities, 212–217

class objects, 221–224
concepts, 212
error message, 214
player class objects, 217–221
set and get member
   functions, 222
Secret class, 171–174
static data member
   activities, 201–204
   class declaration, 200
   contexts objects, 200
   control objects
      state, 204–208
   getCount()/setCount(), 201
   normal/static data
      members, 201

G, H

Gaming application
   actions/interactions, 230
   C++ classes
      Bomb class, 238–240
      building blocks, 235
      coin class, 240–242
      gun class, 242–244
      player class, 235–238
   data members/member
      functions, 230
   implementation
      bombs/guns/coins, 247–251
      game-playing scenario, 244
      main game
         scenario, 252–254

moving players, 251, 252
player observation, 245–247
real-world entities, 229, 230
scenario, 231

I, J, K, L

Inheritances
   access controls, 301–306
   aggregation
      object aggregation, 344–346
      smart applications, 342
      smart devices/object
         composition, 342–344
      testing code, 346–349
   approaches, 294
   base classes, 293, 299
   benefits, 293
   combine/connect objects
      aggregation, 336
      approaches, 335
      composition, 335
   constructors/destructors
      base classes, 306, 309–311
      iconstdestr.cc file, 307
      Special class, 307
      testing code, 308
   existing classes, 292
   handling approaches, 299–301
   hierarchical approach, 298
   multilevel inheritance, 297
   multiple class, 298
   object association methods
      smart devices, 349–353

579

INDEX

Inheritances (cont.)
    versions, 354–360
    object composition
        aggregation, 342–349
        automatic gun
            objects, 337–342
        gaming header files, 337
        gun object, 337
        internal bomb/time bomb
            objects, 338
        SpecialWeapon class, 338
        specialweapon.cc file, 341
        weapon objects, 340
    object composition/aggregation
        concepts, 291
    reduce/reuse principle
        application software, 311
        benefits, 311
        employee profile, 315–318
        personal profile, 312–314
        testing code, 317–319
        trainee profile, 320–324
    redundant/inconsistent
        code, 292
    single-level
        inheritance, 295–300
    software versions
        activities, 323
        automatic guns, 324–326
        Bomb version, 326–328
        scenarios, 324
        version game
            context, 331–335
        version players, 328–330

M, N

Model application entities
    CancelledOrder class, 265–267
    customer/item classes, 255, 256
    DeliveredOrder class, 268–270
    DeliveryPartner class, 259–261
    features, 228, 229
    gaming application (see Gaming
        application)
    principles/concepts, 227
    order class, 261–265
    real-world entities, 255
    Shopkeeper class, 256–259
    shopping application (see
        Shopping application)
    software design, 228

O

Object-oriented programming
    (OOP), 1
    adventurous game, 33
        bomb class, 38, 39
        characters, 33
        grabs bomb, 35
        gun objects, 37
        player/enemy
            interactions, 33–36
        problem scope/context, 33
    algorithm vs. software
        definition, 2
        elements, 3–5
        features, 5

INDEX

problem-solving, 5
procedural-oriented program, 4
procedural programming approaches, 6, 7
programming constructs, 3
requirements, 6
system software, 5, 6
C++ (*see* C++ programming)
classes
    abstraction, 12
    access specifiers, 13
    class structure, 8
    customer entities, 8
    data hiding, 12, 13
    definition, 7
    encapsulation, 10, 11
    gaming application context, 9
    IoT sensor modeling, 9, 10
    member functions, 8
design pattern (*see* Design pattern)
event-driven programming, 467–505
inheritance, 16–18
integration/connecting dots, 20
interface design, 21
learning process, 1
objects
    components, 13
    details, 14, 15
    memory allocation maps, 15
operators, 46–48

polymorphism, 19, 20, 362 (*see also* Polymorphism)
primary concepts, 508
Python (*see* Python programming)
real-world entities
    browsing item details, 29
    canceling order, 31, 32
    customer classes, 26, 27
    customers, 24, 25
    data members/member functions, 22, 27
    delivering order, 32
    hands-on activity, 23
    high-level procedure, 21
    interactions/tasks, 22
    item class, 29, 30
    order class, 30, 31
    problem scope/context, 23
    registration, 26
    shopkeeper interacts, 25, 26
    shopkeeper registration/class, 27, 28
    transactions/tasks, 23
    user interactions, 23
real-world problems (*see* Model application entities)
requirements and design processes, 7
reusable/extendible software components, 20
simplifies modeling, 19
software development (*see* Inheritances)

INDEX

Object-oriented programming (OOP) (*cont.*)
   software development process, 19
   Solidity (*see* Solidity programming)
   transaction class, 20 (*see also* C++ programming)
OOP, *see* Object-oriented programming (OOP)

P, Q

Polymorphism
   definition, 362
   dynamic polymorphism, 363
   function overriding, 363
   generic functions/data structures
      data structures, 388, 389
      data types, 381, 382
      gendatastruct.cc file, 390
      member function/friend function, 382
      template, 389–395
      template functions, 383–388
      template syntax, 381
   operations/tasks/actions, 362
   operator overloading, 362
      benefits, 371
      binary operators, 372, 373
      coin class objects, 374–380
      friend function, 373
      object computation, 371
      operators, 371
      overloadcoin.cc file, 375
      unary operators, 374
   overloading function, 362
      DataAlgorithms class, 364–366
      datalagos.cc file, 367
      member functions, 366
      static/compile-time, 363
   overriding function, 367–371
   user interfaces
      abstract classes, 401–403
      concepts, 395
      dynamic concepts, 403–408
      overriding function, 397
      virtual functions, 396–400
   virtual functions
      abstract classes, 401–403
      definition, 396
      override.cc file, 397–401
      Phone objects, 401
      pointer arguments, 402
Python programming
   concepts, 526
   constructors/destructors, 531, 532
   constructs
      access specifiers, 516
      class keyword, 515
      conditional statements, 512
      destructors, 517, 518
      input() function, 512
      loop statements, 513
      member functions, 516

principles, 511
public member functions, 517
variables/conditional statements/loops/functions, 511–514
development activities, 509
encapsulation, 526–528
features, 509
hiding principles, 528–531
inheritance
    approaches, 532, 533
    base class, 519
    BatsMan class, 534, 535
    Bowler class, 534, 535
    constructs, 519, 520
    derived class, 519, 520
    hierarchical approaches, 520
    multilevel approaches, 520
    multiple/hybrid approaches, 521
    player.py file, 533, 534, 537
meaning, 508
polymorphism methods, 521, 538–540
    abstract classes/methods, 524, 525
    built-in functions, 522
    overloading concepts, 522, 523
    override member functions, 523, 524

R

RAM, *see* Random access memory (RAM)
Random access memory (RAM), 414, 432

S, T, U, V, W, X, Y, Z

Shopping applications
    classes, 233
    customer interaction, 234
    functions, 270–274
    identification, 232
    interaction functions
        application.cc file, 275
        browsing function, 275
        canceling customer, 276
        customer interactions, 274–277
        items/quantity, 275
        simulation activities, 274
    implementation, 234
    interactions, 233
    placeOrder function, 284
    real-world entities, 231
    registration process, 283
    respective functions, 283
    scenarios, 232
    shopkeeper interactions
        application.cc file, 278–282
        delivery partners/dates, 280
        functions, 278

INDEX

Shopping applications (*cont.*)
    tasks, 270
    task simulation, 282–288
Solidity programming
    basic programming
        constructs, 541
    blockchain technology, 510
    constructs, 541
    data type variables, 542
    inheritance
        approaches, 546–548
        MySecretProfile, 563, 564
        multilevel, 548
        overloading, 565
        principles, 562
        Remix browser, 563, 567
        setSecretData function, 564
    meaning, 508
    multilevel inheritance
        approach, 548
    polymorphism
        concepts, 549
        abstract classes/pure virtual
            functions, 549, 568–575
        constructs, 551, 552
        derived contracts, 568
        implementation, 568
        interfaces, 549
        override keyword, 550
        Remix browser, 570, 572
        standard interfaces, 550
        virtual functions, 549, 569
    Remix editor, 553–556
        Internet browser, 552
    single-level inheritance
        approach, 546
    single-line comments, 542
    smart contracts, 510
        definition, 544–546
        inheritance, 562–568
        MySecretData instance, 558
        MySecretData deployment,
            557, 558
        principles, 556
        Remix browser, 559, 561
        storing and retrieving, 556
        test results, 561
        visibility modes, 559
    visibility modes, 543
Starting/stopping software
    applications, 114
    closing application
        activities, 118
        disconnect/stop/remove
            services, 119, 120
        releasing resources, 119
    components, 115
    constructors/destructors (*see*
        Constructors/destructors)
    initialization/configuration,
        115, 116
    resource allocation, 116
    software object startup, 117
    subcomponents/external service
        connectivity, 117, 118
Structural design patterns
    adapter pattern, 429
    bridge pattern, 431

composite class, 430
decorator class, 430
facade pattern
    classes, 429
    every layer, 433
    implementation, 433–439
    protocol stack, 432
    simplified interface, 436
    tasks, 439
flyweight pattern, 432
proxy server pattern, 432, 440–445
reusable solutions, 428
types, 429

Printed in the USA
CPSIA information can be obtained
at www.ICGtesting.com
CBHW060618141024
15807CB00010BA/139